NATURALLY BREWED

A HISTORY 1859 – 2018

NATURALLY BETTER

THE HISTORIC BREWERIES OF DULUTH & SUPERIOR

TONY DIERCKINS & PETE CLURE

ZENITH CITY PRESS
DULUTH, MINNESOTA

147/300

Zenith City Press
Duluth, Minnesota
www.zenithcity.com
218-310-6541

Naturally brewed, naturally better: the historic breweries of Duluth & Superior

Text by Tony Dierckins & Pete Clure
Copyedit by Scott Pearson
Index by Lydia Vanderwerk
Research by Pete Clure, Tony Dierckins, and Timothy Killian
Cover & Interior Design & Layout by Tony Dierckins
Photo Editing by Kelsey Anderson, Mer Eggert, and Tony Dierckins
Modern breweriana photos by Brian Rauvola, HBR Studios, Duluth

First Edition, September 2018

Library of Congress Control Number: 2018906161

ISBNs: 978-1-887317-49-8 (softcover); 978-1-887317-48-1 (hardcover)

Printed in the United States of America by JS Print Group

COVER:
Tin lithograph depicting Duluth Brewing & Malting, ca. 1910.
[TERRY POST COLLECTION]

BACK COVER:
Lithograph of Duluth and Superior, 1910, by Henry Wellge.
[DULUTH PUBLIC LIBRARY]

TITLE PAGE:
Enjoying Northern beer, ca. 1900.
[C. OLSEN COLLECTION]

COPYRIGHT PAGE:
Enjoying Fitger's beer while posing for a novelty postcard, ca. 1905.
[C. OLSEN COLLECTION]

ACKNOWLEDGMENTS PAGE:
Enjoying Fitger's beer on the porch, ca. 1905.
[C. OLSEN COLLECTION]

PAGE IV:
Several brothers enjoying Fitger's & Duluth Brewing & Malting beer, ca. 1905.
[P. CLURE COLLECTION]

CONTENTS PAGE:
Enjoying Fitger's beer while playing cards, ca. 1905.
[P. CLURE COLLECTION]

CONTENTS

PREFACE

My first taste of beer came courtesy of my father, circa 1972. I was about eight years old, and we were in the garage, listening to a Minnesota Twins baseball game on the radio. It was hot outside, cool in the garage, and the beer was cold. He allowed me a sip—it was Hamm's.

It had to be Hamm's—the old man made the stuff. My father, Don Dierckins, worked as a brewer at St. Paul's Theodore Hamm Brewing Co. for roughly twenty-five years beginning in the late 1950s. If you lived on the East Side like we did, on certain days the wind would carry the scent of the Hamm's malt house across town—though we lived miles from the brewery, he was never far from work.

Whenever the brewery laid my father off as it struggled to survive the 1970s—which was annually, up to five months at a time—he augmented his unemployment checks by bartending. When I moved to Duluth in 1984 to attend the University of Minnesota Duluth (UMD), one of my first jobs was bartending at a restaurant inside the newly renovated Fitger's Brewery complex. The symbolism did not go unnoticed by this English major.

Years later I was living in Duluth, writing and publishing books and helping others self publish books when Scott Vesterstein, who with others owns the Fitger's Complex, hired me to produce Clarence "Coopen" Johnson's *Fitger's: The Brewery and Its People*. It would be the first illustrated "coffee table" book I ever designed and, moreover, one of the first projects that gave me a taste for the history of the Head of the Lakes. Sadly, Coopen died before the book was printed, so he never got to see it. To finish the book, I had to become something of a Duluth brewing historian myself. Seven years later I made the choice to focus my work on books that celebrate historic Duluth and the western Lake Superior region.

So I was ready when I finally met Pete Clure in 2015. It seems we should have met years before—we attended UMD at the same time and knew a lot of the same people (Duluth has just one and a half degrees of separation). After Pete showed me his extensive breweriana collection, which also includes a healthy selection of Hamm's items, I knew I had stumbled across both a kindred spirit and a book project. Pete, as you will soon read, has collected breweriana for most of his life. His extensive archive includes six volumes of letters between Fitger president Arnold Fitger and brewmaster John Beerhalter, a unique doctoral dissertation on the history of Minnesota's brewing industry, and other rare items that helped tell a broad yet detailed story.

We had research help from others, of course. In particular we were fortunate to have expert assistance from Doug Hoverson, Midwest brewing historian and author of *Land of Amber Waters* and *The Drink that Made Wisconsin Famous*.

FACING PAGE: MEMBERS OF THE GAGNON AND LUEMERE FAMILIES ENJOYING NORTHERN BREWING CO. BEER IN SOLON SPRINGS, WISCONSIN, 1938. [P. CLURE COLLECTION]

Working together Doug and I discovered information that shed new light on the history of the region's pioneer brewers.

Coopen Johnson helped us out not just with the book he wrote, but also by instilling in his son Rockne a love for Twin Ports breweriana. Many of the images in this book come from their combined collection. We reference Coopen's work often, as much of his information comes from personal diaries left behind by August Fitger and Victor Anneke (Rockne also shared some of that research with us). While our research did not always agree with what Coopen had previously written, his work helped guide us to a much better understanding of Fitger's history.

My favorite part of the research was talking and trading emails with people connected to the region's brewing history, such as Jim Hartel, grandson of Northern Brewery brewmaster Joe Hartel; Bob Byrne, who worked at Northern until it closed in 1967; John Sorenson, who leased the People's brewing facility in the 1960s and met daily with brewery owner Carl Hanson; Eddie Gleeson, whose grandfather was a founder of People's Brewing Co.; and Bill Ralph, a descendant of the Decker family, pioneer brewers of Duluth.

I also had a lot of fun gathering images for this project, and you can read more about those who contributed to the book's expansive collection of breweriana and historic photos on pages 187 and 213. All told we gathered over 750 images and managed to fit over 575 of them on these pages. I just hope you're not so busy enjoying the pictures that you forget to read the text.

I recommend you read this book the same way I like to read books: while drinking a cold, naturally brewed beer made at the Head of the Lakes. Cheers!

— Tony Dierckins, June 2018

My first taste of beer is directly connected to my hobby collecting breweriana. I was eleven years old and had acquired a can from the Walter Brewing Co. of Eau Claire, Wisconsin—but it was full. My friends and I cracked it open and we passed it around.

Can collecting was an escape for me. I started in the summer of 1977 because my friends were doing it. By then my parents had divorced and my father had remarried—twice. His third wife and I did not get along and disagreed about most things—including my collection. Meanwhile, my father simply didn't understand it, and instead encouraged me to collect stamps or matchbooks—something that could be more easily stored out of sight.

I grew up in Fredenberg Township, north of Duluth, where in 1977 it seemed all the kids were collecting beer cans—the hobby was at its height nationally. That summer my dad's cousin Dave Hood took me to the World Wide Beer Can Collecting show in the Twin Cities—my first breweriana trade show. Dave and his son Jeff were founding members of the Nordlagers, a group of Twin Ports breweriana collectors that includes myself, Don Hoaug, Brian "Wrench" Hemming, Steve Korkalo (the godfather of Duluth breweriana collectors), Rockne Johnson (son of Fitger's distributor and historian Coopen Johnson), Dr. John Kress, Chris Olsen, Art and John Pickar, and Bert and Judy Wittington, owners of the historic Northeastern Saloon & Hotel in Cloquet, Minnesota—the Nordlagers' world headquarters.

During high school my friends Daniel J. Lane, Christopher Hermans, and Steve Schafer often accompanied me on my breweriana-hunting expeditions. After high school I moved in with family friends Mona and Ken Knutson, who not only encouraged my hobby but made sure I attended the University of Minnesota Duluth and helped finance my education through jobs as a caretaker and working for Mona's family at the Dougherty Funeral Home.

Other work brought me in closer contact with the brewing business. I spent nine years bussing tables and washing dishes for Steve and Tony Wisocki at Duluth's legendary Pickwick Restaurant, originally built as Fitger's Brewery Saloon. I then worked at the Historic Fitger's Complex doing building maintenance and security from 1995 to 1998.

In 1998, thanks in no small part to the help of Lake Superior Brewing Company's Bob Dromehauser, I was hired by Michaud Distributing as a sales associate, selling beer to accounts in Duluth, Superior, Fredenberg Township, and Proctor, Minnesota (that "gem on the hill"). Michaud is housed in buildings that were once part of the vast Duluth Brewing & Malting complex, so each workday directly connects me to Duluth's brewing past. That job has also put me in contact with Duluth's craft brewing companies, and over the years I've become friends with many of their owners and brewers.

I've also been fortunate to have met several people directly connected with Duluth and Superior's historic breweries and have interviewed many former brewery employees and officers, including Fitger Brewing Company president John Beerhalter Jr., Fitger's owner John Ferris, Coopen Johnson, Duluth Brewing & Malting brewmaster and president Bob Ostern, DB&M secretary Russel Gravelle, and Northern Brewing Co. jack-of-all-trades Dick Hartel (son of brewmaster Joe Hartel). The Ostern and Hartel families even contributed photos and other breweriana to my collection.

My collecting and research has also been influenced by the spirit of Duluth's Walt Pietrowski, who collects just about everything related to the Zenith City—even architectural elements from nineteenth-century brownstone buildings that have met with the wrecking ball. Thanks, Walt, for literally keeping pieces of Duluth history around for the rest of us to enjoy. (And thanks to Gene and Kathy Onchelenko for helping me expand my collection to include the historic and modern breweries of Thunder Bay, Ontario).

I hope you enjoy this book as much as I have enjoyed collecting the resources used to put it together—and don't be shy about raising a glass of naturally better beer brewed with Lake Superior water to the other collectors who have generously shared their breweriana. Prost!

— Pete Clure, June 2018

TWO GUYS WHO LOOK NOTHING LIKE AUTHORS PETE CLURE AND TONY DIERCKINS ABOUT TO ENJOY A FITGER'S BEER AT THE BIG MUSKIE TAVERN, SOMEWHERE IN THE WOODS OF NORTHERN WISCONSIN OR NORTHEASTERN MINNESOTA, SOMETIME IN THE 1940S OR 1950S.
[P. CLURE COLLECTION]

THE HISTORIC BREWERIES OF DULUTH & SUPERIOR

⭐ PIONEER BREWERIES (1859–1885)

1. LUCE/BUSCH BREWERY
(aka J. G. Busch & Co., Duluth's pioneer brewery, Decker Brewery, Vermillion Brewery, M. Fink Brewery, Washington Avenue Brewery, Decker Brothers Brewery, and W. Franke & Co.)

2. LOUIS KIICHLI BREWERY (1st)

3. LOUIS KIICHLI BREWERY (2nd)
(aka Superior City Brewery, Klein & Decemval)

4. SHIELS & SIZER BREWERY

5. GUSTAV KIENE BREWERY
(aka Point Brewery)

6. KREIMER BROTHERS BREWERY
(aka Western Brewery, Camahl & Busse, Fink Brewery)

⭐ SMALL BREWERIES (1889–1909)

1. WEST SUPERIOR BREWING CO.

2. KLINKERT BREWING & MALT

⭐ MAJOR BREWERIES (1881–1972)

1. LAKE SUPERIOR BREWERY/ FITGER BREWING CO.

2. KLINKERT BREWING CO./ NORTHERN BREWING CO.

3. DULUTH BREWING & MALTING

4. PEOPLE'S BREWING CO.

See page 26 for addresses and additional information.

BREWERY LOCATIONS INDICATED BY A *Brauerstern* OR "BREWER'S STAR," WHOSE SIX POINTS ARE THOUGHT TO REPRESENT THE CRITICAL ASPECTS OF BREWING PURE BEER: WATER, HOPS, GRAIN, MALT, YEAST, AND THE BREWER; ITS ASSOCIATION WITH BEER AND BREWING CAN BE TRACED BACK TO THE FOURTEENTH CENTURY. MAP OF DULUTH AND SUPERIOR PUBLISHED IN 1911 BY THE DULUTH STREET RAILWAY COMPANY.

[MINNEAPOLIS STREETCAR MUSEUM]

MAP OF DULUTH (MINNESOTA) AND SUPERIOR (WISCONSIN) SHOWING LINES OF THE DULUTH STREET RAILWAY COMPANY

Copyright, 1911, by Duluth Street Railway Co.

PART ONE
1859 – 1885

THE PIONEER BREWERIES
AT THE HEAD OF THE LAKES

IDNEY LUCE NEVER INTENDED TO LIVE IN DULUTH. In fact, the city didn't even exist when he first arrived at the Head of the Lakes in 1856. He had traveled from Ohio to Superior, Wisconsin, to look after some investments "without any intention of remaining any length of time," according to Luce himself. Yet he accepted a temporary job building houses for $3 a day in Portland, a new township platted at the northwestern corner of the tip of Lake Superior. The carpentry job in Portland allowed Luce to make improvements on his investment—the township itself, which he had helped found along with other Ohioans from Ashtabula County. Despite his original plans to return to Ohio, Luce ended up staying for the next twenty years, becoming one of Duluth's most important pioneers. He also established a business that became the longest-surviving manufacturing concern in the history of the Zenith City, lasting more than 110 years—a brewery.

BREWING BEGINS (1859–1865)

Luce considered himself "not…well-versed in western wildcat ways," so he did not invest in potential copper-mining property like many other pioneers (see "Boom Bust Boom I" on page 5). Instead, he built a warehouse along the lake at the foot of Third Avenue East, anticipating the community's need to store supplies for the coming winter. The Financial Panic of 1857 had brought an end to all development at the Head of the Lakes, and many pioneers left seeking other opportunities. In its wake, Luce reluctantly remained, and he and a handful of others did their best to keep the population from further decline. Luce had an idea that would keep at least four men in town—and bring pleasure to others who remained. As Luce himself would later remember:

SIDNEY LUCE
THE FATHER OF DULUTH BREWING

Duluth pioneer Sidney Luce (pronounced "loose"), the man who first brought brewing to Duluth, was born in Kingsville, Ohio, on September 19, 1819. He spent much of his early life in nearby Ashtabula before taking a job with the county auditor's office in Jefferson, Ohio. There he met and married Harriet A. Wood, a native of Troy, New York. They had one daughter, Katie.

In 1856 Luce (pictured on page 9) moved his family to Superior and soon after to Portland Township, which he had established along with other former Ashtabula residents. Luce built a warehouse at the foot of Third Avenue East along the lake shore—Duluth's first commercial building. His warehouse/home would become the center of the entire Minnesota side of the lake for most of the next twelve years. Until 1871, the *Minnesotian* reported, the building served as "the artery through which the pulsations of the coming city beat; all the business was done or talked over there; in it and around it."

Following the Panic of 1857, Luce served as registrar of the United States Land Office. During this period Luce also served the local municipal government as both a councilor and president. He also passed the time building what the *Minnesotian* deemed "excellent" rowboats. When the Lake Superior & Mississippi Railroad arrived in Duluth in 1870, Luce's warehouse became railroad property and he and his family moved to the base of Minnesota Point. That same year Duluth became a city, and Luce was elected alderman and the municipality's first comptroller.

In 1872 Duluthians elected Luce their third mayor, which surprised him: "In the spring of 1872 I was, during my absence from the city, and without my knowledge, elected mayor, which under the circumstances, while complimentary, imposed great burdens upon me. These I cheerfully assumed and gave my whole time to doing what I could to relieve the city from embarrassment." Historians report Luce's administration was marked by "great progress in city affairs" and he was "faithful, fearless, honest, and ever-ambitious for the city." His motto was "Do it for Duluth!"

Yet Luce resigned his one-year term while still in office and moved to his hometown, but not for long. He returned to take the reins of Duluth's First National Bank, which struggled after the Panic of 1873. When the bank failed in 1876, he went back to Kingsville and took up residence on the farm where he had been born and raised. He visited Duluth just once more.

Duluthians never forgot Sidney Luce. Upon his death in 1912, Luce's friend and fellow pioneer J. D. Ensign told newspapers that "[Luce] was a truly admirable man and citizen, ever ready to assist his neighbors and to further every undertaking to promote the community's welfare. In the days when Duluth was young, energetic kindly spirits like his were needed to meet the problems which beset the place." And the kindly spirits in the beer brewed at his brewery no doubt did their part to help face those troubled times as well.

The season of 1859 was like its predecessor. There was nothing doing to relieve the stringency of the times. Our population was steadily decreasing, and to retain what remained was a matter of anxiety. In canvassing the matter it was found that there were four single men out of employment, one of them being a practical brewer. He suggested the building of a brewery, as the four could do all of the construction and carry it on. As this seemed likely to add a little to our enlivenment I encouraged the project by giving them a location and otherwise assisting. The location was on what was then called Washington Avenue, on a small stream. The company was composed of H. S. Burk, Gilbert Falconer, Harry Fargo and J. G. Busch.

Those men—Henry S. Burk, Gilbert H. Falconer, Harvey "Harry" Fargo, and J. Gottlieb Busch—had not come to the Head of the Lakes to make beer. Burk was thirty-one years old in 1859, a Pennsylvania farmer who lived with Luce and his family. Another Pennsylvanian, thirty-one-year-old Harry Fargo, lived on Minnesota Point "opposite Superior" as early as 1853 and worked as a carpenter and cabinetmaker. Falconer, thirty-seven, came from New York to build boats.

John Gottlieb Busch, who went by his middle name, was the oldest of the bunch. The thirty-nine-year-old had emigrated from Saxony, Germany, and came to Portland after working in Detroit. He was not a practical brewer, as Luce suggests, but a cooper. His barrel-making talents no doubt put him in close contact with beer manufacturers in his native Germany, and he likely picked up some brewing experience. He possessed enough at least to give himself and Luce the confidence to start a brewery during a depression in a community with a quickly dwindling customer base. Starting a brewery wasn't a bad bet. At the time thirty other breweries had opened in Minnesota, most in population centers along the Mississippi and Minnesota Rivers, and all of them had survived the 1857 panic.

With lumber borrowed from Luce and the carpentry skills of Fargo and Falconer, they built their operation between East First and Second Streets along Washington Avenue in Portland Township. Unlike the rest of Minnesota townships at the western tip of Lake Superior, whose streets ran about forty-five degrees to the compass, Portland's streets were platted directly north and south. Washington Avenue began immediately east of Sixth Avenue East and Superior Street and ran along a line that bisected Portland Square. The site was directly adjacent to a stream from which Busch drew water for brewing, and soon thereafter locals began calling it Brewery Creek. The brewery itself was referred to as the Luce-Busch Brewery, and later the J. G. Busch & Co. Brewery, the Washington Avenue Brewery, and sometimes "Duluth's pioneer brewery."

If Luce had canvassed farther west, he may have found himself a more experienced brewmaster. According to the 1860 U.S. census, thirty-one-year-old Louis Kiichli—occupation brewer—lived with his family in Oneota Township, located west of Rice's Point. He had emigrated with his parents from Strasbourg, France, to Canada, where his brother Henry was born in 1847. In 1853 they crossed into the U.S., purchased property in what is now the Duluth neighborhood of Bayview Heights, and logged it clean. The same year Luce helped Busch and his friends get started, Louis and Henry Kiichli opened their own brewery in Superior. It joined about 230 others operating in Wisconsin at the time. Just who started brewing at the Head of the Lakes first— Busch or Kiichli—remains a mystery.

By brewing across the bay, the Kiichli brothers were gambling that Superior, which had a much larger population, had a better chance of surviving the panic than did any of the North Shore communities (they did not officially move to Superior until after April 1860). An advertisement in the August 6, 1859, *Superior Chronicle*, announced Kiichli had set up shop at 346 East Second Street in Superior's Uppertown district as a "manufacturer and wholesale and retail dealer in lager beer." The ad promised that he would have beer, wines, liquors, and cigars "constantly on hand" and that "gentlemen will be furnished with LUNCH, and private rooms at all hours."

Two years later Kiichli moved his brewery to Sixth Avenue East and Third Street or "Near Third Street on L Avenue, now Central Park." Both locations were adjacent to what was called the "big slough," later called Faxon Creek, which now runs underground from Central Park to the bay. Kiichli used water from the slough to make his beer. The new location improved the product, as the *Chronicle* reported that "the beer made there is of much better quality than the last two brewings at the old place."

Superior pioneer John Bardon—son of James Bardon, namesake of Duluth's Bardon's Peak—spoke about Superior's early breweries in 1933 and mentioned their contribution to the struggling local economy: "The industry also stimulated the local growing of hops, rye, and other grains. Wild hops grew on all the local streams and in the valleys and were picked by Indians and whites for ready sale to this new brewery. Hand made kegs gave employment to local coopers, who also had been making kegs for salted white fish and trout." He also mentioned that Kiichli's brewery "was always credited with

LOUIS KIICHLI,
No. 346, WEST 2d STREET, SUPERIOR, WIS.
MANUFACTURER,
AND WHOLESALE AND RETAIL
DEALER IN
LAGER BEER,
KEEPS CONSTANTLY ON HAND, A CHOICE STOCK OF
WINES, LIQUORS, AND CIGARS.
Gentlemen will be furnished with LUNCH, and private rooms at all hours.
Superior, August 6th, 1859.—tf.

Duluth Brewery,
DULUTH MINNESOTA,
J. G. BUSCH & CO.
CREAM ALE,   STOCK ALE,
WHEAT ALE,   PRESENT-USE ALE,
LAGER BEER.
This Brewery is situate upon a pure mountain stream on the North Shore of Lake Superior.
The above articles of Beer and Ale will be shipped to any place on Lake Superior on receipt of order by
D. SCHUTTE,
SUPERIOR, · · · WISCONSIN,
Who keeps a supply always on hand, in barrels, half barrels and kegs.   may 28-tf.
J. G. BUSCH.   D. SCHUTTE.

AD FOR LOUIS KIICHLI'S BREWERY FROM THE AUGUST 27, 1859, *SUPERIOR CHRONICLE* (TOP) AND FOR J. G. BUSCH & CO. FROM THE AUGUST 13, 1864, *SUPERIOR GAZETTE* (BOTTOM), REPRODUCED FROM MICROFILM ARCHIVES.
[ZENITH CITY PRESS]

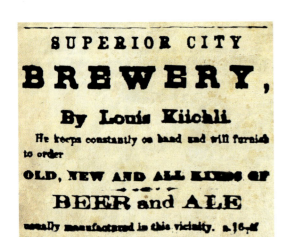

BREWERY,

By Louis Kiichli

He keeps constantly on hand and will furnish
to order

OLD, NEW AND ALL KINDS OF
BEER and ALE

usually manufactured in this vicinity. a 16 tf

Superior City Brewery,

KLEIN & DESEMVAL, *Proprietors.*

WE have recently added extensive and valuable improve
ments our Brewery and are now manufacturing a first
class article of

Lager Beer,

which we will deliver to our customers around the head of Lake
Superior or along the Northern Pacific R. R. in large or small
orders.

We have a large stock on hand which we are selling at lowest
rates. Try us before ordering elsewhere.

apr15tf   KLEIN & DESEMVAL.

An ad for Louis Kiichli's Superior City Brewery that appeared in the *Superior Gazette* in October 1864 (top) and Klein & Decemval's Superior City Brewery that appeared in the *Superior Times* in 1871, reproduced from microfilm archives. Note the apparent typo in the bottom ad; the spelling of "Decemval" varies throughout historic documents [ZENITH CITY PRESS]

turning out a fine product—with plenty of body to it."

Then came war. Residents on both sides of the state line left to enlist in the Union Army, further reducing the local population. Luce hints that during those years, Busch didn't sell much beer: "The enterprise was not a pecuniary success, but it afforded employment as the means of support." The four men he put to work building a brewery stayed as well, at least for a while. Falconer and Burk no doubt helped Luce build rowboats, as the brewery did not produce enough beer to financially support four men. But there was also little demand for new rowboats, and they eventually found other work (see "The Fate of Duluth's First Brewers," page 10).

Busch operated the brewery with little assistance until 1864, when he began working with local liquor dealer Dietrich Schutte to increase sales. Schutte sold Busch's beer by the barrel and half barrel across the bay in Superior. An advertisement in the *Superior Gazette* of August 13, 1864, mentioned the J. G. Busch & Co. offered "cream ale, stock ale, wheat ale, present-use ale, [and] lager beer." The ad also promised that "this brewery is situated upon a pure mountain stream on the North Shore of Lake Superior" and that the brewery would ship its products "to any place on Lake Superior."

Kiichli continued to provide competition for Busch & Co. in Superior without the help of his brother Henry, who had joined the Union Army. In 1864 Kiichli advertised his enterprise as the Superior City Brewery, boasting that he kept "constantly on hand and will furnish to order OLD, NEW AND ALL KINDS OF BEER and ALE." The ad, which ran for several years, indicated he may not have been brewing all that much himself, ending with the statement "usually brewed in this vicinity."

Someone else had also begun brewing beer in Kiichli's vicinity. In the mid to late 1860s, Thomas Shiels and Henry S. Sizer built a brewery along the Nemadji River near the bay in what was then known as Lowertown (the building would have stood roughly at Thirty-First Avenue and Second Street today). Shiels, a native of Scotland, came to the U.S. in 1838 when he was seven years old. He had lived in Buffalo, New York, and Detroit, Michigan, before arriving in Superior sometime after 1860. Sizer was a native of Buffalo, where he and Shiels no doubt became acquainted. In Superior, Sizer made the beer and Shiels kept the books. Sizer also lived in the Shiels household.

Bardon described Shiels and Sizer's product in 1930: "It is said the beer was wonderful. The red iron impregnated waters of the Nemadji imparted to this beverage health giving qualities rivaling 'Ayers Cherry Pectoral,' 'Vinegar Bitters,' or Lydia E. Pinkham's vegetable compound."

Both Superior breweries and Duluth's Busch & Co. also competed with retailers who sold beer shipped from Milwaukee and Sheboygan, Wisconsin. As the Civil War came to an end, their customer base would soon increase dramatically, particularly in Duluth.

A NEW BREWER IN DULUTH (1865–1870)

Those who found their way to Duluth Township following the Civil War included thirty-three-year-old Nicholas Decker. Decker emigrated from Germany to the U.S. in 1852, arriving in New York before setting out first for Michigan's

Pioneers established Superior, Wisconsin, in 1854, the year the second Treaty of La Pointe opened the Minnesota side of Lake Superior to settlement by U.S. citizens. The 1842 Treaty of La Pointe had opened northern Wisconsin and Michigan's copper-rich Upper Peninsula, and prospectors assumed that Lake Superior's North Shore also held large deposits of copper.

In 1856, fortune seekers established more than a dozen "copper towns" along the North Shore—at least on paper. Eleven other townships popped up in today's Duluth, including Bellville (Fortieth Avenue East to Forty-Third Avenue East), Endion (Chester Creek to Twenty-First Avenue East), Portland (Third Avenue East to Chester Creek), Upper and Lower Duluth (today's downtown south to the canal), Middleton (today's Park Point), Rice's Point (including the West End), Oneota (the eastern portion of West Duluth), and Fond du Lac.

Perhaps 1,500 people lived in those townships in 1857, while Superior boasted 2,500 inhabitants. That summer the Panic of 1857—the first international financial depression—crippled development. Meanwhile, copper speculators along the shore had failed to find enough copper to mine. Historian Walter Van Brunt reported that "three quarters of the [Minnesota] population fled" before the year was out. Superior lost 80 percent of its residents.

The 1860 census reported just 406 people living in all of St. Louis County, Minnesota, and 812 in Douglas County, Wisconsin. The townships between Endion and Rice's Point contained just eighty residents, including

brewery financier Sidney Luce. Van Brunt credits them for "[keeping] vigil over the lifeless corpse of Duluth."

The Civil War further decimated the local population. When it ended, just 294 people lived in St. Louis County. In 1868 one resident estimated that just fourteen families lived "at the base of Minnesota Point." That year Philadelphia financier Jay Cooke announced he would terminate his Northern Pacific Railway and Lake Superior & Mississippi Railroad in Duluth. Cooke's agents came soon after, and Duluth's fortunes began to change, as Van Brunt poetically describes: "A glorious resurrection took place; the lifeless corpse [of Duluth], touched by the wand of Jay Cooke, sprang full-armed from the tomb."

That wand was a wad of cash, as Cooke's men spread his money around Duluth building the railroad, depots, docks, and grain elevators as well as hotels, banks, boardinghouses, and even churches. Waves of newcomers flowed into Duluth, eager for jobs provided by Cooke's projects. By 1870 more than three thousand people lived in Duluth, which became a city on March 6. The new metropolis included all eleven 1850s townships. The following April the dredger *Ishpeming* completed the initial cut of Duluth's ship canal, causing problems for Superior as nearly all shipping traffic to the Wisconsin city stopped. Two years later Duluth's population rose to five thousand. While Superior waned, Duluth's future success seemed assured.

And then came September 18, 1873, the day Jay Cooke ran out of money, ushering in the Panic of 1873, another

economic depression. The U.S. economy collapsed, falling hardest at the Head of the Lakes. Without Cooke's money, nearly all work in the Zenith City came to an abrupt stop. In 1877, defaulting on loans and facing mounting debt, civic leaders allowed Duluth's city charter to lapse. The townships between Rice's Point and Portland, with a combined population of roughly 2,500 souls, reorganized as the District of Duluth; in October the district became the Village of Duluth.

Despite this setback, the community was actually on the verge of recovery. Within three years Duluth had found its footing, as the 1880 census showed a population of 3,483. Two years earlier the Red River Valley had blossomed with wheat, and the Northern Pacific began shipping grain to Duluth. By 1881 so much grain moved through the Zenith City local businessmen established the Duluth Board of Trade to rate quality and set prices. At about the same time, the lumber industry shifted from Michigan's Upper Peninsula and northwestern Wisconsin to northeastern Minnesota. Soon large sawmills began popping up along the St. Louis River, from Rice's Point to Grassy Point. Superior, however, did not recover as fast; in 1880 just 655 people lived in all of Douglas County.

When 1881 was over 7,500 people were calling the Village of Duluth home. A year later that number rose to 12,000, and another 2,000 moved to town by the end of 1883, the year Superior recorded 2,500 residents.

When 1885 came to an end, more than 18,000 people lived in Duluth, but Superior housed fewer than 3,000.

Upper Peninsula and very soon thereafter to Superior. In 1856 he married Mary Unden, and the following year the Deckers moved to Oneota Township. They moved again in 1860 when Nicholas was appointed farmer and millwright to the Fond du Lac Band of Lake Superior Chippewa on the reservation in Carlton County.

In March 1866 the Deckers moved once more, this time to Duluth Township where Nicholas jumped into local politics. Already well known, Decker was soon elected the township supervisor and a county commissioner. He also took up a new profession: brewery owner. Duluth's first brewery may have been advertising as Busch & Co.—and J. G. Busch &

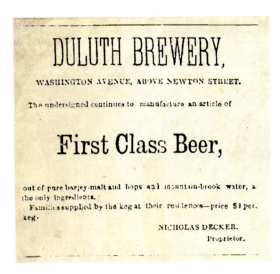

DULUTH BREWERY,

WASHINGTON AVENUE, ABOVE NEWTON STREET.

The undersigned continues to manufacture an article of

First Class Beer,

out of pure barley-malt and hops and mountain-brook water, a the only ingredients.

Families supplied by the keg at their residences—price $3 per. keg.

NICHOLAS DECKER.
Proprietor.

VERMILLION HOUSE

CORNER WASHINGTON AVENUE, AND NEWTON STREET.

DULUTH, ST. LOUIS CO., MINN.

This Hotel, on the direct road to Vermillion Lake Gold Region, is now open for the accommodation of Travelers.

NICHOLAS DECKER,
Proprietor.

ADS FOR NICHOLAS DECKER'S BREWERY AND VERMILLION HOUSE HOTEL THAT APPEARED IN THE *DULUTH MINNESOTIAN* IN THE SUMMER OF 1869, REPRODUCED FROM MICROFILM ARCHIVES. [ZENITH CITY PRESS]

Co. filed federal tax records through 1866—but Luce still owned at least a controlling interest and the land upon which the brewery sat. Luce sold the brewery to Decker, and Busch stayed on for a time as brewer—or so the story goes.

In 1940 Decker's granddaughter, Dorothy Hanson, wrote to the St. Louis County Historical Society at the request of her father, Nick Decker's son Benjamin. She stated her eighty-two-year-old father's memory was still "very keen, especially of his early life" and described a series of owners between Luce and Decker: "John Schutte had a mortgage on the brewery which he sold to my grandfather.... Grandfather Decker was not a brewer but rented it—first to Henry Miller, and then to [Decker's] brother, Bernhard, and later to Gottlieb Busch who was a brewer."

Benjamin Decker was just seven years old in 1866, and by 1940 his memory may not have been as keen as claimed. While Dietrich Schutte was selling Busch & Co.'s beer in Superior in 1864, no one named John Schutte lived at the Head of the Lakes. It may well be that the name of Busch & Co. indicates an ownership change, as it is likely Luce sold the Washington Avenue brewery to Busch and Dietrich Schutte in 1864, and that Schutte financed the venture and then sold the brewery to Decker. If Decker leased the brewery to Henry Miller, Busch likely did the brewing. Miller operated a brewery in Detroit from 1857 to 1879, and there is no indication he ever lived in Duluth, though it does appear that he

and Busch knew one another well. In the late 1870s Busch left Duluth to work for and board with Miller in Detroit. Bernhard Decker indeed ran the brewery for two years, but not until 1870.

Soon after purchasing the brewery, Decker built a hotel about two hundred feet to the west of it, approximately at the northeast corner of today's Seventh Avenue East and First Street—but he had few lodgers. Then Philadelphia financier Jay Cooke announced he was terminating both his Northern Pacific and Lake Superior & Mississippi railroads in Duluth, not Superior, which set off a flurry of construction. The population boom that came with Cooke's investment coincided with a false gold rush at Lake Vermilion, roughly ninety miles north of Duluth. This brought another wave of newcomers to Duluth—prospectors, passing through on their way to wealth. Locals called those who arrived that year the Sixty-Niners, and many of them passed through Nick Decker's hotel on their way out of town.

When prospectors began arriving the only way to get to Lake Vermilion was to follow an old Ojibwe path heading north. The path essentially followed Washington Avenue from Superior Street past Decker's hotel and brewery and eventually to Lake Vermilion. In 1869 noted pioneer George Stuntz turned the path into a road known as the Vermilion Trail. Consequently, Decker's hotel became known as the Vermillion House. The hotel soon brimmed with guests, both lodgers and diners who enjoyed their last meal before hitting the trail served to them by the Deckers' daughters Barbara and Emma.

By May that year the *Duluth Minnesotian,* which released its first issue April 24, was reporting the Vermillion House "continues crowded with guests, the old arrivals departing to find other abiding places, and new ones constantly filling up the gaps." Dr. Thomas Foster, the newspaper's editor (who was once described as "a beer barrel of a man"), was likely happy to run a positive article about one of Decker's businesses, as the saloonkeeper/hotel owner/brewer advertised both of his Washington Avenue businesses in the *Minnesotian* beginning with its second issue.

At the time Decker was handling the brewing responsibilities himself, but the hotel business was getting the better of him. Later that month the *Minnesotian* reported that "Mr. Decker has at length employed a brewer; finding his public house as much as he can attend to, without making beer for the million. We will now have 'first class beer' all the time, or, there will be one brewer taking a bath in the big lake, suddenly." The brewer Foster threatened was likely Christian Spier, then a thirty-seven-year-old German immigrant. In July Decker took on more responsibility by opening a saloon at Thirty-One West Superior Street.

That October the *Minnesotian* reported Decker had sold the brewery to prominent pioneer and real-estate man J. D. Ray for $4,000 and was preparing to build a new home for his family. The sale may have been prompted by news that a competitor was building a new brewery on Minnesota Point. In November Gustav Kiene established what the *Minnesotian* called the Point Brewery "on Minnesota Point, about a mile below Franklin Square"—about Twenty-Fourth Street and Minnesota Avenue today. Kiene was born in Prussia circa 1837 and immigrated to the U.S. in 1852, but how he spent his first seventeen years in the U.S. remains unknown. The newspaper announced that his brewery would soon produce "Lake Superior Ale." Busch and Decker used water from Brewery Creek, Kiichli from Faxon Creek, and Shiels and Sizer from the Nemadji River. Kiene's operation was the first in Minnesota or Wisconsin to brew with water drawn from Lake Superior. He had a batch in the kettle by the second week of December 1869.

The same story that announced Kiene had commenced brewing also mentioned that Decker would continue to

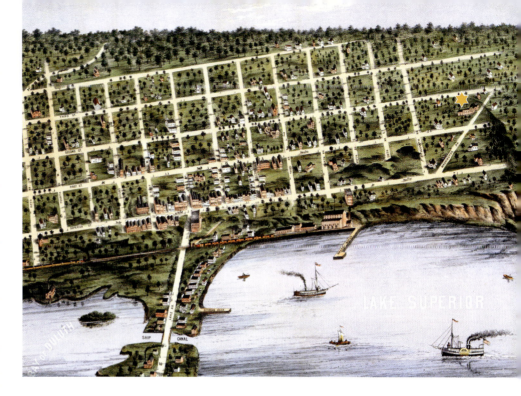

brew out of the "old Vermilion Brewery" until the following June, when Ray would take possession of the property and either continue to operate or dismantle the brewery. But the deal fell through, and Decker was again forced to change brewers. Spier and his wife, Mary, had stayed in Duluth until at least April 1870, when the U.S. Census was taken, but had left before October, when the *Minnesotian* announced Decker had "gotten himself a choice brewer" so there was no need to "import beer any more."

The new brewer's name was not reported. Decker couldn't have rehired Busch, even though they remained neighbors. Earlier that year the *Minnesotian* reported that "that old settler J. G. Busch" had contracted to remove stone quarried along the shore of Lake Superior—and mentioned that "he knows how to work!" The 1870 census shows him employed as a miner and living in Duluth with wife Emma and two-year-old son Augustus. His family is registered just

above the Spiers, who are followed by the Unden family—Decker's in-laws—and the Deckers themselves are listed on the next page. This implies that in April 1870 all four families were living in close proximity to one another at and near the brewery and hotel.

DULUTH BECOMES A CITY (1870–1873)

From all appearances, the deal between Decker and Ray fell through and Decker's brother Bernhard assumed operation of Duluth's original brewery. Perhaps Decker and Ray canceled their agreement because both men were busy helping to run the brand-new City of Duluth, established in March 1870. They, along with Sidney Luce, had been elected to the town's first city council as aldermen.

While Duluth's population had grown to over 3,000, just 1,122 lived in Superior—with Cooke's railroads providing impetus, Duluth had replaced Superior as the promising city at the Head of the Lakes. Louis Kiichli had moved his family back to Duluth in 1869, as had his brother Henry. Louis set up a saloon on Minnesota Point and officials promptly fined him $25 for selling beer on a Sunday. He had sold his Superior brewery to Jacob Klein and Victor Decemval in 1869, and the 1870 census listed Kiichli as a "laborer." Obscure mentions of a Klein & Kiichli brewery operating in Superior in the 1860s indicate that Klein had worked with Kiichli prior to purchasing the brewery.

Like Kiichli, Jacob Klein came from France. By 1860, when he was twenty-five years old, he was living in Superior with his brother Joseph, a saloonkeeper. During the 1860s he married Margaret Decemval, also a native of France, and they had two daughters.

When Margaret's brother Victor first came to the Head of the Lakes, he settled in Oneota where in 1860 he worked as a carpenter and would have been well acquainted with the Kiichli family. In May 1869 the *Minnesotian*—which described Decemval as "irrepressible and enterprising"—reported he was setting up a sawmill outside of Oneota. The following year Victor Decemval was in Superior helping his brother-in-law run the former Kiichli brewery—and improve it.

In October 1870 the *Superior Times* reported that Klein & Decemval had "enlarged and added many improvements to their brewery in Uppertown. They have built, with stone walls and arched roof, the largest basement cellar at the head of the lake, to be used for storage purposes." By April the following year they had named their operation the Superior City Brewery. The *Times* reported that Klein and Decemval "thoroughly understand the business of brewing, are accommodating and straight-forward business men [*sic*], and we bespeak for them a liberal share and custom for dealers of foaming beverage in this vicinity."

In the same issue they advertised that they were "manufacturing a first-rate article of Lager Beer, which we will deliver to our customers around the head of Lake Superior or along the Northern Pacific Railroad" and asked consumers to "try us before ordering elsewhere." That October the *Times* reported that Klein & Decemval were "clever gentlemen and make an excellent quality of beer." An article in December 1871 also reminded readers that Klein & Decemval produced "an excellent article of beer" and told readers that "if the people at the head of the lake don't produce as many articles as they ought to, it is some satisfaction to know that they manufacture enough beer for home consumption."

Meanwhile, Shiels & Sizer's Nemadji Brewery appears to have struggled. In April 1870 the brewery began running a classified ad to sell a fifteen-horsepower portable engine that it owned for only three months. In September the *Times* announced that Henry Sizer had died on the seventeenth, but did not provide a cause of death. On the last day of 1870, the *Times* reported that the brewery had been leased to thirty-four-year-old John Walbourne, a German brewer from Detroit, and that Walbourne had "made many valuable improvements in and about the establishment, and those who know pronounce his beer first class."

Almost exactly a year to the day after Sizer died, Walbourne was dead as well. The *Times* reported that while he was preparing to go duck hunting on the Nemadji River adjacent to the brewery, his gun discharged as he was setting it in his boat. "It went off, the entire charge lodging in his bowels, and he fell to the ground immediately." Described as a "good, steady and upright citizen," Walbourne left behind a wife and two young children.

Across the bay, Bernhard Decker had brewed 579 barrels of beer in Duluth's first fiscal year as a city, and the new city's population continued to rise. The brewery seemed destined for expansion. In May 1871, the *Minnesotian* reported that the "Pioneer brewery of Duluth has been leased by Mr. Decker

to Kramer & Co. for three years," but there is little evidence that anyone named Kramer made any beer at the brewery along Washington Avenue. In fact, Bernhard Decker kept brewing, producing 1,179 barrels between May 1871 and May 1872—more than double the previous year's output.

In early August 1871 Gustav Kiene's brewery on Minnesota Point was destroyed by fire. Kiene lost everything but "the blankets on which he was sleeping," the *Minnesotian* reported, including his entire stock of beer. The *Duluth Tribune*'s report said that the fire had started in the chimney and spread quickly—only the barking of Kiene's dog alerted the brewer to the blaze, likely saving his life. The *Minnesotian* declared Kiene's property loss at $2,500 and mentioned it was insured for $1,200, but the *Tribune* said the loss amounted to $1,200 and that Kiene had insured his property for $750. Whatever the case, it would take Kiene over two years to get his operation back up and running.

The *Brewer's Register* mentions a third brewery operating in Duluth between May 1870 and May 1872. The register shows a firm called Schutz & Miller produced 1,170 barrels of beer in 1870-1871 and 527 more by May 1872. It also provides a partial address—Washburton Avenue—and lists Alexander Schutz and Henry F. Miller as its proprietors. Miller—no apparent relation to Detroit brewer Henry Miller—was a saloonkeeper in Duluth throughout the 1870s and 1880s. Schutz was an accountant, but his name does not appear in Duluth or Superior records until the 1880s. Duluth has never had a street called Washburton Avenue—which could easily be a typesetting mistake intended to be Washington Avenue. Further, Duluth newspapers make no mention of this third brewery operating in Duluth in the

THE MAYORAL PORTRAIT OF SIDNEY LUCE, THE "FATHER OF DULUTH BREWING" AND THE CITY'S THIRD MAYOR, ELECTED IN 1873 WHILE HE WAS OUT OF TOWN AND UNAWARE HE WAS A CANDIDATE. HIS MOTTO WAS "DO IT FOR DULUTH!"
[DULUTH PUBLIC LIBRARY]

After Henry S. Burk, Gilbert Falconer, Harvey Fargo, and J. Gottlieb Busch built what would become Duluth's oldest and longest-lasting industry in 1859, only Busch worked at the brewery after the onset of the Civil War, and he stopped brewing just as the conflict ended.

Henry S. Burk lived with brewery financier Sidney Luce and his family until at least 1870, when his occupation was listed in the federal census as carpenter. A decade later he was a married father of three children, working a farm in Hudson, Wisconsin. Research revealed no further information about Burk.

On Luce's recommendation, boatbuilder Gilbert Falconer was appointed postmaster in 1861, but he didn't exactly take to his new job. "The entire management and control of the office was left with me," Luce recalled, "and I continued to act for him for some years." Falconer's years as postmaster ended in 1868, but he remained in Duluth until at least 1875. He purchased land in Bayfield, Wisconsin, in December 1869, but lived in both Superior and Duluth until at least 1875. Falconer had moved to New York City by 1880, the same year he married Lillian A. Hoyt. He was still at work as a carpenter in 1889, but died some time before the century ended.

As postmaster, Falconer hired Harvey Fargo to handle the weekly fifteen-mile route between Duluth and Fond du Lac. Historian Walter Van Brunt wrote that Fargo "used to travel the route in all weathers, it not being difficult in summer, by water, or in winter over

the ice, but, between seasons, when the ice was too thin for use by pedestrians, and too thick for navigation in a boat, the Indian trail had to be taken."

Judge John Carey recalled Fargo's last day as mail carrier during the early spring of 1863: "When crossing the ice on the easterly side of Rice's Point, [Fargo] broke through the crust on the snow, and got his moccasins and feet wet. He was able to travel but little after that." Three years after he froze his feet, Van Brunt reports, Fargo was "murdered by [Ojibwe], to whom he refused more whiskey, in a logging camp in Wisconsin." Historian Dwight Woodbridge implies that the Ojibwe then set the facility on fire and states that Fargo's body "burned with the camp."

In 1875 the census showed fifty-five-year-old J. Gottlieb Busch living next to the brewery he started in 1859—alone. No records could be found of the deaths or departure of his wife and son Augustus, who would have been just seven years old.

An 1890 article in the *Duluth News Tribune* provides a description of Busch that casts all other records of his otherwise stalwart life in Duluth in another light, and may provide a clue as to his family's fate. Rather than a struggling cooper turned brewer turned industrious miner, the article describes Busch as "very prosperous in the early days and recognized as the richest man in this section." The article credits Busch, not Decker, as the proprietor of the Vermillion House and implies

Busch had made a fortune before he was swindled out of it:

> Time passed on and reverses set in against Mr. Busch. His prosperity eventually slipped away from him. The story would seem like a novel. Did he keep the lands that were once his at the Head of the Lakes, who could compute his wealth today? But it has been with him, alas, much the same as the stories that are too often told of some of our great inventors. They lose their rights through the trickery of some scheming investor, or sell them for a song, when half developed, and die in want in poverty while others are living in the luxury that is afforded them from the products of the inventor's hand.

The passage ends, "Charity forbids saying what became of Mr. Busch—suffice it to say that he is among the living and in St. Louis County." It was highly doubtful he was in St. Louis County—or even alive—when the article was written. By 1880, according to census reports, sixty-year-old Gottlieb Busch was in Detroit, listed as a cooper and living in the home of seventy-two-year-old brewer Henry Miller. Busch's marital status is listed as "widower." His relationship to the head of the household, Miller, is recorded as "servant." Records, however, indicate Miller's brewery closed in 1879, a year before the census. When Busch died, and what happened to his wife and son, remains a mystery.

early 1870s, which would have been big news in a growing community. Together the Decker Brewery and Shutz & Miller's outfit reportedly produced 1,735 barrels of beer in 1871 and 1,643 in 1872, remarkably consistent numbers. Perhaps both Bernhard Decker and Shutz & Miller brewed together at the same facility but sold their product to separate accounts under the name of whomever made the sale.

Flames threatened another Duluth brewery in 1872. Kreimer's Brewery—also known as the Western Brewery and the Kreimer Brothers' Brewery—is first mentioned by the *Minnesotian* in late October 1872 in an article about a fire in "the woods surrounding Duluth." Historian Walter Van Brunt, then the foreman of the city's volunteer fire department, concluded it was "not necessary to put up a stream" as the brewery was in no danger of burning. The story locates the facility at Fourth Street and Eighth Avenue West. This seems to be supported by Bardon, who wrote in 1933 that one of Duluth's early breweries was located "at about Seventh Avenue West and Fourth Street on a sparkling cascade which still trickles down near the foot of Mesaba Avenue."

Researchers have suggested that the equipment used in this new brewing operation may have come from Louis Kiichli's original 1859 brewery in Superior. However, Klein & Decemval, who purchased Kiichli's Superior City Brewery in 1869, advertised its beer in Superior newspapers as late as March 1875. It is more likely that the Kreimers got their equipment from Superior's Shiels & Sizer Brewery, which produced no beer after 1872.

A few weeks after the fire, the *Minnesotian* reported that the Kreimer Brothers Brewery had opened for business: "The first beer from the new Western Brewery, of August Kreimer & Brothers, situated on the corner of Fourth Street and 12th Avenue West, will be brought out on Tuesday morning. Mr Kreimer informs us that it will be equally good for the palates of Grant men as well as Greeley men. You who drink beer, keep this in mind."

The article alluded to the forthcoming presidential election, in which Democrat Horace Greeley faced Republican Ulysses S. Grant. Within a month the *Minnesotian* had supplied two similar addresses for the brewery, four blocks apart—both adjacent to the address later supplied by Bardon. There are no maps of Duluth's streets in the 1870s, and there was very little developed between Seventh Avenue West and Rice's Point, making it impossible to identify the brewery's precise location. A later report places it "above Rice's Point," and both locations mentioned by the newspaper are indeed directly north of the point. Buckingham Creek crosses Fourth Street just west of Twelfth Avenue West, placing its most-likely location at Fourth Street and

Twelfth Avenue West. Buckingham Creek no longer trickles down near the foot of Mesaba Avenue, as it has been diverted underground at First Street.

August and Paul Kreimer—listed as the brewery's owners in 1873—were brothers of Duluth grocer Charles D. Kreimer and likely the same "Kramer & Co." that the *Minnesotian* reported having leased Decker's brewery in 1871. The Kreimers came to the U.S. from Hanover, Germany, in the 1850s. By 1870 Charles had established himself in Duluth as a merchant, selling flour, feed, pork, and fish on

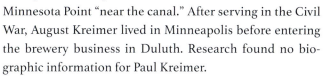

Minnesota Point "near the canal." After serving in the Civil War, August Kreimer lived in Minneapolis before entering the brewery business in Duluth. Research found no biographic information for Paul Kreimer.

ANOTHER PANIC TAKES A TOLL (1873–1877)

Another financial panic struck the nation in 1873, and few U.S. communities were hit harder than nascent Duluth. The population began to dwindle, dropping to roughly 1,300 by May 1874—and as it fell, so did the market for beer. While Duluth newspapers between 1872 to 1875 referred to the facility along Washington Avenue as Decker's Brewery, the brewery itself did not advertise during that time and production may have ceased. August and Paul Kreimer don't appear to have produced much beer at all in the panic's wake. They leased the facility to an outfit named Camahl & Busse in 1874, but *Shade's Brewery Handbook* reports that firm did not produce any beer.

For Sale Cheap.

Brewery at Duluth;

Also, a Kaestner Grind-Ing Mill, with 24-Inch Parls Stone;

A Bolting Chest, 20 feet long;

A Saw Bench, 16 feet long.

Enquire of

C. D. Kreimer,

DULUTH, MINN.

AN ADVERTISEMENT PLACED BY CHARLES KREIMER ADVERTISING THE SALE OF THE BREWERY HIS BROTHERS ESTABLISHED IN 1872 THAT APPEARED IN THE *LAKE SUPERIOR NEWS* IN 1880 AND 1881, REPRODUCED FROM MICROFILM ARCHIVES. [DULUTH PUBLIC LIBRARY]

Charles Kreimer took possession of his brothers' brewery and shuttered it after Camahl & Busse left in 1875. August had already returned to Minneapolis, where he moved into a boarding house; there his life took a steep decline. In September 1876 the *Minneapolis Tribune* reported that before August Kreimer left Duluth he had transferred his interest in the brewery to Charles to prevent his estranged wife from collecting alimony. The paper described August as "a man much given to intellectual pursuits [who] read a great deal"—hardly the image of a frontier brewer. The article explained that August had recently visited Duluth, hoping Charles would give him back his brewery investment, which he valued at $4,000—worth over $93,000 in today's economy. It is doubtful the entire unproductive brewery, let alone August's share, was worth a fraction of that. With his retail customers fleeing town in the wake of the panic, Charles Kreimer likely didn't have the money on hand. Angry, disappointed, and empty handed, August headed back to his rooms in Minneapolis where he was overheard remarking that he "had one shot for his brother and then one for himself."

A few days later he failed to kill himself by swallowing laudanum, a tincture of opium commonly found in households at the time. Two days after doctors saved him, his fellow boardinghouse residents heard "a noise described to be like the falling of a window sash and shortly afterwards he was found stretched upon the floor dead, with a bullet hole through his head, and the revolver with which the deed had

been done near by." Following August's suicide, Charles Kreimer retained possession of the brewery, but it sat idle for most of the remaining 1870s and into the 1880s.

It seems the only person making beer in Duluth following the panic was Gustav Kiene. Despite the economic depression, *Shade's Brewers Handbook* reports Kiene produced 197 barrels of beer in 1874 and 1875 combined. By then he had married, and he and his wife, Pauline (called Lena), had also produced two boys, Joseph and Herman. They soon left Duluth for Kittson County in the northwest corner of Minnesota and eventually moved to Ohio.

The depression affected already-struggling Superior as much as Duluth, if not more so. In the year after the panic, 290 ships visited Duluth's outer and inner harbors while not a single vessel passed through the Superior Entry. Neither Superior brewery survived the Panic of 1873. There is no evidence that Shiels leased or operated his brewery after Walbourne's death in September 1872. Shiels moved his family to St. Paul in 1876 and established the Shiels & Heymel Saloon. An 1882 article in the *Times* reported that the brewery had been empty for some time, while another source claimed that the brewery "operated off and on until it was destroyed by fire in 1884," but no known records verify this.

Klein & Decemval's Superior City Brewery—Louis Kiichli's original operation—advertised until March 1875, but Victor Decemval wasn't working much at the brewery. In 1873 Superiorites elected Decemval as town supervisor, and he had contracted to repair the Military Road between Superior and St. Paul. The following year, after the *Times* called him a "political thief," Decemval was elected chairman of Superior's town board as well as Douglas County sheriff, a job he held until 1877, the same year the local school district and fellow Superiorite V. Roy both sued him for failure to pay a debt.

The authors would like to thank:

Emily Aldrich, Kent Aldrich, Denny Anderson, Kelsey Anderson, Sally Anderson, Jeff Andrews, Noel Boelter, Mark Brandt, Bob Byrne, Heidi Bakk-Hansen, Wes Berntson, Milissa Brooks-Ojibway, Doug Davis, Douglas Fitger Donnelly, Mer Eggert, Ron Finstad, Scottie Gordonio, Greg Grell, Jim Hartel, Bryan "Wrench" Hemming, Roland F. Hoch III, Nate Hooper, Doug Hoverson, Sandra Immerman, Aaron Isaacs, Coopen Johnson, Rockne Johnson, Timothy Killian, Pat Lapinski, Jeff Lemke, Ken Malz, Eric Mathison, Hollis Norman, Maryanne C. Norton, Chris Olsen, Steve Osterman, Jody Otto, Darby Patterson, Scott Pearson, John Pickar, Terry Post, Bill Ralph, Brian Rauvola, Pete Sommerness, John Sorenson, Tobbi Stager, John Steiner, Tami Tanski-Sherman, Lydia Vanderwerk, Madeleine Vasaly, Scott Vesterstein, Bert Whittington, and Joan Wilson.

The entire Reference Department staff of the Duluth Public Library; Aimee Brown, Mags David, and Pat Maus of the University of Minnesota Duluth Kathryn A. Martin Library Archives and Special Collections; Kathryn Montgomery of the Douglas County Historical Society; Teddie Meronek of the Superior Public Library; Shana Aue of the University of Wisconsin Superior Jim Dan Hill Library Archives and Special Collections; Mary Leb of the Fond du Lac Public Library, Fond du Lac, Wisconsin; and Bob Pirie of the American Breweriana Association.

Laura Mullen and Max McGruder of Bent Paddle Brewing Company, Brad Nelson of BevCraft, Brian Schanzenbach of Blacklist Artisan Ales, Ben Starbeck of Boathouse Brewpub, Erik Lietz of BoomTown Brewery, Ken Thiemann of Borealis Fermentery, Paul Kaz and Kristen Grant of Canal Park Brewing Co., Rick Boo and Eddie Gleeson of Carmody Irish Pub & Brewery, Maddy Stewart of Castle Danger Brewery, Mike Maxim and Mark Dexter of Dubh Linn Irish Brew Pub, Bob Blair of DuBrue, Tim Nelson of Earth Rider Brewing Co., Paul Gecas of Gunflint Tavern & Brewpub, Laura Hoops of Hoops Brewing Co., Rod Raymond and Teri Gemblin of JTA, Andy Klockow of Klockow Brewing Co., Dale Kleinschmidt and Lisa Blade of Lake Superior Brewing Co., Bo Bélanger of South Shore Brewery, Steve Knauss of Thirsty Pagan Brewing Co., Ben Hugus of Ursa Minor Brewing Co., and Sue Prom of Voyageur Brewing Company.

For everyone who has ever enjoyed a beer brewed at the Head of the Lakes with chemically pure Lake Superior water.

The 1880 census lists Decemval's wife, Jennie, as a widow. That year her brother Jacob Klein and his family lived in Houghton in Michigan's Upper Peninsula, where he worked as a cooper, having likely become skilled at making and repairing barrels for his former brewery. He later returned to Superior where in the 1880s he and his son both worked making barrels, but not for local beer—roughly 230 breweries operated in Wisconsin in 1880, down 20 percent from the state's all-time high of 289 in 1870, none of them in Superior. The family later moved to Menomonie, Wisconsin.

Nicholas Decker developed tuberculosis—often called "consumption"—in late 1874 and died on the first day of the new year. His funeral was held at the Sacred Heart Roman Catholic Church on Fourth Street, where, according to the *Minnesotian*, Duluth's German population turned out "en masse." Both the church's choir and the local Liederkranz Society, which celebrated German heritage, sang hymns and dirges before the procession traveled east on Fourth Street to the original Forest Hill Cemetery along Chester Creek, where another dirge was sung before they laid Decker to rest. The newspaper reported that an intensely cold wind kept others from participating in "this last sad rite to an old and respected Townsman." Decker was just forty-five years old when he died. His death left his widow Mary and their four children—Benjamin, Barbara, Nicholas, and Emma—with a brewery to run. Benjamin, the oldest, was just seventeen at the time and could not take over the business, so it sat idle.

In a letter dictated to his daughter in 1940, Benjamin Decker reported that, following Nicholas Decker's death in 1875, his mother sold the property to a Henry Kuetchlie. He likely meant Henry Kiichli, but there is no evidence that he or his brother Louis ever purchased the brewery. Since moving to Duluth, Henry Kiichli had worked as a surveyor, built bridges and coal docks, managed a sash-and-door company and a soap factory, and done the books for a grocery store, but he hadn't made any beer. In 1875 he didn't even live in Duluth and was serving as the acting keeper of the Outer Island Lighthouse in the Apostle Islands, with his father Antoine acting as second assistant. Louis was also no longer in Duluth when Nick Decker died. In 1872 he had moved his family to Oneka Township, Minnesota—now the town of Hugo   where he built a store, hotel, and saloon.

Two years after Decker's death, Duluth had run out of money and lost its city status, reverting to village status—but fortunes would turn before the decade ended. In the meantime, as in the 1860s, the faithful remained to wait out the financial crisis. Gustav Kiene and his brewery were gone, the Kreimer Brothers' facility unoccupied, and Duluth's pioneer brewery idle.

DULUTH BOUNCES BACK (1877–1883)

Michael Fink came to the U.S. from Germany in 1867 when he was twenty-seven years old. According to 1881's *History of the Upper Mississippi Valley*, Fink almost immediately made his way to Minnesota, first living in Chaska, where his brother Conrad established a large farm in the 1850s. After two years in Chaska, he spent a year in St. Paul and then moved to Stillwater where he first entered the beer brewing business.

In 1873 he became a partner in Stillwater's Wolf, Tanner & Company Brewery, which later became the Joseph Wolf Company. Two years earlier he had married Catherine "Cattie" Fetz. Like clockwork, every two years between 1872 and 1882 the Finks added another child to their family, first Agatha, then Elisa (called Lizzie), Mary, Conrad,

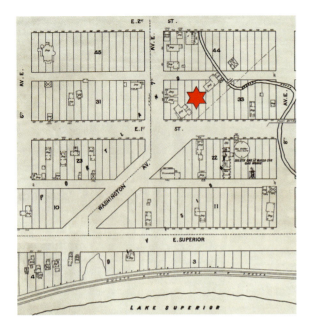

A PORTION OF A SANBORN INSURANCE MAP PUBLISHED IN 1888 SHOWING THE LOCATIONS OF DULUTH'S ORIGINAL BREWERY AND DECKER'S VERMILION HOUSE HOTEL ALONG WASHINGTON AVENUE. THE STRUCTURE ABOVE AND TO THE RIGHT OF THE BREWER'S STAR IS THE BREWERY; THE HOTEL IS THE STRUCTURE JUST BELOW AND TO THE LEFT OF THE STAR.

[ZENITH CITY PRESS]

Theresa, and Loraz. The family moved to Duluth in the summer of 1875, and that October the *Times* reported that Fink had rented the Kreimer Brothers Brewery and promised to produce a "top quality lager beer"—yet there is no indication he ever used the Kreimer facility. In 1876 Fink not only leased the pioneer brewery from Mary Decker, he also moved his family next door to the Decker and Unden families.

Johnson reports that eighteen saloons operated in Duluth in 1877, and Fink sold beer to most of them as well as "thirty private accounts." Outside of being a beer factory, the brewery on Washington Avenue was the centerpiece of an enclave of three German-American families, the Deckers, the Finks, and the Undens. Mary Decker's brother Jacob's family included his wife, Emma, and five children under fourteen years old, including a son named Charles. Charlie Unden—also called Spike—was eleven years old when the Finks moved next door. He had grown up playing at the brewery with his cousins Benjamin and Nick Decker Jr. and would work in the brewing industry until he retired in 1937 at seventy-one years of age. In a speech honoring Spike Unden at his retirement, an unnamed childhood friend provided the following description of life at the convergence of Washington Avenue and Brewery Creek circa 1877:

> The brewery was a one-story building that was built on the crest of [a] rather long hill. The front part was the brewer's home; the rear upstairs was the mill and malt storage; then down a flight of stairs to the kettle which

was situated over a large brick fireplace heated by cord wood. The mill was operated by horsepower—that is where we kids used to get a free ride "round 'n' round." The mash tub was way down on the ground floor.... One novel feature they had was quite an improvement over the old way of carrying beer up in buckets to the kettle or hand pump—they invented a water wheel. They had a long trough up the creek; water running down would turn the wheel which pumped the beer up into the kettle.... The cord wood pile served as seats for the visitors. In cold winter weather, they would heat a poker and stick it into the mug of beer; that is where the name of "Poker Beer" came from. You should have seen the beer cellar! It was in a dug-out—a regular tunnel. That was the old way of building breweries—up against a hill. They also had an ice house that stood...at 115 North Seventh Avenue East. We kids used to have lots of fun playing in the sawdust. Another interesting place at the old brewery was where the kegs were pitched. We were always welcome to roll the kegs back and forth. Of course, we got a drink of beer for doing that.

The rustic facility may sound romantic, but it soon gave Mike Fink a headache. In March 1878 rising waters of Brewery Creek compromised a cold-storage addition attached to the brewery. The structure collapsed, dumping 180 kegs of beer into the creek. The *Minnesotian* reported Fink lost $400 and finished the story with a terrible pun: "We warn Good Templars and Blue Ribbon folks [i.e., temperance types] not to go fishing on Brewery Creek below the brewery as it would look suspicious; possibly that brook may now start a bar at its mouth."

Minnesota brewing historian Charles Dick reports that despite the loss, Fink sold 1,180 barrels of beer in 1878. Fink's brewery was one of 114 operating in Minnesota that year, and the northernmost as well. The following year sales reached just 614 barrels, a drop of nearly 50 percent, yet in 1880 Michael Fink was among the village's top property-tax payers,

While the sale of liquor on Sundays was illegal in Minnesota starting in 1856, Duluth's early history shows a revolving-door policy regarding adherence to the statute even though the city paid keen attention to liquor issues from its start—the very first ordinance passed by Duluth city officials regulated the "trading in intoxicants."

On July 21, 1870, "Professor" F. E. McBain, owner of the Zenith Bowling Saloon, wrote a letter to the Duluth *Minnesotian* complaining about a new city law forbidding liquor-license holders from selling on Sundays. "After granting said license for one year," McBain wrote, "they then pass an ordinance forbidding us to sell any liquor on 52 days of said year." Duluth was only a few months old, having become a city in March. McBain's letter implies that Sunday liquor sales had been allowed dating back as far as the 1850s when pioneers first established the townships that became Duluth. McBain must have had support, for Duluth's liquor dealers were selling on Sundays again by the spring of 1872—and not everyone was happy about it. Outgoing Duluth mayor Clinton Markell ordered the end of Sunday sales in April, 1872, as the *Minnesotian* explained:

> On Sunday last quite a number of individuals appeared on our streets in a state of intoxication, with indecent exposure in one instance. Upon this, Mayor Markell immediately determined that liquor selling on Sunday must be stopped, and his proclamation or order in reference thereto in our advertising columns will be strictly enforced tomorrow.

The paper added that incoming mayor Sidney Luce would undoubtedly uphold the new ordinance as well. Four years after the Markell-imposed ban, liquor dealers petitioned the common council for "the privilege of selling liquor on Sunday." The newspaper failed to follow-up on the issue, and there is no indication that the liquor dealers won the day.

After the city's financial collapse led to its reorganization as a village in 1877, the new community's laws included a ban on Sunday liquor sales, even though the state law already strictly forbade it. In 1880, a cash-strapped St. Louis County experimented with issuing licenses for Sunday beer gardens in order to raise money, but it was quickly shut down (see "A Killer of a Beer Garden," page 20).

In 1884 Duluth had been ignoring both the state and village prohibition of Sunday sales for at least two years. That year mayoral candidate J. D. Ensign, a pioneer attorney of St. Louis County, promised that if elected he would strictly enforce the village's ordinance against Sunday liquor sales. His immediate predecessors, Joshua B. Culver (who had also served as the city's first mayor back in 1870) and C. H. Graves, later U.S. Ambassador to Sweden, had not.

Ensign won, much to the chagrin of alderman and brewer Mike Fink, who had told newspapers that Sunday was "day of all the week, the best" for selling beer. Fink, a German immigrant, was likely thinking of *Frühschoppen*, the German tradition of meeting in a tavern

or tent for a liquid brunch following Sunday church services. The brewer introduced an amendment to the liquor ordinance "providing that on Sundays *front* doors of the saloons shall be closed, but implying that the *back* or *side* doors may be kept wide open." The *Duluth Tribune* added the italics.

Not only did the measure fail, but in 1885 Duluth codified its village ordinances, including its liquor law. It strictly forbade Sunday sales. In fact, Mayor Horace B. Moore was elected in 1885 on a platform that included strict adherence to the law. The Sunday after Moore's inauguration, the *News Tribune* noted, all of Duluth's saloons were "closed up tight." When Duluth regained its city status in 1887, the new city constitution retained the village law prohibiting Sunday sales. It didn't last. By 1889 Duluthians were drinking on Sundays again.

Duluth newspapers published between 1890 and 1920 contain hundreds of stories of saloonkeepers violating the law. Following Prohibition, new liquor laws allowed restaurants and taverns to serve beer and liquor on Sundays, but banned the retail sale of packaged alcohol. Wisconsin had no such law, and for decades Duluthians who forgot to buy beer on Saturdays crossed the bay to stock up on beer on Sundays.

That state law was repealed in 2017, although in Duluth drinking establishments holding a full liquor license must also offer food prepared on-site if they want to open on Sundays. (See "Duluth's Post-Prohibition Liquor Laws, 1934–2016," page 122.)

an indication that the brewery had been profitable enough for him to invest in real estate. He had also become involved in local politics and was appointed a Democratic delegate to that year's state legislative session. By then most of Duluth's pioneer brewers were gone. Gilbert Falconer, Henry Burk, Thomas Shiels, Jacob Klein, and Gustav Kiene had left the

region. Harvey Fargo, Henry Sizer, Victor Decemval, and August Kreimer were dead. Louis Kiichli, Superior's original brewer, would die before the year was out and Duluth's pioneer brewmaster, Gottlieb Busch, was in Detroit apparently fixing barrels for a brewery that no longer made beer (see "The Fate of Duluth's First Brewers," page 10).

This adveritsement for Mike Fink's Lake Superior Brewery appeared in Duluth's 1882 city directory.
[LIBRARY OF CONGRESS]

In 1880 there were 2,741 breweries operating in the U.S., including 130 in Minnesota and 155 in Wisconsin, but only one was making beer at the Head of the Lakes. Fink's crew at the brewery included the Decker boys, Charlie Unden, thirty-year-old John Nepp, nineteen-year-old George Tischer, and forty-six-year-old Louis Fetz, Fink's brother-in-law.

With the ascension of the grain trade and the lumber industry's migration to northeastern Minnesota, the population was increasing at the Head of the Lakes—but Fink continued to operate with no local competition. In fact, Charles Kreimer was trying to dispose of his brothers' shuttered brewery. In August 1880 Kreimer started running an ad in the Lake Superior News that began, "For Sale Cheap. Brewery at Duluth." He had no takers. The brewery was still for sale in October 1881 when the newspaper reported that "a gentleman from the east" had visited Duluth, interested in the brewery—but had left town without coming to an agreement with Kreimer.

Mike Fink had a very good, and very busy, 1881. In February he harvested one thousand tons of ice from Lake Superior to keep his beer cold. The Duluth Weekly Tribune commented that "Lake Superior ice, like Lake Superior fish, is of prime quality." March found Fink building a twenty-five by fifty-foot house to store his ice that the Tribune called "new

and model." It was divided into three cells. The center cell held beer stored in hogsheads and ice was packed into the compartment on either side. More ice was packed above the center compartment.

In April Duluthians elected Fink to a two-year term as an alderman of the village's second ward. Near the end of May the Tribune, now a daily paper, announced Fink would "erect a substantial business building on the site of the Dramatic Temple," which stood at 213–215 West Superior Street—but it did not mention the nature of the business. In June the newspaper stated that Fink reportedly paid $300 in tax stamps—a sign of prosperity, as the newspaper suggested when it quipped "that's business, revenue, and beer for you." The story also mentioned that Fink and a business partner were building a sidewalk "in front of their property on Rice's Point."

Before 1881 Fink sent a freight car of ice to Winnipeg at $5 a ton, and Duluth brewing historian Coopen Johnson reports that the brewer also sold some real estate that year. Besides making beer, Mike Fink engaged himself in all sorts of business—his own and the village's. And the village was getting busy; by year's end over 7,500 people lived in the Village of Duluth.

Another sign of the brewery's prosperity came in May 1881 when Fink began advertising in the Weekly Tribune, calling his brewery "An Old Reliable Establishment." The advertisement coincided with a story in the Tribune on July 9 that reported that the previous month "2,853 kegs of Duluth lager beer were consumed in this place, besides the bottled beer and beer furnished from Milwaukee and St. Paul, to say nothing of stronger liquors."

The Tribune may have been coyly helping a new advertiser, but editor Robert Mitchell seemed to genuinely like Fink, often running articles on the aspects of Fink's life that fell outside of business and politics. Mitchell was a consummate Duluth booster, strongly supportive of the Zenith City's civic leaders—and as alderman, Fink had joined their ranks. In 1881 Mitchell's was the only daily newspaper in town, and Fink the only brewer; it was good business for both.

On July 24 Fink celebrated his forty-first birthday with a "large number of friends." He was serenaded by the Duluth Glee Club and toasted by his friend and fellow pioneer John Rakowsky. The *Tribune* joked that while the German immigrant "smashed the Queen's language considerably" his speech brimmed with energy and good will. Rakowsky credited Fink's great success to his "spunk" before espousing Duluth's own prosperity of the past few years; to Rakowsky, Fink's rise in Duluth was symbolic of the city's own resurrection. Fink, the paper reported, was a good sport and "stood the speech well."

A week later Fink made the paper again when the *Tribune* reported that a raid on a storage building on Park Point "occupied by a gang of tramps and hoodlums" turned up "a dozen kegs of lager beer stolen from Fink." Fink's beer was so good people were stealing the stuff—perhaps it was time to expand. On September 11 the *Tribune* reported that Fink had nearly "completed his arrangements for the erection of a large, new brewery" which would stand on Superior Street between Fifth and Sixth Avenues East.

The newspaper reported that the brick building would be seventy foot square and stand three stories tall, though it would appear only two stories high along Superior Street.

Fink hired fellow German-Americans to help build his new brewery, including mason Charles Yager and excavator Louis Meining. Jacob Unden, Mary Decker's brother and Charlie Unden's father, did much of the carpentry. Fink told the paper it was his intention to "put up a building that shall be second to none in the state for the purpose intended, and will furnish it with all the improvements known to modern-brewers." He promised to hire a large group of men so he could move in by mid-November. Indeed, by mid-October newspapers reported that a "large force of men" had erected the new facility's stone foundation. Fink kept pressing, now expecting to be brewing by November 1.

He missed his self-imposed deadline, and meanwhile the rushed construction nearly caused great injury to Jacob Unden. He fell through a "scuttle hole" in the roof of the new building, hitting a joist on his way to the floor, but fortunately did not break any bones. The same issue of the *Tribune* that reported Unden's accident also mentioned that Fink had entered the county commissioner race. "If Fink makes as good a commissioner as he does an alderman, he

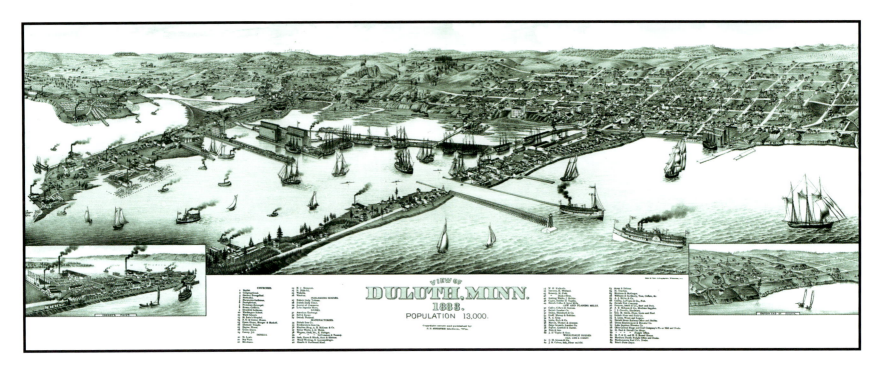

VIEW OF
DULUTH, MINN.
1883.
POPULATION 13,000.

will be a good one. Under his shaggy light hair he has a big amount of plain common sense." With Mitchell's endorsement, Fink easily won the commissioner's seat.

During the first week of December, construction began on a large icehouse adjacent to the new brewery, described in the press as "nearly as large as the brewery itself." On the twenty-ninth of December the paper again reported Fink's plan for a "mammoth" icehouse to accommodate the "wants of the man who when summer's sun oppresseth him, cools his feverish blood with 'good old l-a-g-e-r.'" But as Fink's busy 1881 came to an end, construction of his new facilities appears to have stalled before workers even started to apply the brewery's brick façade.

Fink's new duties as a St. Louis County commissioner began on January 3, 1882, ushering in another red-letter year for Fink, though it came with its share of frustrations. There was no news on the progress of his new brewing facilities

until February, and that was news of yet another innovative approach Fink had brought to building icehouses:

M. Fink, the brewer, has a novel scheme to filling his large new ice house. The house is built with a number of water-tight compartments, into which water is pumped by an engine stationed near the lake and allowed to freeze. Between ice storage boxes are other compartments for the storage of beer. This method is considered less expensive than cutting the ice from the lake. Unfortunately the mild weather of the present winter is not favorable to the success of Fink's scheme, and he may yet be compeled to haul ice from the bay.

Fink's scheme indeed failed, at least that first winter. Before February ended, the paper reported that Fink was cutting ice on the lake near the foot of Fourth Avenue East. In March "half a dozen men" scrambled to fish a "valuable cow" out of the lake—it had fallen in where Fink and his crew had harvested ice. Four days later Fink had already packed two thousand pounds of frozen Lake Superior water and planned to keep cutting until he had six thousand more. But there was no news on the progress of the brewery, and he must have been feeling pressure to get his operation up and running, as in April the *Tribune* announced that August Hohman, a St. Paul brewer "of many years experience in Germany, France, and this country, arrived here last night, and has determined to build a brewery here next season." Hohman likely recognized the growing market: the Village of Duluth now had sixty saloons operating between the brewery and Rice's Point—a 333 percent increase over 1877, when Fink had but eighteen drinking establishments to serve.

Fink was brewing—or had at least moved out of the Washington Avenue brewery—even before Hohman's announcement. In early May advertisements for Decker Brothers Brewery began appearing in the *Tribune*. Nicholas Jr. and Benjamin Decker, likely with the help of Charlie Unden, were brewing beer at the brewery they had grown up in and lived next to their entire lives. And if they were selling beer in May, they must have brewed it well before that.

Weeks after the Decker brothers began selling beer, Fink obtained a liquor license so he could sell beer through the new facility's bierstube, called the Brewery Saloon. The paper made no announcement that Fink was brewing at the new facility, but it did mention that he had a potential new employee: "Arrived, Tuesday in the family of M. Fink, a young brewer, weight 12 pounds." Loraz Fink, the youngest child of Michael and Cattie Fink, was born on May 16, 1882.

Fink was likely brewing by June, when a reporter from the *St. Paul Daily Globe* visited Duluth and Superior and wrote an article comparing the two communities. The story described a shiny, prosperous Duluth and a worn-out, broken-down Superior. The reporter mentioned he was "surprised at the increase of the brewing business in the last

year or two. One establishment, that of M. Fink, who made last year over 3,000 barrels of beer, was farely [*sic*] crowded out of his old quarters and has a large veneered brick [brewery] on Superior Street.... His capacity is fifty barrels per day." The article was partially speculative—Fink's brewery had not yet been dressed in its brick façade, and while Fink's brewery may have been operating that June, Fink wasn't. On the twenty-third the newspaper mentioned he was "still confined to his room with acute rheumatism."

According to Coopen Johnson, Fink's new brewing outfit—the M. Fink & Company Lake Superior Brewery—sold its first beer in August, packaged in kegs that held about four gallons or an eighth of a full barrel. Fink sold 2,501 of the small kegs that first month, which Johnson described as a "very good start." A history of early brewing in Duluth prepared in 1973 by the St. Louis County Historical Society described the interior: "The major portion of the building was used for brewing—the basement was used for storage and a part was used to house the brewery saloon. On the second floor were offices and sleeping quarters for the help." The report agreed with the *Daily Globe* that the brewery's

THIS DETAIL FROM THE MAP ON THE OPPOSITE PAGE SHOWS BOTH THE 1859 PIONEER BREWERY (YELLOW BREWER'S STAR) AND THE 1881 LAKE SUPERIOR BREWERY (RED BREWER'S STAR). [ZENITH CITY PRESS]

As one might imagine, where beer goes drunkenness often follows, and that can lead to trouble. Subsequently, Duluth's pioneer brewers often found themselves at the center of conflict. In fact, the Zenith City's first murder—the 1869 stabbing of George Northrup—resulted from an argument that started in brewery owner Nicholas Decker's Superior Street saloon.

Since the town had no jail, the accused—Philadelphian Thomas Stokely and friends—were incarcerated in the cold caves dug behind Decker's brewery where the beer was aged, perhaps the most secure and best protected facility in town. The *Atlantic Monthly*'s John Townsend Trowbridge happened to be in town and wrote that the suspects were "imprisoned in a lager-beer brewery...where they spent a thirsty night—lager, lager everywhere, and not a drop to drink. To prevent a rescue, the streets are patrolled after dark by a strong guard of citizens.... 'Who goes there?' is the challenge. 'Lager!' is the bold response; followed by the rather unmilitary rejoinder, 'Advance, Lager, and give us a drink, will you?'" Duluth's first brewery was also its first jail. Stokely, the son of Philadelphia Republican mayoral candidate William Stokely, was convicted—and then set free. In the wake of the Civil War even the victim's father, notoriously reckless Indian fighter Ans Northrup, thought it in the best interest of the Republican Party that scandal not interfere in the upcoming election. Stokely won.

In 1880 St. Louis County experimented with issuing licenses for Sunday beer gardens as a way to raise money.

The 1880 county ordinance restricted Sunday liquor sales to outside the borders of the Village of Duluth, which then extended to about Twenty-First Avenue East. The Urs and Elizabeth Tischer family had established a farm immediately east of the mouth of a creek named for them. Their son John purchased a license, and on a Sunday in late June many Duluthians, particularly those of German extraction, headed to Tischer's Beer Garden. Those in attendance included brewery owner Michael Fink and Nicholas Decker Jr., whose family leased the brewery to Fink. Decker and Fink supplied the beer. Also in attendance was their friend Herman Oppel, son of prominent pioneer grocer Christian Oppel.

According to one witness, there was also "a good deal of drinking going on there." James Brennan, an official with the St. Paul & Duluth Railroad, quarreled with Alexander McGinnis. The *Lake Superior News* reported that Brennan's brother Edward tried to break up the feuding pair when Oppel, "partially under the influence of liquor and apparently desirous to have the fight go on, followed up a threat against the separation by striking [Edward Brennan] behind the ear with a loaded cane.... He fell and three minutes later was dead."

Oppel was arrested the next day and sent to St. Paul for a brief incarceration—authorities couldn't very well hold him at his good friend's brewery. But they did delay his trial for almost two years. St. Louis County's Sunday liquor license experiment was stopped. Daniel Cash and J. D. Ensign, both respected pioneers of the St. Louis

County judicial system, defended Oppel at his January 1882 trial, arguing that he had struck Brennan in self defense. Witnesses said Brennan had unlinked his shirt cuffs, preparing for a fight. He approached Oppel, who warned him to keep back. Brennan kept coming. Oppel struck him a one-handed blow close to the left ear. Brennan stumbled backward and fell. The blow had only raised a bruise—since there were no lacerations or broken bones it was highly doubtful it could have killed Brennan. (We know much more about head injuries today than we did in 1882.)

A jury of land-owning males—most of whom traded with Christian Oppel and had known Herman since he was a boy—came back with a verdict of not guilty. Days later the *Duluth Weekly Tribune* announced that Oppel had finally married Mary Mannheim, whose faith in Oppel's innocence never faltered. Since he could have been hanged for murder, they had postponed their wedding until after the trial.

The murder at Tischer's Farm occurred on June 27, 1880. In 1903 Chester Congdon purchased the Tischer farm site and built his grand estate, Glensheen, on the grounds. On June 27, 1977, the bodies of the Congdon's daughter Elisabeth and nurse Velma Pietila were discovered at Glensheen. Like Hermann Oppel, suspect Marjorie Congdon Caldwell—adopted daughter of Elisabeth Congdon—was acquitted of the crime. Like Thomas Stokely, Caldwell's husband, Roger Caldwell, was found guilty and later released.

new equipment could produce five thousand barrels of beer annually—ten times the capacity of the Decker Brewery. Fink would need it, as that year the local population grew to an estimated twelve thousand.

By early September Fink was back on his feet and regularly attending village council and county commission meetings. His friend John Tischer had joined the operation as keeper of the Brewery Saloon, and in September he was granted a license to operate a billiard table in the brewery. That same month Fink announced he was going to make his own malt and had already set Charles Yager to work building the new facility's furnace—but the brewery still had no

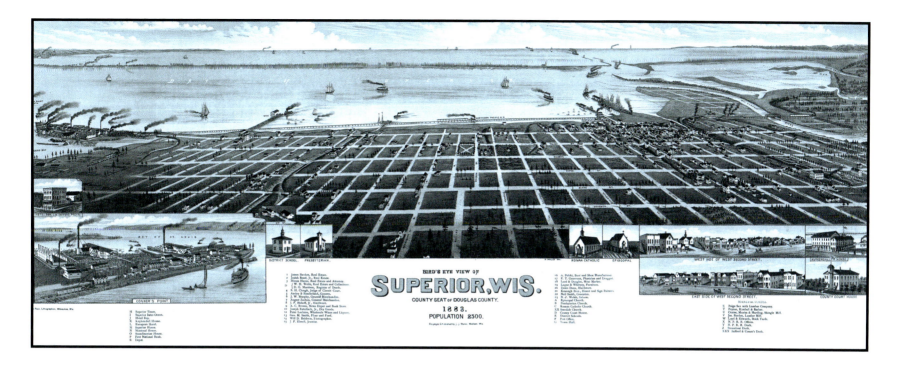

bricks. Fink's operation was becoming a great success, and consequently he became more and more busy, which added to his already heavy load as businessman, village alderman, county commissioner, and father of six.

To keep up the growth, Fink needed to delegate more responsibility. He had hired a new brewer in the fall of 1882, though the local newspapers made no mention of the change until February 9, 1883, when the *Daily Tribune* wrote that its staff was "indebted to M. Fink for a sample keg of his new beer, made by a brewer he lately engaged in Milwaukee and they pronounced it excellent." The brief article failed to mention the brewer's name.

Duluthians reelected Alderman Fink in April 1883, and before the year ended he had one thousand more citizens to serve and sell beer to as the population reached thirteen thousand. Despite Duluth's population boom, only Fink and the Decker Brothers were making beer for commercial

sale on either side of the bay. Superior had not grown along with Duluth; just 2,500 souls occupied the Wisconsin city, and none of them were making beer. They were drinking Fink's, who shipped it to thirty-three accounts on the other side of the bay as he busily worked to expand his business.

In July he hired Bert Marshall, formerly of McGowan's Saloon, as an agent and collector—essentially a salesman, or in today's nomenclature, an account manager. That month the brewery reported producing 667 barrels of beer—well beyond its capacity—and selling 5,950 kegs. But the papers still had not mentioned the name of Fink's new brewer from Milwaukee.

The news that summer focused on the village's continued growth, and Fink spent much of it traveling. Johnson reports that, with a new brewer handling production at the plant and Marshall handling local sales, Fink set to work expanding his reach. He opened accounts in nearby Thomson

A PERSPECTIVE MAP OF
SUPERIOR IN 1883 PUBLISHED
BY HENRY WELLGE.
[LIBRARY OF CONGRESS]

and Northern Pacific Junction (now Carlton) and as far away as the booming logging town of Grand Rapids. He also sold to accounts at Lake Vermilion and a new town called Tower, named for Charlemagne Tower, who that summer began shipping iron ore from his newly opened mines on what became known as the Vermilion Iron Range. The Duluth & Iron Range Railroad carried ore from Tower to Agate Bay—today's Two Harbors—where Fink sold to thirteen saloons that popped up in a four-acre parcel that became known as Whiskey Row. The Lake Superior Brewery delivered its beer in kegs using horse-drawn wagons, boats, and railroad cars. Fink, Johnson reports, mostly used the railroad to visit these accounts once a week, but took a boat to Agate Bay.

The Decker Brothers, meanwhile, struggled to keep their brewing operation alive. In October the *Daily Tribune* used just one sentence to sum up their situation: "The Decker Brothers contemplate the sale of their brewery." The same month that Nicholas Jr. and Benjamin Decker were thinking about selling theirs, Fink finally got around to facing his, hiring Meining & Yager to apply a veneer of white bricks from Brainerd, Minnesota. They trimmed the corners, windows, and doorways with more traditional red bricks. Perhaps Fink was spurred into action by fear of fire, for that same month the *Daily Tribune* mentioned that he and brewery accountant Bert Marshall had "organized a private fire company" at the brewery. The brickwork was completed in mid-November.

When Fink and company closed the books on 1883, according to Johnson, they had sold over 5,200 barrels of beer—more than their brewery was supposed to be capable of producing. At the same time, increased competition

had come to town as breweries in Milwaukee, St. Paul, and Minneapolis opened accounts in the region. The newspapers still had not mentioned the name of the brewer Fink had hired a year earlier, but the local population certainly enjoyed his beer.

THE FALL OF ALDERMAN FINK (1883–1885)

As 1883 turned to 1884, Fink's fortune, it seems, began to turn as well, and he found himself in court as February began. C. P. Byam had been arrested for assault after slapping Fink with the back of his hand, and witnesses stated that the brewer had been using abusive language while arguing with Byam; others said he had not. Byam was fined ten dollars and court costs, and the newspaper implied that Byam would likely "cause the arrest of Alderman Fink on the charge of using language calculated to provoke an assault." Fink did not face charges, but his proclivity for inflammatory speech was beginning to show another side to him—a side that would emerge as the year played out.

February ended badly not only for Fink, but for several of his fellow aldermen on the Common Council as well. A representative of Duluth's Chamber of Commerce had accused them of engaging in "skull-duggery" regarding a right-of-way franchise the chamber hoped to use to lure a railroad to town. The franchise held "all the available dock room in the village [between Rice's Point and Minnesota Point]." Fink and his fellows members, it was charged, had already given away the franchise to a company that existed on paper only.

This action, though completely legal, was characterized by the *Tribune* as "not fair, decent, honest or acting in good faith toward the public." If allowed to succeed, the newspaper said, the aldermen would have "swindled [the village] out of a most valuable property...which would go into the hands of a few men to fatten their purses enormously." As had the Chamber of Commerce, the paper suggested a conspiracy was afoot. "The woodchuck that is holed is one of rare size and...should be smoked out." The paper claimed that the franchise, by the action of Fink and the other four aldermen, had "been raped, prostituted, [and] debauched."

Fink and his fellow aldermen had fallen from the grace of *Tribune* editor Robert Mitchell, until then a big supporter of Fink. The newspaper's position was clear, and Mitchell would be relentless in his criticism of those who voted in favor of selling the franchise to the phantom company, Fink in particular. The issue dragged on into the next election, with Fink offering a horse to anyone who could put up a decent mayoral candidate who would support him and the "franchise men." Meat-packer John B. Sutphin accepted the challenge. Fink, who still had another year left of his two-year term as alderman, promised the *Tribune* he would work to elect Sutphin "if it takes his whole brewery to do it." Mitchell's paper then chastised the alderman:

> We would inform our Teutonic friend that he has taken a bigger contract than he can carry out, and bitten off more than he can chew. There are perhaps some men in those wards whose votes that eminent law giver Fink can purchase for a few glasses of beer...[but] there are a good many men who drink beer and who sell beer, men who think for themselves and do not intend to let Alderman Fink *run* them.

Sutphin lost the election to attorney J. D. Ensign, the community's final rebuff of the franchise crowd. Moreover, the *Tribune* no longer found Fink's celebrated spunk charming. During Fink's next twelve months as alderman, the newspaper worked to ridicule him at every opportunity. In an article recounting the mayoral election results, the paper reminded readers of Fink's prediction and then added that Fink "doesn't know as much about politics as he does about beer." Two days later the paper implied Fink freely

passed out liquor licenses, a conflict of interest due to his business as a brewer. Several days after that the paper was quick to point out that Fink, a maker of beer, had objected to the local Good Templars request for permission to install a drinking fountain at Lake Avenue and Superior Street.

In May Fink once again stirred things up on the Common Council. The state of Minnesota forbade the sale of liquor on Sundays, a law not always enforced in Duluth over its history (see "Sunday: 'Day of All the Week, the Best!'" page 15). The village had a ban on Sunday liquor sales as well, but Ensign's predecessors had not enforced it. Ensign—later a beloved district court judge—expected to see that the law was enforced during his tenure as mayor. Fink tried to circumvent the law by introducing a new ordinance that would allow saloons to operate on Sundays if the front door was locked, no matter if side or back doors were flung wide. The newspaper reminded its audience that Fink made his living selling beer and asked, "Does the moral element of this community desire the passage of Alderman Fink's ordinance?"

Duluth's Common Council tabled any vote on Fink's ordinance in late May and again in early June. At the council meeting on June 10, Fink made a grand effort to pass his ordinance, arguing that many other such legal restraints were not being enforced in booming Duluth. Cows and horses, for example, were blocking intersections when the law said they could not roam at large.

He then targeted the new mayor by comparing Ensign to his predecessors, who Fink characterized as "gentlemen

M. FINK.   A. FITGER.
M. FINK & CO.,
Lake Superior Brewery,
DULUTH, MINNESOTA.
OUR BEER IS CONCEDED THE PUREST ARTICLE MANUFACTURED.

D. DECKER,   N. DECKER.
DECKER BROS.,
Duluth Brewery.
All Orders Promptly Attended To.
may-2-3m

TOP: THIS AD FROM THE 1884 DULUTH CITY DIRECTORY IS THE FIRST NOTICE THAT AUGUST FITGER WAS BREWING IN THE ZENITH CITY, PUBLISHED TWO YEARS AFTER HE FIRST ARRIVED.

BOTTOM: THE DECKER BROTHERS' ADVERTISEMENT FROM THE 1883 DULUTH CITY DIRECTORY.
[ZENITH CITY PRESS]

who did not stick their nose into business." Since the ordinance was a matter of conscience to Ensign, Fink suggested, perhaps "the mayor might allow his conscience more latitude" by passing along Fink's amendment.

The *Tribune* reported that Ensign replied to Fink "in a spirited manner that he was the keeper of his own conscience" and called for a vote. The measure, and Fink, failed, 4–2. Two days later the paper mentioned that the brewer told reporters he thought their portrayal of him during the meeting was "written in an unfriendly manner." But Mitchell was just getting started.

Two days before his complaint turned up in the newspaper, Fink attended the funeral of brewery employee Peter Nepp, who died of undisclosed causes. At the time, Johnson reports, Nepp and others would have been working with Joe Wargin and Andy Haller, who boarded at the brewery along with that unnamed brewer from Milwaukee, who oversaw all production.

By then Duluth's population was approaching 16,500 citizens. Eighty-three saloons were serving them beer, and Fink had a relative monopoly on sales of local brew—Benjamin and Nicholas Decker Jr. stopped brewing that summer and Nick went to work for Michael Fink as an agent

and collector. Still there was competition in town from outside brewers, including Milwaukee giant Phillip Best Brewing Company (which became Pabst), who sold to saloons and retailers.

The Decker Brothers leased the 1869 brewery to twenty-eight-year-old bookkeeper William Franke, who had help making beer from Louis Eischstadt and Charlie Unden, who was then eighteen. They organized as W. Franke & Company and were listed in Duluth's city directories from 1884 to 1886, but the outfit produced little beer and would be gone by 1886. By the time the decade was out, Duluth's pioneer brewery—active for twenty-seven years—would be a memory.

Fink probably didn't worry much over Franke & Co. in 1884. He was busy fighting with a newspaper, not a competing brewer. On July 3 the Common Council met to discuss whether to press charges against the village marshal based on allegations published in the *Tribune*. Fink, who considered the investigation a waste of time, spoke against it. The *Tribune* reported that "Fink had made a wild speech, sworn a little, and sat down without any body knowing what he was trying to say." The council passed the measure. The vote couldn't have upset Fink too much—the next day he and his crew drove a decorated wagon loaded with kegs of beer to the community's Independence Day celebration.

A few days later, however, Mitchell set his sights on Fink again, and with good reason. The day before, the local YMCA secretary had registered a complaint that Fink had sold beer at his brewery on the preceding Sunday. The newspaper also revealed that the brewer had recently paid a fine for selling on another Sunday. The same issue of the *Tribune* suggested that Fink had once again become upset at the most recent Common Council meeting: "We think that all who attended the meeting of the council last night will agree with us that Alderman Fink is not only a blatherskite, but that he sometimes can make an egregious ass of himself."

The following day the paper recounted Fink's weekly visit to Northern Pacific Junction to see after his accounts. He had missed the passenger train, and the conductor of a freight train refused to allow him to ride in the caboose during its twenty-mile journey to Duluth, which was forbidden. After the conductor refused to be persuaded with payment, the "little alderman" succeeded in bribing a brakeman, who let Fink hide in a boxcar. The brakeman then went to the conductor and said, "There's a little Dutchman back here stealing a ride on us in a box car, shall I kill him?"

The conductor spared Fink, but threw him off the train at Fond du Lac, still roughly fifteen miles from his destination. Fink, according to the newspaper that despised him, supposedly yelled, "I gif you den tollars of you let me ride to Duluth mit you in your tamned old kerbooses!" Fink was forced to sleep in the railroad's freight house until the passenger train came the next day. Mitchell was taking every available opportunity to paint Fink a fool.

Fink had a better day on the twelfth, when he was acquitted of his most recent charge of violating the Sunday liquor sale ordinance after testifying he had served his guests ginger ale, not beer. Later in the week the newspaper ran a humorous column under the headline "What Duluth Wants to Know." Among the questions posed was "whether Alderman Fink appreciates the fact that he makes a laughing-stock of himself every time he opens his mouth in the council chamber." Throughout the summer the paper would use phonetic spelling to mock Fink's thick German accent and continued to call him an ass at every opportunity.

The paper mocked Fink's apparent hypocrisy regarding issuing liquor licenses in August. Fink, the paper said, had always liberally signed off on liquor license requests as he was in the business of selling beer, but when a saloonkeeper who owed Fink money applied, Fink tabled the request for further review. In November he introduced an ordinance

BEER!
OR DOWN COMES THE HOUSE!

In mid-January 1884 a group of Duluthians of German extraction objected to the marriage of "the ancient and much married" Peter Arimond, a seventy-one-year-old five-time widower, to a twenty-four-year-old German immigrant named Louise, who lived in St. Paul. It would take beer made with pure Lake Superior water to calm a raging mob.

Arimond, also a native of Germany, had arrived in Duluth in 1867 with his thirty-four-year-old wife, Margaret, and six children between the ages of one and fifteen. He began working as a stone mason and plasterer and they settled in at 120 Tenth Avenue East, just two blocks east of Duluth's first brewery. Margaret died by 1875, when the state census lists Arimond as a widower, as does the 1880 national census. It is unclear whether Margaret was his first wife or the mother of all six children, and research uncovered no information about his other four marriages.

But in 1884, someone in Duluth believed that those marriages didn't end well. The day before the wedding, Louise received an anonymous letter suggesting that Arimond had caused the deaths of his previous wives. She abruptly packed and tried to return to St. Paul, but Arimond caught up with her at the railway station and persuaded her to stay. They were married the next day.

But that night about fifty men, described as mostly "Dutchmen" (then another term for "German"), stood outside Arimond's home and held an old-fashioned *charivari*. In this old European custom a community's disapproval of a marriage was expressed by a mob making as much noise as it could in order to disrupt the couple's coupling. But rather than the traditional banging of pots and pans, Duluth's Dutchmen shouted as they threw stones, breaking doors and windows. Arimond told the newspaper that it was as if "all the devils of hell have broken loose and come on earth for the special purpose of making trouble for me."

Arimond asked what he could do to make them go away, and they shouted "Beer!" More precisely, they wanted five dollars so they could purchase some of the beer. And not just any beer, but specifically the beer Mike Fink's crew was cooking up at the Lake Superior Brewery. Arimond told the crowd he would order two kegs from Fink and have it sent to the mob the next day if they would just "leave him alone in his glory." The crowd countered, demanding five kegs. Arimond said no. The group spokesman then demanded, "Five kegs of beer, or down comes the house!" Arimond gave in.

The crowd dispersed, but the next day Arimond told Fink to delay the beer delivery until the mob had paid for the damages to his house. Unable to retrieve their beer, the crowd returned to Arimond's home and raised "a bigger racket than before." Fink's men rushed two large kegs of beer to the scene and the crowd dispersed.

Peter and Louise moved to Anaheim, California, in 1890 for Arimond's health. He was eighty-nine when he died suddenly in 1902 on his way home to Louise from the post office.

PIONEER BREWERIES AT THE HEAD OF THE LAKES

DULUTH:

LUCE/BUSCH BREWERY (1859–1866)

ALSO CALLED: J. G. Busch & Co., Duluth's pioneer brewery

LOCATION: Washington Ave. & 1st St.

OWNER(S): Sidney Luce, August Busch

LESSEE(S): Possibly leased to Dietrich Schutte and Henry Miller, ca. 1865

DECKER BREWERY (1866–1875)

ALSO CALLED: Vermillion Brewery

LOCATION: Washington Ave. & 1st St.

OWNER(S): Nicolas Decker

LESSEE(S): Possibly leased to Alexander Schutz and Henry F. Miller, 1870–1872

M. FINK BREWERY (1877–1881)

ALSO CALLED: Washington Avenue Brewery

LOCATION: Washington Ave. & 1st St.

OWNER(S): Mary Decker

LESSEE(S): Michael Fink

DECKER BROS. BREWERY (1882–1884)

LOCATION: Washington Ave. & 1st St.

OWNER(S): Nicholas Jr. & Benjamin Decker

W. FRANKE & CO. (1884–1885)

LOCATION: Washington Ave. & 1st St.

LESSEE(S): William Franke

GUSTAV KIENE BREWERY (1869–1876)

ALSO CALLED: Point Brewery

LOCATION: 2400 Minnesota Ave.

OWNER(S): Gustav Kiene

KREIMER BROS. BREWERY (1872–1874)

ALSO CALLED: Western Brewery

LOCATION: 4th St. & 12th Ave. W.

OWNER(S): August & Paul Kreimer (1872–1874); Charles D. Kreimer (1875–c. 1881; inactive)

LESSEE(S): Camahl & Busse (1874; owners' first names unknown; produced no beer); Fink Brewery (1875; Michael Fink, prop.; produced no beer)

M. FINK & COMPANY'S LAKE SUPERIOR BREWERY (1881–1885)

LOCATION: 528–540 E. Superior St.

OWNER(S): Michael Fink (1881–1885); M. Fink & August Fitger (1882–1885)

SUPERIOR:

LOUIS KIICHLI BREWERY (1859–1869)

ALSO CALLED: Klein & Kiichli, Superior City Brewery

LOCATION: 346 E. 2nd St (1859–1861); 6th Ave. & 3rd St. (1861–1869)

OWNER(S): Louis Kiichli; Jacob Klein (1866–1869)

KLEIN & DECEMVAL BREWERY (1870–1875)

ALSO CALLED: Superior City Brewery

LOCATION: 6th Ave. & 3rd St.

OWNER(S): Jacob Klein & Victor Decemval

SHIELS & SIZER BREWERY (ca. 1865–1872)

ALSO CALLED: Nemadji Brewery

LOCATION: 31st Ave. & 2nd St.

OWNER(S): Thomas Shiels & Henry S. Sizer

LESSEE(S): John Walbourne (1872)

> **SEE MAP FACING PAGE 1 FOR BREWERY LOCATIONS**

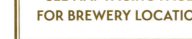

"providing for the indiscriminate transfer of liquor licenses." When the ordinance failed, he told the newspaper he "won't vote with any of the other aldermen after this when they introduce ordinances."

Fink's woes continued into 1885. In January he found himself embroiled in two lawsuits and seemed to be picking petty arguments with his fellow aldermen and making unnecessary objections, prolonging meetings. Yet in February the newspaper predicted Fink, according to his fellow aldermen, would run for mayor that April as the "poor man's" candidate. Instead, in March he announced he intended to retain his alderman seat.

Fink faced popular young newcomer F. B. Dougherty in a battle the newspaper described as "a hard one," yet Dougherty prevailed by a substantial margin, 308 to 161. Fink did not take it well. When Mayor Ensign and the Common Council met for the final time in April 1885, Fink didn't bother to show up. He told the *Tribune* that "the time was when the council elected the chief of police; now the chief of police elects the council." The newspaper didn't use phonetic spelling to mock Fink. Apparently now that Fink was down for the count, Mitchell had no appetite to kick him. On the tenth the *Tribune* politely reported that Fink told them "he is now out of politics, and he's glad of it."

He was also out of the beer business. In March the *Tribune* had made the following announcement: "Yesterday M. Fink sold his interest in the Lake Superior Brewery to Mr. Anneke, of Milwaukee, lately bookkeeper of Schlitz & Co., in that city. It is not expected Mr. Fink will leave Duluth." Unbeknownst to most of Duluth, back in 1882 Fink had sold half of the brewery to his new brewer. Together the bookkeeper and brewer—Percy Anneke and August Fitger—developed a company that would dominate the brewing industry in Duluth, Superior, and throughout the region for nearly the next ninety years.

THE RISE OF THE
MAJOR BREWERIES

DESPITE HIS APPARENT SUCCESS SELLING BEER, Michael Fink must have been financially stressed by the spring of 1883. His new brewery was nearly a year old, yet the much-touted brick building still had not been faced with bricks. Between the spring of 1881 and fall of 1882 Fink had built the brewery and two icehouses and, on November 11, 1882, hired August Fitger as his brewmaster. Perhaps Fink had severely over-extended his financing, or perhaps Fink was just trying to get out of the brewing industry. Whatever the case, only six months after Fink hired Fitger, the new brewer purchased half of Fink's Lake Superior Brewery for $18,000. What's more, the deal involved a third party, Fitger's friend Percy Anneke, a salesman for Milwaukee bottling company Voechting, Shape & Co. Anneke agreed to buy the other half when he had enough money, and in the spring of 1885 he was ready to invest.

FITGER'S FORMS (1885–1890)

Carl George August Fitger was seventeen years old when he left his hometown of Delmenhorst in Germany's Lower Saxony region to emigrate to the U.S. in 1871. Fitger—who went by his third name—began his new life in America at his sister Elfrieda's home in Kiel, Wisconsin, about sixty-five miles north of Milwaukee. After trying his hand in the lumber business, in 1874 he moved to Milwaukee and took a job with the Phillip Best Brewing Company. He left Milwaukee in 1876 for Munich, Germany, where he attended the Weihenstephan Brewing School. After apprenticing in Germany, he returned to Milwaukee in 1879 to work as the "first brewer" at Best's Southside Brewery. Despite reports, Mike Fink likely didn't find his "Milwaukee brewer" in Milwaukee. In 1880 Fitger was in St. Louis, Missouri, working in the Samuel Wainwright & Co. Brewery's

Friends described Fitger & Co. cofounder Percy Anneke as a shrewd businessman, civically active, extremely generous, and having a keen interest in politics. That regard for politics came from his parents—not just their opinions, but their actions as well.

Anneke's mother, Mathilde Giesler, was born into a successful mining family in Westfalia, now part of Germany, in 1817. She received an excellent education, but her father lost the family fortune. Mathilde married a wine merchant who promised to help with the family's finances. But he drank as much wine as he sold, and they divorced in 1841.

A single mother of two, Mathilde supported her family writing for newspapers. Biographer Joe Horsley reports she also attended "liberal Rhineland debate clubs...where she discussed ideas with other dissidents." There she met Friedrich "Fritz" Anneke, an idealistic Prussian artillery officer. In 1846 his "democratic activities" earned him a dishonorable discharge. The Annekes moved to Cologne, where Fritz joined his friends Karl Marx and Friedrich Engels as leaders of the Communist movement. There he and Mathilde founded the "pro-working class" newspaper *Neue Kölnische Zeitung*. Mathilde also published *Frauen-Zeitung*, described by Horsley as "the first feminist women's newspaper in Germany."

As founder of the Cologne Workers Organization, Fritz spent six months in jail for political crimes. Upon his release Fritz joined the democratic rebels as an artillery officer in the German Revolution of 1848. Horsley reports that Mathilde, "a skilled horsewoman, followed [Fritz] into battle as his orderly and mounted courier." When the revolution was crushed, the Annekes fled to America with thousands of other Germans who became known as Forty-Eighters. Their family now included infant Friedrich, born while his father sat in prison, and Mathilde was pregnant with Percy. It does not appear that Mathilde's children from her first marriage, Alfred and Fanny, made the leap to America. The Annekes landed in Milwaukee, where Percy was born, and blended into its large German population. Mathilde delivered a series of lectures and wrote for German-language newspapers before starting the *German Woman's Newspaper*. She continued the paper after the family moved to Newark, New Jersey, where Fritz started the city's first daily German-language newspaper. Along the way they had three more children, twins Irla and Herta and another child who died in infancy.

FRITZ ANNEKE, , cA. 1861. [PUBLIC DOMAIN]

MATHILDE ANNEKE, , cA. 1835. [PUBLIC DOMAIN]

Mathilde Anneke stopped publishing her newspaper in 1858 after smallpox killed Friedrich and Irla. Two years later, Mathilde and Fritz separated but remained close. Fritz went to Italy to fight in the Italian Revolution, but ended up working as a war correspondent. Mathilde, Percy, and Herta returned to Milwaukee to live with poet Mary Booth, wife of noted abolitionist Sherman Booth. Mathilde and Mary Booth shared the next six years together, raising their children in what was then referred to as a "Boston marriage"—two women living together financially independent of men in a relationship that "may involve both physical and emotional intimacy." Fritz had found his way to Switzerland by 1860, and at his urging Mathilde, Mary Booth, and their children joined him in Zurich. Six months later Fritz returned to America to fight another war, leaving the others behind to join the Union Army as a full colonel.

Booth returned to the U.S. in 1864 and died the following April of heart disease. By then Mathilde and her children had already spent five months living in Paris with a young teacher named Cecilie Kapp. They all moved to the U.S. in 1865, and Kapp established a German-language girls school later called the Milwaukee Academy for Young Ladies. She left two years later to teach at Vassar; Mathilde kept the school running for eight more years.

Fritz, meanwhile, had again been dishonorably discharged from the army in 1863—perhaps, Horsely suggests, because he carried on a same-sex relationship of his own. He then bounced around the Midwest before moving in with Mathilde after Kapp left. In 1872 he visited Chicago, trying to cash in on the rebuilding that followed the Great Chicago Fire. He fell into a partially built building foundation, landed on his head, and later died.

Mathilde lived until November 1884. Her obituary in the *Milwaukee Herald* praised her while suggesting that the world (and the notice's author) was not quite ready for women like Mathilde Anneke: "She was one of the most cultivated, highly gifted and noblest women, although the world, we should hope, will never recognize her unpractical ideas with regard to women's equality." Someone else did take note of those "unpractical" ideas about feminism, as Susan B. Anthony once said, "It was through the influence of a German woman, Madame Mathilde Franzika Anneke, that I became a suffragist." In 1988 Germany honored Mathilde Anneke with a postage stamp.

malt house. He had worked his way up to brewer by 1882 when Fink lured him to Duluth.

Percy Shelley Anneke, named by his feminist mother for the British poet, was born in Milwaukee in 1850 after his parents fled the German revolution of 1848 (see "Percy Anneke's Radical Roots," page 28). In 1865 fifteen-year-old Anneke began attending Milwaukee's Spencerian Business College. The following year he accepted the first of a series of teller and bookkeeping jobs at various firms, including R. G. & Dun Co., known today as Dun & Bradstreet. In 1880 he began work for Voechting, Shape & Co., who bottled the beer brewed by Milwaukee's Joseph Schlitz Brewing Co. Anneke's work as a traveling agent took him outside of Milwaukee.

Fitger and Anneke, it has been long assumed, met in Milwaukee, but that may not be the case. Until 1880 Anneke had no association with the brewing industry, and by the time he went to work for Voechting, Fitger had moved to St. Louis. The pair could just as easily have met in St. Louis as Milwaukee, perhaps more so. Anneke's work may have brought him to St. Louis, and an aunt lived in St. Louis, as did his future wife. Wherever they met, by the fall of 1882 Fitger and Anneke trusted each other enough to enter into a very speculative business agreement. Duluth brewing historian Coopen Johnson records that the 1883 Fitger-Anneke agreement was made with a handshake and not actually written and signed until 1892.

While Fitger began quietly making beer for Fink, Anneke divided his time traveling for the bottling company and taking care of his aging and ailing mother, who died on November 25, 1884. After her estate was settled, Anneke settled with Fink. The brewing outfit then became known as the A. Fitger & Co. Lake Superior Brewery.

August Fitger and Percy Anneke had a very busy 1885. Anneke started the year in St. Louis, where on January 15 he married twenty-nine-year-old German immigrant Lydia

Spaeter before the pair moved to Duluth. In September Fitger traveled to Sheboygan and wed twenty-four-year-old Clara Kirst. A month later Lydia and Percy Anneke welcomed a son, Marcel.

Marcel Anneke, his parents, and Clara Fitger weren't the only new arrivals in Duluth that year. The population would rise to over eighteen thousand in 1885, and Fitger and Anneke had a monopoly on locally made beer at the Head of the Lakes. Their first move to increase sales relied on Anneke's experience with Voechting: bottled beer.

In the 1870s Anheuser-Busch popularized bottled beer for home consumption—it stayed fresh longer and, unlike the traditional galvenized pail (or "growler"), bottles didn't spill on the way home from the brewery. More and more breweries began bottling. Bottling became so important to a brewery's success that Anneke's former boss, Christian Voechting, became the president of the Joseph Schlitz Brewing Co. the same year Anneke left for Duluth.

Johnson reports that bottling came with unique challenges. Because of complicated tax laws, beer could not be

A. FITGER & CO. LAKE SUPERIOR BREWERY EMPLOYEES, CA. 1889.
[C&R JOHNSON COLLECTION]

TOP: THE A. FITGER & CO. LAKE SUPERIOR BREWERY, CA. 1890, SHOWING THE 1881 BREWERY (LEFT) AND 1886 STOCK HOUSE (RIGHT).

BOTTOM: THE FIRST NEWSPAPER AD FOR FITGER'S BOTTLED BEER, NOVEMBER 2, 1885.

[C&R JOHNSON COLLECTION]

bottled "anywhere on the brewery or warehouse premises." So to begin bottling their beer, Fitger and Anneke first built a temporary bottling facility. After waiting six months for their beer to age they rolled tax-stamped kegs from the brewery over Superior Street, then turned around and rolled them back across Superior Street and into the bottling works, satisfying the law's mandate that the beer be carried over "a public highway." After that the bottles were filled, pasteurized, corked, and packed into wooden boxes.

The Lake Superior Brewery began selling bottled beer in November 1885. The brewery ran a classified ad to assure beer lovers that they did not use rubber stoppers in their bottles, which was "injurious to beer." Like other brewers, Fitger & Co. called their bottled beer an "Export Beer," which then meant it was pasteurized for longer shelf life—and therefore could be shipped or "exported" to customers farther away. Their first advertisement boasted that the beer had been "brewed especially for bottling purposes" and was so wholesome and palatable they recommended it for invalids. They promised to deliver twelve- or twenty-four-bottle cases of quarts or pints throughout Duluth.

The brewery had about eight thousand more potential customers to ship their export beer to in 1886, when the Fitgers and Annekes rented houses side by side at 613 and 627 East Superior Street, across the street from their brewing operation.

The year began with the election of Republican John B. Sutphin as mayor of the Village of Duluth. Sutphin, a New Jersey native of German extraction, came to Duluth in 1868 and eventually established a successful meat-packing business located along the Minnesota Slip, near today's Sutphin Street in the Canal Park Business Disctrict. The *Duluth Daily Tribune* reported on the celebration that followed Sutphin's victory: "Jay W. Anderson, H. C. Kendall, Percy Anneke, August Fitger, with the mayor-elect and others, early in the evening hired a band and carriage and drove to Rice's Point, where everybody was serenaded and the visitors cheered lustily."

Fitger and Anneke had both joined the Kitchi Gammi Club and would also later become members of the Duluth Boat Club and Northland Country Club. And, like all good German-Americans, they belonged to the city's Turnverein Society, which celebrated fitness and German culture. Both shrewd businessmen, they knew making the right connections was as important as making the best beer—and theirs had already gained an excellent reputation. In early September one local newspaper ran a story that read more like a sales pitch than objective journalism:

> A. Fitger & Co. have rendered proof that lager beer can be manufactured in Duluth as well as anywhere else. They employ only skilled brewers. Their beer vaults are the finest in the country, and their storage capacity is so large that no beer is put on the market until it is well aged. A. Fitger & Co. uses the finest material, Minnesota barley, *the best in the world*, [and] Washington Territory and Bohemian hops. Every nickel spent for outside beer counts against the growth of Duluth.

Eighteen thousand people lived in the Village of Duluth in the summer of 1885, the year August Fitger and Percy Anneke's friend and fellow native German John B. Sutphin was elected mayor. Eight thousand more would arrive over the next year. By the end of 1886 Duluth had enough money to pay off its debts, and in 1887 state legislation reinstating Duluth's city status passed on March 2, and the Zenith City was once again a city.

Duluthians retained Sutphin as their chief executive, making him the last mayor of the Village of Duluth and first mayor of the second City of Duluth. He served through 1890, a period of considerable population growth and physical expansion. During Sutphin's administration, historians wrote, "the city enjoyed much prosperity."

Housing developed above the business district from Point of Rocks to the border at Chester Creek, filling in the empty space below the crest of the hillside. Endion Township became a Duluth neighborhood, stretching the Zenith City's eastern border to Twenty-First Avenue East. The city's western border remained at Thirty-Third Avenue West, the border with Oneota Township. In 1889 the Village of Park Point rejoined the city.

New "streetcar suburbs" began growing at the outskirts. To the north Hunter's Park and Woodland developed along Woodland Avenue. Kenwood, Duluth Heights, and Piedmont Heights appeared above the hillside crest. East of the city, New London at Fortieth Avenue East had become Lakeside, and east of that Lester Park filled the gap between Fifty-Third Avenue East and the Lester River.

As industry continued to develop west of Point of Rocks, immigrant populations began filling up the West End, where unskilled laborers could walk to work to the mills, elevators, docks, and warehouses. In 1888 Oneota Township officials and a group of developers incorporated the Village of West Duluth, which promised to be the "Pittsburgh of the Northwest." They lured several steel-fabricating firms to the new community. More immigrant labor followed the steel industry to West Duluth.

Superior didn't enjoy the same level of success Duluth had during the 1880s. By 1887, when Duluth's population soared past 27,000, fewer than 3,500 people called Superior City home—but they had new neighbors.

In 1883 General John H. Hammond and Robert Belknap formed the Land and River Improvement Company and began developing the adjacent Village of West Superior. (Hammond's grandson and namesake, a music producer and civil-rights activist, is credited for discovering Billie Holiday, Aretha Franklin, Bruce Springsteen, and native Duluthian Bob Dylan.)

As the St. Louis River's shore became crowded with industry along its Duluth banks, Hammond lured new ventures to the Superior side, and soon West Superior hummed with its own coal docks, grain elevators, lumber and flour mills, and other improvements made possible by Hammond and Belknap. On March 25, 1889, the Village of Superior (aka Superior City) and the Village of West Superior joined to become the City of Superior. The following year's census recorded its population at 11,983 and the new city had a new nickname: "The Eye of the Northwest," coined by Superior statistician and historian Frank A. Flower. (It didn't catch on.)

In the early 1890s, the Merritt family of West Duluth opened the Mesabi Iron Range, and giant ore docks were built first in the Superior neighborhood of Allouez and later at the foot of Thirty-Third Avenue West in West Duluth. Meanwhile, in 1891 the Zenith City had added the neighborhoods of Duluth Heights, Piedmont Heights, Kenwood, Hunter's Park, and Woodland; Lakeside and Lester Park, briefly the City of Lakeside, joined January 1, 1893.

Another financial panic struck the nation in 1893, and the Village of West Duluth fared poorly. The panic closed most of the metal manufacturers, and to save the village it merged with Duluth. Over the next three years Bayview Heights and the land that would become the neighborhoods of Riverside, Smithville, Morgan Park, Gary, and New Duluth—essentially all the land between old Oneota and Fond du Lac—became part of Duluth. Fond du Lac itself came back into the fold in 1895. Fortunately, Duluth was soon back on its feet, and by the turn of the century nearly all of the shuttered factories had reopened.

As the century came to a close, nearly 50,000 people lived in Duluth. Meanwhile, Superior's population had grown to over 31,091 people, making it the second largest city in Wisconsin. The two communities grew in stride with one another, as the same industries served both cities. Over the next ten years 25,000 more people would move to Duluth, 10,000 more to Superior.

The brewery grew right along with Duluth. That year Fitger and Anneke broke ground on a stock house with enough room to comply with bottling laws. Johnson describes the building as a two-story structure with a gabled roof, forty by seventy feet. The architect, Chicago's Fred Wolfe, used local bluestone called "Lake Superior basalt" on the building's façade.

Once the stock house was completed, Fitger altered his brewing process. He used the 1881 building to make the wort (a liquid made from mashed hops, essentially unfermented

beer), but moved the brewing kettles to the stock house, where the beer was brewed and aged. The space created at the former brewing facility became the bottling department—since wort contains no alcohol, beer could be bottled under the same facility that produced the wort.

By September the Lake Superior Brewery was running out of the storage space the *Tribune* had celebrated just weeks earlier. On the seventeenth Fitger and Anneke announced they would build a three-story storage facility, but instead built a two-story facility with a large basement. The new building, also faced with basalt, would double the brewery's storage capacity.

At the St. Louis County Agricultural Fair that October, the *Tribune* gushed over the brewery's display—and its beer: "A. Fitger & Co.'s brewery exhibit...is both unique and interesting; it consists of an enormous vat encircled by a wreath of barley, and surrounded by pyramids of varnished kegs, ornamented by bottles of the famous beer of Fitger & Co. Some cases of bottled beer also grace the front of the exhibit and tantalize the passer by who is cognizant of its excellence and purity."

As Duluth regained its city status in 1887 due in part to its expanding population, the Fitger and Anneke families were themselves expanding. Margaret Anneke joined her brother Marcel and parents in January, and on June 28 Clara Fitger gave birth to Wilhelmina, called Molly. The following year Fitger built a small house at 119 Seventh Avenue East where his in-laws joined him and Clara and newborn Molly.

Work at the brewery continued to progress as Fitger and Anneke worked to keep up with the city's growing population. The brewery added a dedicated bottling facility designed by W. Griesser—the brewery needed more room in the 1881 facility to make more wort. In 1889 Fitger and Anneke hired J. S. Pearce to build a stable and barns behind the brewing facilities: more business meant more deliveries, which meant more wagons to haul more beer and more horses to pull the wagons.

As the decade came to an end, there seemed to be no end to Duluth's, or the brewery's, continued success. Outside of beer brought in from out of town, Fitger and Anneke still enjoyed no local competition in Duluth. In 1887 the *Tribune* had reported that Milwaukee's Joseph Schlitz Brewing Co.—essentially Anneke's former employer—had purchased eight lots on Superior Street a block east of Fitgers for "a large brewery." The same article mentioned that brewer John Gund of La Crosse, Wisconsin, intended to visit Duluth to scout sites for a brewing facility. By the end of 1889 neither project came to fruition. Of Minnesota's 101 breweries, only one operated in Duluth. Across the bay in Superior, however, things were beginning to brew.

BREWING RETURNS TO SUPERIOR (1889–1891)

In 1889 the Village of Superior, Wisconsin, merged with the Village of West Superior, established in 1883 by General John Hammond (see "Boom Bust Boom II," page 31). This marriage of the two communities created the City of Superior, with a local population of over thirteen thousand. It also brought brewing back to Duluth's rival across the bay.

The same year, forty-one-year-old Bernard Schwanekamp and his forty-seven-year-old brother-in-law, Joseph

Hennes, spent $16,000 to build a three-story brewery at 215 Hammond Avenue on Conner's Point. They named their operation the West Superior Brewing Company. By the time the brewery opened in 1890, it was one of about 190 making beer in Wisconsin, roughly 40 fewer than 1880, a decrease of nearly 18 percent.

Little is known about Schwanekamp, a native of Hamburg, New York. He spent much of his younger days in Centerville, Wisconsin, where his Prussian parents established a farm. No records indicated where Schwanekamp lived and worked during the 1870s and 1880s, but he was in Houghton, Michigan, in 1876 when he married a local woman, Rosala Scheuerman. Two years earlier, Rosala's sister Elisabeth had married Johan Joseph Hennes.

BERNARD SCHWANEKAMP'S
WEST SUPERIOR BREWING CO.,
PHOTOGRAPHED, CA. 1889.
[ZENITH CITY PRESS]

Hennes, who went by his middle name, had immigrated to the U.S. from Saalhausen, Germany, in 1854. Ten years later he attended business college in Detroit before resettling in Houghton in 1867. There he went to work for his brother Louis, who operated a large mercantile. Joseph eventually became partners in the business and by 1889 was fairly well off. He appears to have never lived in Superior and was likely just a financial partner and business advisor to Schwanekamp. With his mercantile and eight children at home, Hennes had plenty of other matters to keep him busy in Houghton. Schwanekamp and Hennes set up a rather modest operation housed in one three-story, wood-frame building. It had the capacity to brew nine thousand barrels of beer per year but, as brew historian Doug Hoverson notes, "there is no evidence production ever reached that number."

Schwanekamp had barely begun brewing when another beer manufacturer set up shop in Superior because North Dakota became a state on November 2, 1889. By a narrow margin its counties voted to prohibit the sale and manufacture of alcohol. Beginning July 1, 1890, every saloon, distillery, and brewer in North Dakota would be out of business. This included Fargo's Red River Valley Brewing Company, owned by John Klinkert and Louis Rueping. John J. Kraenzlein had established the brewery in 1881, and Klinkert had bought in for half the following year. Two years later, Rueping bought out Kraenzlein. They then built a malt house and competed with Joseph Prokosch's Fargo Brewery until statehood brought an end to both outfits.

In 1865, when he was just sixteen years old, Klinkert had emigrated from Hesse-Darmstadt, Germany, to the U.S. Several years later he returned to Germany to attend the Brewers Academy in Frankfurt. Back in America he found

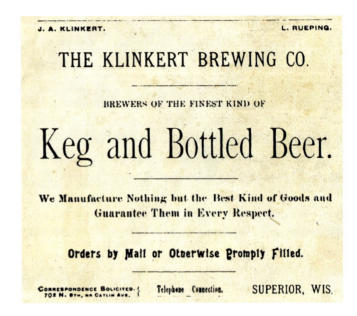

employment in Milwaukee working for a number of breweries, including Phillip Best Brewery, which became Pabst in 1889. He married Emilia Pabst in 1870 and while that sounds like a marriage made in beer heaven, there is no evidence that she belonged to the Milwaukee brewing family.

Seven years later Klinkert invested in Racine, Wisconsin's City Brewery, which became known as Schilling & Klinkert. Schilling left in 1878 and two years later he sold the outfit to his brother Ernst and headed to the Dakota Territory. By the time North Dakota dried up, the Klinkerts found themselves parents to eight children, sons Albert and Ernst and daughters Alice, Louise, Caroline, Lena, Anna (called Molly), and Lilly.

We know less of Louis Rueping. He too was a native of Germany, born in Prussia in 1839. He immigrated to the U.S. in 1854 and by 1880 he was living in Fond du Lac, Wisconsin, working as a leather tanner and, with his wife, Ida, parenting four children. Hoverson reports that the Rueping family also owned a malt house in Fond du Lac, an ideal complement to the brewery business. Censuses indicate Rueping never lived in North Dakota or Superior, and just how Klinkert and Rueping first got together remains a mystery.

When brewing went bust in North Dakota, Rueping was likely aware of Superior's population explosion and that only one brewery served the booming community. Klinkert moved his large family to Superior. Rueping remained in Fond du Lac, tanning hides, making malt, and providing financial support.

Klinkert set up shop at 702 North Eighth Street and boarded nearby at 815 Catlin Avenue. When the brewery opened in 1891, his sons joined in; Albert took on bottling duties and Ernest acted as engineer. Several early descriptions of the facility, estimated to cost $50,000, painted a picture of success. By 1893 it would consist of five buildings powered by an eighty horse-power power plant, including an ice machine that produced thirty-five tons a day. Water was drawn from an artesian well, and the malt came from their malt house in Fargo. Between fifteen and twenty men worked at the plant, producing twenty-five thousand barrels of beer in four varieties—lager for kegs and an export, wiener, and "special stock" in bottles. (Wiener beer is an amber lager, darker, heavier, and less hoppy than a pilsner.)

Early on the brewery had established "a very large local trade...with the leading families and saloons." An 1892 report in the *Superior Citizen* claimed Klinkert's trade "extends to all cities and towns tributary to Superior, and does a big shipping business in the territory west of Fargo, on the Northern Pacific and Great Northern railroad lines."

In the meantime the West Superior Brewing Company had responded to the competition by expanding, adding

a pair of two-story buildings and increasing the staff to seven. While West Superior remained smaller than Klinkert, Schwanekamp made enough money to not only expand his operation, but also pay off his brother-in-law, who does not appear on company records after 1892.

FITGER'S EXPANDS (1890–1896)

Across the bay, Fitger and Anneke's Lake Superior Brewery continued to grow along with a reborn Duluth while the 1859 brewery Gottlieb Busch built alongside Brewery Creek became a memory. As development continued above the business district, only a portion of Washington Avenue below the brewery remained as a reminder that the streets of Portland once ran north and south. By 1888, Washington Avenue was little more than a forty-five-degree truncation of Seventh Avenue West between First and Superior Streets. The only buildings positioned along the former path of

FITGER'S 1890 BOILER HOUSE.
[C&R JOHNSON COLLECTION]

Washington Avenue were the brewery and the hotel and the home the Deckers had built in the 1860s, and the brewery sat dormant.

It was hardly a shame brewing had stopped at the pioneer facility, as the waters of Brewery Creek were no longer "pure as a mountain stream." With more and more houses going up on the hillside above it, and without a sewer system in place, more and more waste material from humans—and the cattle, chickens, goats, and pigs many kept in their yards—washed into Brewery Creek (and, ultimately, Lake Superior). The brewery's source of beer's most important ingredient—water—had been fouled. In May 1890, the brewery, along with the house and hotel, came down to make room for tenement flats.

A block or so away at the Lake Superior Brewery—where a pipe that stretched out into Lake Superior far from the mouths of polluted creeks provided water for brewing—Fitger and Anneke had a building boom of their own. By then their brewery was, according to an 1890 advertisement, "the largest in the state of Minnesota outside of the Twin Cities." That year they built a boiler house designed by Oliver Traphagen and his new partner, Francis Fitzpatrick.

"It's FITGER'S lager,
Fresh and cool,
That makes us feel so queer,
We'll sing and hop,
We'll never stop,
'Till we run short of beer."

Then Duluth's premier architects, Traphagen & Fitzpatrick designed the majority of Duluth's grand Romanesque buildings faced with brick and sandstone built in Duluth by the dozens between 1885 and 1895.

Fitger & Co. added an engine house at the same time. It generated DC electricity that not only powered the entire brewing operation but, according to Johnson, also carried electricity to the Fitger and Anneke homes before the city had a power grid. The engine house contained a very important device: the first ice machine put to use in a Minnesota brewery.

In 1892 Traphagen & Fitzpatrick delivered to Fitger's plans for a new brewhouse (which contractors completed the following year), Clara Fitger delivered Arnold Kirst Fitger in May, and Lydia Anneke delivered Victor Anneke in December. Marion Fitger was born in 1893, the same year

the Fitger family moved into their home at 629 East First Street, just west of the tenements that replaced the Vermillion House, and the Annekes moved a block west of that to 523 East Second Street. Just a year earlier the book *Pen & Sunlight Sketches of Duluth* contained the following description of Fitger and Anneke's beer-brewing complex:

> The Lake Superior Brewery has developed a reputation for the manufacture of a fine grade of lager beer that has become so popular as to have an enormous demand at all seasons of the year.... The plant covers over 61,000 square feet of ground and is complete in every detail, having the most approved machinery and all the latest discovered conveniences. The buildings are one, two, and three stories in height and are constructed of stone, comprising a brewery proper, stock house, ice house, machine house, boiler house, stables, office, etc. The plant has two very large engines, one being 135 horse power. The ice machine used is the first erected in Minnesota, and has a capacity of 50 tons of ice daily. The brewery has facilities for the manufacture of 25,000 barrels of beer each year, and the bottling department 150,000 bottles of beer each year. Only high grade lager beer is made; a specialty being the Pale Bohemian beer for bottling purposes. Over thirty persons are employed, and six teams are utilized.

Another publication from the same era also had high praise for Fitger's beer: "The Pale Bohemian Export beer brewed and bottled by A. Fitger & Co. has achieved a reputation far beyond the borders of Duluth, while the fact that Fitger's beer is largely used at home where it is best known speaks in flattering terms of its qualities. It is safe to say there is no more delightful beer known than Fitger's and none that is more steadily acquiring greater fame throughout the country." ("Bohemian" was another term for "pilsner.") Things couldn't have been going better for Fitger and Anneke. They had no competition in town, the breweries across the bay couldn't come close to their capacity, and their beer's reputation was growing well beyond the borders of Duluth.

The Lake Superior Brewery even survived the Panic of 1893 without too much trouble, as did Duluth. In 1896, while other businesses struggled, the Lake Superior Brewery again hired Traphagen & Fitzpatrick, this time to design a settling room. That same year competition came to Duluth.

THE A. FITGER & CO. LAKE SUPERIOR BREWERY PHOTOGRAPHED FROM LAKE SUPERIOR IN THE 1890S. [C&R JOHNSON COLLECTION]

THE 1893 FITGER HOUSE. [ZENITH CITY PRESS]

THE 1893 ANNEKE HOUSE. [C&R JOHNSON COLLECTION]

After living rather modestly during the 1880s, as both their brewery and their families began to expand, Percy Anneke and August Fitger each moved into homes in Ashtabula Heights, what was then Duluth's most fashionable neighborhood. A number of pioneers came to Duluth from Ashtabula, Ohio, and during the 1880s and early 1890s many of them built opulent Victorian homes roughly from Second Avenue East to Sixth Avenue East and from First Street to Fourth Street in much of what was originally Portland Township.

August and Clara Fitger built their home technically just outside of Ashtabula Heights at 629 East First Street in 1893. Fitger hired architect Oliver Traphagen, who had designed several of the brewery's buildings in the 1890s, to design a large but relatively modest three-story house on the corner lot. It cost $10,661, or just under $300,000 in today's dollars. Stained-glass windows along the avenue featured hops on the vine, and the library window looked out over Lake Superior and, more importantly to its

first owners, the Fitger's brewing complex. When the Fitgers moved permanently to California in 1928, the house was purchased by Dr. Thomas Shastid, a prolific writer once called "America's forgotten historian of ophthalmology." His 1937 memoir *Tramping to Failure* contained the sketch above, showing the view from the library. The house still stands, but it has been subdivided into nine apartments.

The Fitgers also built a farm with a cottage along the Lester River in Lakewood Township beginning in 1899. Fitger named the farm Elmhurst, a reminder of his boyhood in Delmenhorst, Germany, and later built a summer home along the river. Like the house, Fitger sold the farm to Duluth pioneer George Barnum, namesake of Barnum, Minnesota, when he left Duluth in 1928.

THE 1909 ANNEKE HOUSE ON MINNESOTA POINT. [ZENITH CITY PRESS]

Percy and Lydia Anneke's Ashtabula Heights home stood at 523 East Second Street, but it isn't clear if they built the house or moved into an existing home. In 1908 the health of their son Marcel, born in 1885, prompted the Annekes to build a summer home on Minnesota Point. Marcel suffered from chronic tuberculosis, and the air off Minnesota Point was considered so clear that in 1900 Duluth had become home to the Hay Fever Club of America. So the Annekes built a 2,390-square-foot home with six bedrooms at 4500 Minnesota Avenue, still the southernmost home on Minnesota Point. Sadly, Marcel died in November 1908.

We do not know how much time the Annekes spent in their home on the Point. In 1911 they built another home at 1801 East Second Street, a two-and-a-half-story Craftsman-style house designed by Duluth native Arthur Hanford. Lydia Anneke lived in the house until her death in 1927, and Percy remained there until he died the next year. Both houses the Annekes built in Duluth still stand today.

DULUTH BREWING & MALTING SETS UP SHOP (1895–1899)

Like August Fitger and many others before him and after, Reiner Hoch (pronounced "hoke") also fell into brewing when his parents settled in Milwaukee after emigrating from Prussia, Germany, where he was born in 1852. Two of Hoch's brothers followed the same path, as did Carl Meeske—born in Germany in 1850—and two of Meeske's brothers, Otto and Gustav. When Hoch was twenty-one years old, he and the Meeske brothers tried to start a brewery in Milwaukee that specialized in weiss (wheat) beer. By 1875 Otto and

Gustav had set out on their own, and Hoch and Carl Meeske (pronounced "mess-key") made enough money to purchase another brewing outfit far from the heady competition of Brew City.

Hoch and Meeske moved their families to Marquette on Michigan's Upper Peninsula in 1878, when it was home to copper and iron mines and the center of the nation's timber industry. The pair had purchased George Rublein's Concordia Brewery, and soon after they expanded the operation by purchasing the J. J. Kohl & Co. Brewery in Negaunee, eleven miles west. They renamed both breweries Meeske & Hoch and

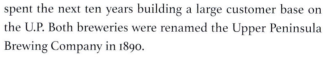

spent the next ten years building a large customer base on the U.P. Both breweries were renamed the Upper Peninsula Brewing Company in 1890.

Four years later Hoch & Meeske put the finishing touches on a new brewing facility in Marquette, a project they had begun in 1887. At its center was a four-story brewhouse designed to look like a castle. In 1896 they closed the Negaunee facility, likely due to both the panic and a shrinking customer base. In the early 1880s the timber industry began moving into northeastern Minnesota, centered on Duluth. Minnesota's Vermilion Iron Range opened in 1883, and the Mesabi Range opened less than ten years later. By the mid-1890s, despite the national depression, the growth of Duluth and its surrounding communities had created a much larger market than could be found in northern Michigan. Hoch and Meeske set their sights on the Zenith City.

LEFT: DULUTH BREWING & MALTING CO-FOUNDER CHARLES MEESKE, CA. 1905. [ZENITH CITY PRESS]

ABOVE: MEESKE'S BUSINESS PARTNER REINER HOCH, DATE UNKNOWN. HOCH RAN THE DULUTH BREWERY WHILE MEESKE STAYED IN HOUGHTON, MICHIGAN, TO SEE AFTER THEIR UPPER PENINSULA BREWING CO. [R. F. HOCH III COLLECTION]

The *Duluth News Tribune* first announced Hoch and Meeske's plan for a brewery in Duluth in October 1895, when both men—along with renowned Chicago brewery architect August Maritzen—stayed in Duluth's Spalding Hotel while reviewing five potential sites for their new facility. They told local newspapers they would likely employ thirty to thirty-five men. Hoch added, "We have long had an eye on Duluth and believe it to be one of the best brewing points in the country...we will begin work at once and push the brewery to completion."

Hoch moved to Duluth while Meeske remained in Marquette. Hoch would act as president of the Duluth brewery and Meeske its vice president. Meeske assumed the role of president of the Marquette brewery and Hoch its vice president. Capitalists Edward M. Breitung and N. M. Kauff, investors in the Marquette brewery, helped with the financing.

In early November they had settled on a site at Twenty-Ninth Avenue West and Helm Street in Duluth's West End. Maritzen's plans were published in the *News Tribune* on November 10, 1895, showing a brewhouse and malt house. Like the Marquette Brewery, both had castle-like features. Most of the buildings were to be faced with red brick made in West Duluth and brownstone pulled from Chambers Quarry in Fond du Lac. The six-story brewhouse itself would be capable of producing fifty thousand barrels of beer a year— about twice what Fitger's could produce at the time.

The facility, which in the end cost $90,000, would also include an ice-machine house, a boiler house, a cellar house, a wash house, a shipping house, a bottling house, an office building, an ice-storage house, and a stable and barn capable of housing twenty horses, but it would take several years before the entire complex was complete. The proposed malt house would produce 250,000 bushels of malt annually, and employ roughly another thirty men. It would be one of just two Minnesota breweries that made its own malt. The other, St. Paul's Theodore Hamm Brewing Company, was the state's largest brewery. The malt house would not be complete until 1902, but the fact that they planned to make their own malt was evidence that the ambitions of Hoch and Meeske's stretched well beyond the Head of the Lakes.

The investors broke ground on November 21, 1895, after which contractor William Lavanway and his crew set to work building the brewery. Construction was well underway in March when Hoch announced that the new brewery—now called Duluth Brewing & Malting—would open with a brand new copper kettle with a capacity of 125 barrels, allowing the brewery to reach its goal of 50,000 barrels a year by brewing one batch of beer each day of the week, except Sundays. Only the finest ingredients would be used, including water drawn from an artesian well.

While his brewery was under construction, Reiner Hoch was making friends. The *News Tribune* reported that not only did the neighbor children all know him, they lay "in wait for his coming.... When he leaves or approaches the brewery they swarm about him and from the tiniest tot to the boy or girl of six or seven they begin to cry, 'a penny Mr. Hoch?'" Hoch told the reporter he didn't mind, but noted that it was "embarrassing to forget to provide oneself with pennies" and disappoint them.

He made more friends by inviting all of Duluth to visit the plant after an informal dedication on September 9, 1896. They would be given a tour of the brewery and provided lunch, "the choicest of cigars," and samples of the "best beer the company can make." He promised two styles, standard and wiener. The "nourishing" standard or malt beer, he promised, was a "rich and mellow brand, full of vim and bounce...an invigorating tonic splendid for family use." Meanwhile the "favorite" wiener was "Unequalled! Bright! Sparkling! A delightful beverage.... A pale beer with hosts of

friends. A pleasing beverage for the home. A beer that gives universal satisfaction."

The *News Tribune* also heralded the event in an article, writing that "manifold assurance is given of the undoubted success of the Duluth Brewing & Malting Company, and the public waits with eager anticipation the first fruits of the enterprise." The next day a lengthy article not only described the facility, but explained how the entire brewing process would work at the new plant. It was outfitted with the most modern equipment yet devised, including an ice machine that did not make ice but instead fed liquid ammonia through pipes and condensers to keep storage facilities at a steady thirty-six degrees Fahrenheit. More than three thousand people showed up for free food and beer and a tour of the plant by Hoch himself.

DULUTH BREWING & MALTING FACILITIES, CA. 1902, AFTER THE CONSTRUCTION OF THE MALT HOUSE (FAR LEFT) WAS COMPLETED. [PUBLIC DOMAIN]

The brewers of Duluth and Superior didn't just compete with one another, they also had to contend with large, well-known breweries from other cities who established depots and operated tied houses (see page 50) in both communities at Lake Superior's westernmost point.

In the 1860s, when he didn't have enough of his own beer on hand, Superior brewer Louis Kiichli sold beer made in other Wisconsin cities—the breweries were seldom named. In 1870, when the City of Duluth was just a few months old, the *Minnesotian* advertised that saloon-man John Bruchner had "forty kegs of Sheboygan beer" that compared "formadably [*sic*] with the best Milwaukee beer" while dealers Hakes & Co. were selling beer brewed in Chicago. By the end of the summer, merchant Joseph Mannheim had become Duluth's exclusive agent for a Chicago brewery and two in Milwaukee.

As the 1880s began, brewers started bottling beer, and sales became brand specific. William Dambruck's liquor and cigar wholesale operation sold Budweiser all the way from St. Louis—Anheuser-Busch began using refrigerated rail cars shortly after they were introduced in the late 1870s. Local bottlers also started getting in on the actions. Michael Pastoret's Duluth Bottling Works on Lake Avenue was putting up Schlitz from Milwaukee in quart and pint bottles. Jay W. Anderson came to Duluth in 1882 to sell beer made by Milwaukee brewer Phillip Best, predecessor to Pabst. He sold kegs to saloons and hired W. N. Pollock's Zenith Bottling Works to package the beer for the "home trade." (In 1885 he also helped organize Duluth's first professional baseball team.)

Milwaukee's Valentin Blatz Brewing Company (commonly called Val. Blatz) bypassed local agents and built its own branch—essentially a depot—at the corner of Lake Avenue and Railroad Street along the rail line at the base of Minnesota Point. Within a few years it was flanked by depots belonging to Pabst and Miller. In 1889 Blatz constructed the Canal Block at 340 South Lake Avenue, known today as the home of the Green Mill restaurant. The Maine Hotel occupied its entire second floor, and the first floor originally featured five store fronts; one opened to the hotel entrance, another to a restaurant, and the others to three separate saloons—all tied houses that exclusively served Val. Blatz beer.

Many other Duluth tied houses belonged to brewers from Milwaukee, St. Louis, and St. Paul's Theo. Hamm Brewing Co. During this period several Milwaukee breweries—Miller, Pabst, and Val. Blatz—established depots in Superior, as did John Gund Brewing of La Crosse, Wisconsin.

In 1905 Jay Anderson began selling for Hamm's, and that year the St. Paul brewery expanded operations in both Duluth and Superior, building depots and buying hotels and real estate on which to build saloons. Anderson's territory extended west to Grand Rapids, south to Hinckley, and all along Lake Superior's North and South Shores. He told the *Superior Evening Telegram* he remembered that when he first came to the Head of the Lakes, the "Hamm brewing company was my only competitor." A year after Anderson went to work for Hamm's, Duluth and Superior were home to four breweries and another was organizing, and the *Duluth News Tribune* ran full-page ads for Budweiser. Schlitz had begun advertising in the *News Tribune* as well.

By 1910, as the temperance movement picked up steam and the nation marched toward Prohibition, Duluth's Fitger Brewing Co., Duluth Brewing & Malting, and People's Brewery competed with eight outside breweries. In Superior, Northern stood alone against eight foreign brewing agencies—including Fitger's and DB&M. The battle continued in both communities until Prohibition. Following repeal, those same large outside breweries would become even larger, leading to the demise of most of the nation's small regional brewers.

FITGER'S RESPONDS (1896–1900)

Before 1896 had ended, ads declared DB&M was delivering beer to accounts in "Duluth and West Superior and at all the adjacent towns thereto, and on the Iron Ranges." The ads also promised that "you can make no mistake, by drinking the beer of our make" and offered both wiener and standard at two dollars a case in quart or pint bottles. They sold 8,257 barrels of beer in their first four months. Two years after it opened, the brewery expanded, installing fifteen new tanks, five each for fermenting, cleansing, and storage. By then it employed eighteen men. By the end of the century DB&M

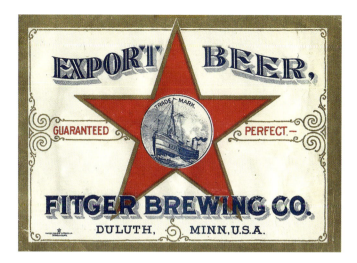

would spend $150,000 on its Duluth facility alone—a nearly $4.5 million investment today.

August Fitger and Percy Anneke responded to the new local competition by expanding their own advertising program. On January 1, 1896, nine months before DB&M filled its first keg, the A. Fitger & Co. Lake Superior Brewery began advertising aggressively in local newspapers. The first ad contained more than a dozen superlatives, as if they couldn't decide on a slogan. They declared the beer "Duluth's regaling and refreshing beverage," "the Zenith product of the Zenith City," "the superior beer of Lake Superior," "the beer that made itself famous," "the beer that stands without peer in the Northwest," "a delicious beverage brewed after the most approved methods," "the American queen of bottled beers; nothing better on the market," and "a standard superb beer of high merit." They further stated that the beer had been "awarded first place in the tastes of the masses" and that there was "no beer more refreshing" and "no beer more nourishing."

The same issue of the paper contained a lengthy description of the brewery and praise for its Pale Bohemian lager. A month before DB&M opened, offering two styles of brew, Fitger & Co. introduced a Bavarian beer, which had "a full body and rich flavor, and is highly recommended as a nourishing beverage. It is liquid bread, and builds up the system."

Since 1885 Fitger & Co. had identified its bottled beer with labels featuring an image of the *City of Duluth*, a wooden steamship launched in 1874, surrounded by a wreath of wheat and hops. In 1898 a redesign placed the image of the ship within a hole in the center of a red star—a symbol that would later come to be identified with Fitger's beer. Coopen Johnson states that Fitger redesigned the label himself.

A year after the new label was introduced, the *News Tribune* reported that Fitger's had remained the largest brewery in Duluth and that "over half of the beer consumed in Duluth is brewed by this firm." The Lake Superior Brewery's success was on display the following year, when it built another stock house—also designed by Traphagen—in order to keep up with demand. That July Fitger's alma mater, Germany's Weihenstephan Brewing School, awarded him a medal for his twenty years of experience in the brewing industry. The *News Tribune* reported that it was the first time the medal had been given to an American.

LEFT: A NEW LABEL DESIGN FOR A. FITGER & CO. WAS INTRODUCED IN 1898. THE LABEL SHOWN IS FROM 1905, AFTER THE COMPANY'S NAME WAS CHANGED TO FITGER BREWING CO.
[K. MALZ COLLECTION]

RIGHT: THE SKETCH FOR THE LABEL DESIGN IS THOUGHT TO BE THE WORK OF AUGUST FITGER HIMSELF.
[FITGER'S COMPLEX]

IRON RANGE BREWING ASSOCIATION LABEL, CA. 1898.
[K. MALZ COLLECTION]

IRON RANGE BREWING ASSOCIATION LABEL, CA. 1905.
[K. MALZ COLLECTION]

After Michael Fink sold his brewery in 1885, he remained "retired" until becoming a health inspector in 1888. In October 1891, newspapers announced he had purchased five acres of land on the Vermilion Iron Range intending to build a brewery. Investors included his wife, Cattie, and majority stockholder Philip M. Graff, a lumber baron. Charlie "Spike" Unden, nephew of pioneer Duluth brewer Nick Decker Sr., joined Fink in Tower, Minnesota, to make beer. Brewing historian Doug Hoverson reports that Fink's operation found itself on unstable financial footing almost from the start, and after just two years, "sold the brewery to a group of investors from Duluth." Fink returned to Duluth and set up a farm on Maple Grove Road. He died in 1899 of tuberculosis, the same disease that killed Decker. Fink's obituary mentioned that he had "scores of old friends, and many expressions of regret were heard yesterday when the news of his death had spread." Unden began working as a brewer for A. Fitger & Co. in 1895 and remained there until retiring in 1937.

The investors reorganized the operation as the Iron Range Brewing Co. A few years later ownership changed hands again. The *Duluth News Tribune* reported in 1897 that Samuel Owens, George Hunter, and William H. McQuade—all Tower residents—purchased the brewery and reorganized it as the Iron Range Brewing Association. Its first bottled beer was a pilsner. While the brewery bottled and shipped beer throughout the Iron Range, it remained small—in 1904 the operation employed just four men. Reports indicate the brewery could produce about three thousand barrels a year. The brewery later labeled its beer under the name Prima. Reports indicate that when Prohibition became law, the brewery briefly made a cereal beverage called Iron Beer before closing its doors.

In April 1904, Duluth and iron range newspapers announced that investors had organized a "co-op brewery" for the Mesabi Iron Range. The new brewery hoped to attract the business of half the saloons on the Range, despite fear of opposition from the "large brewing companies whose sales on the range are now enormous." Organizer Albert Olson previously worked on the Range as a sales agent for Duluth's A. Fitger & Co. The group chose to locate the brewery in Virginia in 1905. Hardware-store owner and three-time Ely mayor Patrick "Paddy" R. Vail, along with A. D. Ellefson, Nels Anderson, and saloon owner Alex Pakkala, incorporated the Virginia Brewing Company and announced the construction of a brewery on the bank of Silver Lake. Later that year the *News Tribune* briefly mentioned that "Virginia is going to have a new brewery and will have an opportunity to drown its sorrows in home made beer."

A POSTCARD OF THE VIRGINIA BREWING COMPANY BREWERY, CA. 1905.
[ZENITH CITY PRESS]

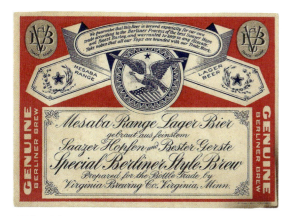

TOP: VIRGINIA BREWING COMPANY (VBC) LABEL, CA. 1905.
CENTER & BOTTOM: THE BREWERY'S "VIRGINIA BUD"
LABELS WERE PRINTED IN BOTH ENGLISH AND GERMAN.
[K. MALZ COLLECTION]

Hoverson reports that Chicago brewery architect Bernard Barthel designed the facility, expected to cost $150,000 including both buildings and equipment. It would have the capacity to produce 25,000 barrels of beer per year, and the new company tapped August Teisse to serve as its first brewmaster.

When Virginia Brewing delivered its first beer Christmas week 1906, it had already opened nine accounts in Virginia and six more in Eveleth. The brewery aggressively pursued sales, as Hoverson notes, building depots in six Iron Range cities within a year after opening and later adding a fifty-thousand-barrel storage facility. Researcher Jay Bago reports the brewery produced Old Bavarian, Old Virginian, Pride of the Range, and a "Berliner style" beer named Mesaba Range Lager Bier. In Virginia, beer drinkers called the lager "Virginia Budweiser" not for its taste but because its label looked nearly identical to that of Anheuser-Busch's flagship brand. The label came in two versions, one in English and the other in German. In 1908 Anheuser-Busch sued the Virginia Brewing Co. for $5,000 and demanded it stop using the design. For reasons unrecorded, Anheuser-Busch dropped the lawsuit. The issue was likely settled out of court.

In January 1912 a drunken customer shot Pakkala dead in his own saloon. Just over a year later Paddy Vail, who had gone on to serve as a state representative and senator, also died. Newspapers reported he had recently visited several health resorts seeking relief from "general derangement" and smallpox had hastened his demise.

The next few years found the brewery embroiled in various lawsuits, most involving liquor licenses and missing money. Several reports indicate that Virginia Brewing Co. closed its doors in 1918 when St. Louis County elected to go dry. However, a label for its Gold Crown Temperance Beer declared the beverage "less than 1/2 of 1%," which meant it was made after January 1920 and the company had briefly attempted to survive Prohibition.

Neither the Iron Range Brewing Association nor the Virginia Brewing Company reopened after the repeal of Prohibition. The Virginia Brewing Company brewery, currently unoccupied, is listed on the National Register of Historic Places. Most of the Iron Range Brewery is gone, but its ice house—the home of Margie's Iron Range Bar from 1955 to 2011—still stands.

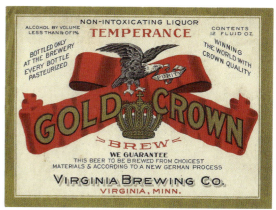

TOP: THE LABEL FOR VBC'S PRIDE OF THE IRON RANGE NOT ONLY INLCUDED AN IMAGE OF THE BREWERY, BUT ALSO ILLUSTRATIONS OF BOTTLES OF ITS MESABI RANGE LAGER (AKA "VIRGINIA BUD") AND OLD VIRGINIAN BRANDS.
BOTTOM: GOLD CROWN, VBC'S NEAR BEER, COULD NOT HELP THE BREWERY SURVIVE PROHIBITION.
[K. MALZ COLLECTION]

THE CELEBRATED SPECIAL BREW LAGER BEER
NORTHERN BREWING CO

NORTHERN BREWING CO.
EMPLOYEES IN FRONT OF
THE BREWERY, CA. 1898.
[P. CLURE COLLECTION]

A RESHUFFLING IN SUPERIOR (1894–1900)

As things came together for Hoch and Meeske and Fitger and Anneke in the Zenith City of the Unsalted Seas, in the Eye of the Northwest Klinkert and Rueping were falling apart. The Panic of '93 had taken a toll, and in July 1894 the *Superior Evening Telegram* mentioned that Louis Rueping had applied for receivership of the firm, implying it stood on very unstable financial footing. Yet the following September the same newspaper ran a lengthy, glowing description of the brewery, calling it "one of Superior's thriving industries." It mentioned that Klinkert operated its own cooperage to make barrels and that "as far as the process of making beer is concerned the Klinkert plant can be surpassed by none in the state." One innovation employed by the brewery was a magnetic fork placed at the feeding end of the grinding mill to catch "nails or pieces of steel wire which may be scattered in the grain."

The story mentioned that the brewery, of course, sourced none but the finest ingredients, including hops and malt from California. Klinkert had also begun to use maize instead of raw corn or rice "for sweetening the beer" and added that maize "gives the beer a lighter color and is much pleasanter to the taste... [and] does away with the use of sweet malt." Klinkert suggested that he enjoyed "large retail patronage" because he never let beer leave his brewery before it had aged six months, boasting that "I have always made it my business to see that no beer leaves my place until it is well seasoned." Shortly thereafter, Klinkert announced his retirement from the brewing business, and for a brief time the brewery was called L. Rueping & Co.

The *Superior Inland Ocean* announced on February 19, 1898, that "the old Klinkert Brewing Company has been entirely reorganized under the name Northern Brewing Company. The incorporators are L. Rueping, Frederick Rueping, Fred J. Rueping and L. A. Erhart. The capital stock is $150,000. Mr. Erhart is the manager and is now living in Superior. He was formerly the mayor of Fond du Lac, Wis." Hoverson suggests Louis Erhart actually resigned his position as mayor to run the new brewing operation in Superior. Besides managing the plant, Erhart also served as the company's secretary and treasurer. There is nothing to indicate Erhart had any experience operating a brewery; in Fond du Lac he had owned and operated L. A. Erhart Cigars. Northern first labeled its bottled beer as Northern Special Brew.

Klinkert had sold his interest in the brewery to Rueping, but news of his retirement was premature. In fact, a month before the old Klinkert Brewery became Northern, he had leased the former Kenyon Woolen Mill at Twenty-Fourth Street and Scranton Avenue and traveled to Chicago to purchase brewing machinery. In May the *Superior Inter-Ocean* ran this description of the repurposed facility, to be named Klinkert Brewing & Malt:

> The old woolen mill building...has been thoroughly remodeled and equipped with the latest machinery for the manufacture of beer. The capacity of the plant at

46 | NATURALLY BREWED, NATURALLY BETTER

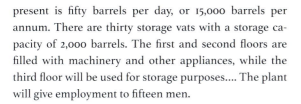

present is fifty barrels per day, or 15,000 barrels per annum. There are thirty storage vats with a storage capacity of 2,000 barrels. The first and second floors are filled with machinery and other appliances, while the third floor will be used for storage purposes.... The plant will give employment to fifteen men.

Klinkert spent $30,000 turning the woolen mill into a brewery. The facility's capacity of just fifteen thousand barrels a year indicates that Klinkert did not intend to compete with the two large Duluth breweries and hoped to carve out enough of the Superior market to feed his family and workforce, which were one and the same. The Klinkert clan made the new brewery a family affair. Ernest and Albert had worked at the old brewery in various capacities, from engineer to bottler to bookkeeper. With the new facility, John managed the plant while Albert served as head brewer, and Ernest as secretary and treasurer while Lillian did the bookkeeping. John Klinkert's brother-in-law Frank Pabst came onboard as vice president. Pabst had been in Fargo with Klinkert and made the move to Superior where before joining the new Klinkert brewery he operated the Exposition Saloon at 1222 Tower Avenue.

As the century came to a close, three breweries operated in Superior and the city's population had grown to over 36,000 people, making it the second-largest city in Wisconsin (but still far behind Milwaukee). Smaller Wisconsin communities had many more breweries, but they did not have two large commercial breweries making beer just across the state line. Fitger & Co., DB&M, and several large breweries in Milwaukee and La Crosse, Wisconsin, all operated saloons in Superior (see "Breweries and the Saloon Business," page 50).

The West Superior Brewing company struggled to keep up with increased competition, and Bernard Schwanekamp could no longer turn to his original financial benefactor, brother-in-law Joseph Hennes. The Houghton businessman, described as "one of the greatest merchants of the copper district," died in October 1897; he had broken his back when he was knocked out of his carriage by a branch as he drove beneath an overhanging tree. He left his widow and eight children $250,000—about $7.3 million today—but little or none, apparently, went to his brother-in-law.

On the first of November 1900, the *Evening Telegram* reported a merger between the West Superior Brewery and Northern Brewing. The article quoted both Schwanekamp and Erhart, who cited several reasons, including a rise in labor cost and the federal tax on beer, which had doubled from one to two dollars a barrel. But the main reason was outside competition and the local saloon men who operated

LEFT: Label for beer bottled by the West Superior Brewing Company in the 1890s.

RIGHT: Labels for beer bottled by the Northern Brewing Company, ca. 1898–1906.

[J. STEINER COLLECTION]

their tied houses. Schwanekamp said that together West Superior and Northern, including its days as the first Klinkert Brewery, had together lost about $65,000 in the previous ten years, including West Superior's entire original investment. They weren't the only Wisconsin breweries that suffered through the Panic of '93. Between 1890 and 1900, more than 20 Wisconsin breweries had closed, dropping the state's beer manufacturers to about 170, a decrease of nearly 12 percent.

Consolidation would reduce labor and management costs. Brewing would move to Northern and the West Superior facility would be used for cold storage. Schwanekamp would focus on expanding business in Superior. Erhart assured the public the operation had plenty of capital to work with, but asked for its help as well, explaining that the company desired "to make the industry a success, but in order to do this it must have the solid support of the citizens and saloon men to accomplish these results." That year Erhart hired John R. Kuehlthau as brewmaster. At about this same time Northern started bottling its flagship beer, Blue Label.

NORTHERN GROWS & KLINKERT CLOSES (SUPERIOR, 1901–1909)

Northern found the support it was seeking from Superior's booming population, and in 1901 announced that a Milwaukee architect was busy at work on plans for a "fine brick and stone building for brewing purposes" that would double Northern's capacity. Newspapers reported that the new, "much larger" brewery along Catlin Avenue would be "modern in every detail." Plans changed the next year, calling for an addition to the brewery and the construction of a large warehouse.

The brewery promised its revamped facility would be "the best in this section of the country." It could produce 25,000 barrels a year and would employ thirty-five men. The *News Tribune* reported that while Northern had a sales branch in Fond du Lac, Wisconsin, and its beer was sold from southern Wisconsin to western Minnesota, the "major portion of the product of the brewery is consumed in Superior."

With the expanded plant, the old West Superior Brewing Company's Hammond Avenue complex was no longer needed for storage. In 1902 Northern sold it to National

Boiler Works, which refit the facility to make and repair boilers. (National later became Whitney Boiler works; today the site is home to Allstate Peterbilt of Superior.)

Despite the bigger brewery, Northern couldn't keep up with demand. The next year it grew again, adding a new, five-story brick brew-and-mill house and a three-story malt house, with a corner tower, on the site of the old bottling house. When complete, the new facility stretched 510 feet along Eighth Street and 160 feet along Caitlin Avenue. Its owners boasted that it would be capable of producing 100,000 barrels a year and would likely employ sixty men when operating at its peak. (Other reports put the brewery's annual capacity at 20,000 barrels). The brewery said it had invested $700,000. In the end, the brewhouse stood four stories high and the malt house was never built.

Within three years market growth required a new storehouse and another addition. The firm also purchased property for a new bottling works along Eighth Street, but construction was delayed for several years. When it was complete, the brewery installed glass-lined storage tanks purchased from Anheuser-Busch.

Besides its equipment, Northern invested in real estate, buying up Superior properties "suitable for saloon purposes" for its own tied houses. Beginning in 1906 the company went on a spending spree, buying up Superior hotels and saloons and building even more saloons. By 1909 Northern owned so much real estate it had become Superior's largest depositor of property tax.

As Northern expanded its size and market, Klinkert Brewing & Malt appeared content to stay small and local. Both the business and the family took a hit in April 1904 when Albert unexpectedly died at thirty-two years of age.

The brewery remained a true family business, as daughters Juliette and Molly and son Adam began working for the brewery, and they all lived in a house next door. Frank Pabst, while still serving as the brewery's vice president, had moved to Montgomery, Alabama, to work as brewmaster for the Montgomery Brewing Company.

While his children helped run his business, in 1905 John Klinkert began having trouble with the local constabulary. That April he was charged with selling liquor to minors, specifically "one eighth of a keg of beer for $1 to six boys whose ages range from 14 to 17 years." Klinkert pleaded guilty and paid a $25 fine.

The next year Klinkert purchased the property and buildings he had been leasing since 1898, planning to increase the plant's capacity, but he couldn't keep out of trouble. In January 1907 Klinkert was again charged with providing liquor to a minor, even though the keeper of one of

LITHOGRAPHIC POSTCARD OF SUPERIOR'S NORTHERN BREWING COMPANY, CA. 1905. [HARTEL FAMILY COLLECTION]

American saloons prior to Prohibition were often unclean and unsavory places. While some saloons, particularly those within upscale hotels, could be rather posh affairs adorned with expensive furnishings and artwork, most were much more modest, working-class affairs housed in poorer sections of a city.

Since most communities banned women from saloons, men didn't feel the need to be on their best behavior. They cursed, and fought, and spit—chewing tobacco was popular, and spittoons were everywhere. At the turn of the century many saloons installed long, trough-like spittoons along the bottom of the bar, some with running water. Patrons often used them as urinals.

Duluth allowed women in saloons until 1897, but they had to inconspicuously enter through a side door, as unescorted women in saloons were often assumed to be prostitutes. It also provided direct access to the back room to purchase beer or liquor and take it home. Some stayed and socialized, but did not enter the bar room, where they were generally unwelcome. After the law changed, women found in saloons faced a fine of up to $100 or ninety days in jail.

Since much of their product was sold in saloons, brewers found owning saloons quite lucrative. Nearly every brewery had its own attached "brewery saloon" for retail sales, and most also built or purchased saloons throughout their sales territory. Until laws changed, an agent working for the brewery purchased the liquor license, and a saloonkeeper was brought in to operate

the establishment, often as brewery employee. These were called "tied houses."

Independent saloon owners could find themselves tied to a brewery as well. Some entered agreements with breweries that provided a deep discount but demanded the saloon sell no other brand. If patrons didn't like the beer, the saloon had little recourse. Those saloons that remained truly independent paid higher wholesale prices for beer than did tied houses.

In 1902 nearly half of Duluth's 164 saloons operated as tied houses. That June the *Duluth News Tribune* reported that the city had denied liquor licenses to agents of breweries in an attempt to "prevent breweries from owning saloons to the detriment of the independent saloon man who has his money invested in his business." A measure ruling that only those who owned a liquor license could operate a saloon failed in council.

Duluth's liquor license issue came to a head in 1908. Republican Roland D. Haven, who ran an antisaloon campaign, won the mayor's seat by defeating Emil A. Tessman, the choice of the "saloon men of Duluth." Soon thereafter a study revealed that a dozen brewery agents owned half of Duluth's saloon licenses. To end this "monopoly" Duluth passed an ordinance declaring that "no liquor licenses shall be granted to employees or agents of any brewery." It had little effect. While saloonkeepers purchased their own liquor licenses, breweries often covered the fee and maintained ownership of the facility and its furnishings. The saloonkeeper leased everything

and owned nothing more than the license and the clothes on his back, thus remaining obligated to serve only the brewery's beer.

In Superior, breweries could still buy liquor licenses, and breweries in Milwaukee, St. Louis, St. Paul, and Duluth purchased most of the 154 the city handed out in 1908. By then Superior's Northern Brewing Co. owned so many saloons it paid more property tax than any other business in town. A new law restricted liquor licenses to businesses incorporated in Wisconsin and Michigan's Upper Peninsula, forcing out Fitger's, Hamm's, and the St. Louis brewers. Duluth Brewing & Malting, whose investors all hailed from Marquette, had filed its incorporation papers in Michigan, making it exempt from the law.

During the first fifteen years of the twentieth century, local elections on both sides of the bay often centered on temperance issues, pitting Wets against Drys. Dry factions accused breweries and saloons of engaging in political meddling; similar scenarios played out across the nation.

In 1911 the number of Duluth saloons peaked at 187 when the population stood at 78,466, below the state regulation of one saloon per 500 residents. In 1916, when Duluth voted itself dry, that number was down to 148. Superior had 40,384 residents and 161 saloons at its peak in 1912, just over the Badger state's limit of one saloon for every 250 citizens. When Superior first went dry in 1916, it closed 145 saloons. Only 66 opened in 1917, and in 1918 the city dried itself out again.

Klinkert's six tied saloons had actually poured the drinks. He was acquitted after a witness failed to appear. In July he was arrested for selling beer direct to consumers, and soon after Arthur Zimmerman, a Klinkert employee, was arraigned on the same charge. Zimmerman had actually been set up, selling beer to undercover police on a Sunday. Superior had

recently enacted an ordinance prohibiting saloons from operating on Sundays. Zimmerman's trial would be a test case in the argument over whether breweries could sell direct to consumers and if so, should the same Sunday prohibition apply to brewery sales. Zimmerman was fined $50, but the brewery appealed. The following January police again arrested Klinkert for selling beer direct to a consumer on a Sunday. But while Zimmerman had waived his right to a jury trial, Klinkert decided to place his fate in the hands of his peers. On the stand Klinkert admitted he did not have a liquor license and had sold beer on a Sunday.

His attorney argued that Klinkert would have obtained a proper license if he could have applied for one, but another new ordinance forbade the city from issuing new liquor licenses until 1911. The city attorney countered that even if a brewery had a retail license, it would be unfair to saloon-keepers to allow breweries to sell on Sundays. Despite his own testimony the jury found Klinkert not guilty, but the larger issue remained unresolved. To stop Sunday sales, Superior slapped an injunction on the brewery.

The day before his acquittal, Klinkert lost a lawsuit brought by a saloonkeeper William Thompson for misrepresenting the ownership of a retail liquor license. That summer, Superior's city council reviewed all of the municipality's liquor licenses and refused to reissue licenses to four saloonkeepers, including Thompson, forcing Klinkert to close the Iowa Avenue saloon Thompson operated.

John Klinkert must have grown weary of liquor laws when the Northern Pacific Railway offered to buy his brewing complex two weeks later. The railroad was expanding its Superior yards and had purchased land adjacent to the brewery. The *News Tribune* reported NP had offered Klinkert $60,000—worth over $1.6 million today. If the deal went through, the fifty-nine-year-old brewer would retire.

Instead, according to the *Evening Telegram*, in January 1909 NP paid Klinkert about $35,000 for the facilities and property, and Duluth Brewing & Malting purchased the brewing equipment, horses, wagons, and saloons for $25,000. In June, workers demolished the former brewery and woolen mill. The Northern Brewing Company stood alone as Superior's only commercial brewery.

"I never had such a good apetite before in my life."

said a gentleman the other day and gives as his reason for it that he was drinking

Klinkerts Beer

three times a day.

Guaranteed to be brewed from MALT and HOPS only.

Superior's

Home Brewed Beer

Almost exactly a year after Klinkert Brewing & Malt closed, Frank Pabst, who had severed his ties with the brewery in 1907 following the death of his wife, Margaret, killed himself in Montgomery. He was forty-three years old. Alabama had just gone dry, but breweries could still make beer to sell in other states. Loss of their local audience forced Alabama's breweries to make drastic budget reductions, including cutting its highest-paid staff. Pabst's ongoing despair for the loss of his wife and an unstable financial future, *News Tribune* speculated, led to his suicide. He left behind a thirteen-year-old son, Henry, who was raised by relatives in Hibbing.

John Klinkert died in 1915 of complications following surgery. He was eulogized by his fellow Elk Solon Perrin, who said that "in Germany, [Klinkert] was a German. In Milwaukee, he was a German-American. After he came to Superior in 1890, he was a just an industrious, successful American."

LEFT: A NEWSPAPER AD FOR KLINKERTS BEER, CA. 1905. [ZENITH CITY PRESS]

ABOVE: ERNEST KLINKERT, SON OF BREWERY FOUNDER JOHN KLINKERT, POSES BEFORE A FALSE BACKDROP WHILE DONNING A DANDY FUR COAT AND SMOKING A CIGAR, DATE UNKNOWN. [J. ANDREWS COLLECTION]

FITGER'S KEEPS GROWING (1900–1909)

When the century turned, nearly fifty thousand people lived in Duluth, and before the decade was out that number would rise to just shy of 78,500, which greatly expanded the beer market. Fitger & Co. and Duluth Brewing & Malting both responded by expanding their operations to keep up with demand and competition from large breweries in Milwaukee and St. Paul. St. Paul's Theo. Hamm Brewing Co. was particularly aggressive at the Head of the Lakes, and Milwaukee's Val. Blatz Brewing Co. built several buildings in Duluth. As the century began, Minnesota was home to eighty-five breweries. A. Fitger & Co.'s capacity had reached 75,000 barrels a year, making it the fourth largest in the state. At 45,000 barrels a year, about 5,000 less than the company claimed, DB&M was the seventh largest. Twin Cities' giants Hamm's and the Minneapolis Brewing Co.—which later became Grain Belt—topped the list with 500,000 barrels each, followed by Gluek's, another Minneapolis brewer, at 150,000.

Fitger & Co. started out the century with a construction project that would turn out to symbolize the renovations that marked the next ten years—and still stands today as the landmark brewery's most recognizable feature: a 135-foot chimney the *News Tribune* described as "two stacks in one." While the paper assured readers Fitger's was not the tallest smokestack in Duluth (that honor fell to the 208-foot metal chimney of the Great Northern Power Company, predecessor to today's Minnesota Power), its design was the most innovative. Using 160,000 bricks, masons built two chimneys, one encircling the other. Single-wall chimneys were exposed to heat on the inside and cold on the outside, which over the years produced cracks and leaks. Since the outer chimney was not exposed to heat, it could last longer without cracking. A gap of several inches separated the two chimneys, allowing the outer layer to sway during heavy winds without damaging the inner layer. (See photos page 97 and 180.)

TOP: FITGER'S EMPLOYEES IN FRONT OF THE BREWERY, CA. 1900.

RIGHT: PERCY ANNEKE (LEFT) AND AUGUST FITGER IN THEIR OFFICE, 1903.
[C&R JOHNSON COLLECTION]

The next year the Lake Superior Brewery spent $22,840 on a new four story brew and mill house along Superior Street. Drawn by Chicago architect Louis Lehle, the plans called for an all steel-and-concrete structure faced with local bluestone and trimmed with brownstone to match the stock house. Lehle and his sons specialized in breweries and designed facilities for more than sixteen beer manufacturers, including the Minneapolis Brewing Co.

The new brew-and-mill house was built adjacent to the original 1881 brewery, and its equipment was upgraded at the same time. Improvements included a new 240-barrel copper kettle which the newspaper described as being "as shining and bright as a brand new copper penny—inside as well as outside." The kettle had a diameter of nearly fifteen feet and, when covered, stood seventeen feet tall.

With a new brewing facility, Fitger and Anneke decided it was time they invested in a new brewmaster. The pair had already gone through four brewmasters—including John Beier, Joseph Besser, and Richard Sippel—dismissing them, according to Johnson, "for being too bossy, conceited, lazy, or impish."

They found John Beerhalter working in a brewery in St. Louis, just as Fitger had done. Beerhalter was born in Germany in 1874 and immigrated to the U.S. in 1891 after spending a few years working for a German brewery. He attended Chicago's Wahl-Henius Institute of Fermentology and excelled academically, reportedly earning the highest scores the school had ever recorded. After graduating, he took a job with Anheuser-Busch. He came to Duluth as a twenty-eight-year-old widower and the single father of seven-year-old William, four-year-old Clara, and three-year-old Richard. While his surname seemed to symbolize his profession, it actually translates to "berry holder."

Johnson describes Beerhalter as a puzzle solver: "He had a knack for finding problems in the brewing process

Top: Fitger's after the new brewery and stock house was built and the original brewery was turned into the bottle house.

Left: August and Clara Fitger photographed in 1907. [C&R Johnson Collection]

and remedying them." He must have found many issues with the Lake Superior Brewery, because during his first four years the company remodeled both stock houses, the boiler house, and even the new brew-and-mill house. Along

FACING PAGE: TOP LEFT, THE 1901 BREW KETTLE; TOP RIGHT, THE STEAM WORKS;
BOTTOM LEFT, THE AGING VATS; BOTTOM RIGHT, THE DC POWER PLANT.
THIS PAGE: TOP LEFT, THE 1908 OFFICE; TOP RIGHT, THE 1908 BOTTLING WORKS;
BOTTOM LEFT, THE WASH HOUSE; BOTTOM RIGHT, THE COOPERAGE.
[ALL IMAGES C&R JOHNSON COLLECTION]

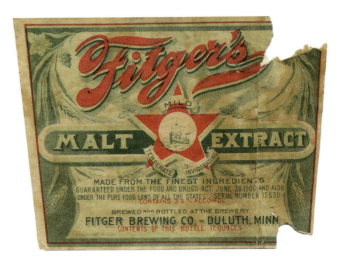

the way they added a wash-and-racking house, again designed by Lehle.

During all the remodeling, Fitger and Anneke incorporated their operation and changed its name from the A. Fitger & Company Lake Superior Brewery to the Fitger Brewing Company. On January 1, 1904, Fitger was named president and Anneke secretary and treasurer; Benjamin Grimm, who had been managing the brewery's sales for seventeen years, became vice president. That year a railroad spur was extended to the Fitger campus. Since the brewery no longer had to truck beer to the railroad cars, Johnson explains, the company saved thousands of dollars in labor and kept its beer cold.

A few months later the *News Tribune* reported that in 1904 Fitger's sold 50,000 barrels of beer, though it now had the capacity to brew 100,000 barrels per annum. That new railroad spur also made it easier to ship beer to the more

than twenty-five agencies it operated on the Iron Range and in northwestern Minnesota. The firm would soon start building hotels in Bemidji, Bovey, Ely, Tenstrike, and Virginia, where they also planned a one-thousand-seat opera house. In 1905 Fitgers built a cold-storage facility in East Grand Forks on the North Dakota border.

Shipping more beer meant moving more ice, and in 1906 the company built a new three-story wooden icehouse designed by prominent Duluth architect William A. Hunt. The next year contractors began building a three-story bottling house designed by Lehle and faced with the same brownstone and bluestone used for the brew-and-mill

house. Three large glass-lined aging tanks were delivered in September; the *News Tribune* story heralding their arrival included this lofty statement:

> The brewers of this country are under a moral and conscientious obligation, to give to the great American people, for consumption in their homes, and for their children, as well as for themselves, a healthful and natural brand of beer—a home beer. Such beer will develop brain and body, might and mind, in the coming generation. It must be brewed and aged in honor, not merely in advertising. A beer which will retain every article of the pure food values contained in the barley grains. In short, an ideal health drink.

ABOVE: A TIN LITHOGRAPH SIGN ADVERTISING FITGER'S BEER, CA. 1908, WHEN THE ZENITH CITY HOSTED THE FOURTH ANNUAL NATIONAL SKI TOURNAMENT OF AMERICA. [C&R JOHNSON COLLECTION]

TOP LEFT: A FULL-COLOR FITGER'S LOGO, CA. 1905. [FITGER'S COMPLEX]

BOTTOM LEFT: A FITGER'S BEER LABEL, CA. 1908. [K. MALZ COLLECTION]

AUGUST FITGER'S ARTISTIC BROTHER ARTHUR

August Fitger came from a large family, one of ten children raised by postmaster/innkeeper Peter Fitger and his wife, Clara, in Delmenhorst in the Grand Duchy of Oldenburg, Germany—and the brewer-turned-businessman wasn't the only one to make a name for himself. His older brother Emil, born in 1848, walked away from a business career to pursue journalism, becoming editor-in-chief of *Weser Zeitung*, a politically driven daily newspaper published in Bremen, just a few miles west of Delmenhorst (the Weser river flows through Bremen; *zeitung* is German for newspaper). His ideas about liberal business practices made the newspaper internationally important until his death in 1917.

Another older brother, Arthur, also became a writer, but was better known for his painting. Born in 1840, Arthur Fitger studied art at the Munich Academy and moved between Antwerp, Paris, and Rome, studying and painting while financed by a scholarship from the Grand Duke of Oldenburg. In 1869 he returned to his homeland and established a studio in Bremen. In Bremen he earned a reputation for painting large works depicting scenes from history and mythology and was commissioned to paint large murals in important public buildings, including Bremen's Ratskeller, where wine has been stored and sold since 1405. (Ratskeller means "council's cellar"; Americans changed it to "Rathskellar" to avoid connotations with rodents.) During the 1870s and 1880s Fitger employed both brush and pen, working as a playwright, poet, critic,

DETAIL FROM A POSTCARD FOR THE BREMEN RATHSKELLER. [C&R JOHNSON COLLECTION]

and translator. His plays include 1873's *Adalbert of Bremen*, 1875's *Here Empire! Here Rome!*, 1878's *The Witch*, 1884's *From the Grace of God*, and *The Roses of Tyburn*, completed in 1888. His poetry includes the 1871 short epic "Roland and the Rose" and two collections, *Traveling Folks* (1875) and *Winter Nights* (1881). As an art critic, Fitger was known for his conservative views and opposition to "artists who followed fashions that were modern at that time." In 1893 Arthur Fitger submitted a four-by-six-foot painting of a scene from Greek mythology titled *Diomedes Wounds Aphrodite* to the Chicago Columbian Exhibition (aka the World's Fair). It was awarded the Gold Prize. When August Fitger's new brewery office was completed in 1908, the painting was hung above its fireplace. When the St. Louis County Courthouse opened in 1910, August Fitger loaned the painting to the county to be displayed in the courthouse's art gallery. Arthur's painting of Bacchus, Roman god of wine, was installed over the mantle in the office building's boardroom. The painting is said to have disappeared during a 1983 redevelopment of the brewery complex; a sketch of the painting hangs in its place today.

Prior to his death, Arthur Fitger drew a sketch for a proposed statue his brother August intended to install in a rooftop garden in a proposed addition to the brewery that was never constructed. The statue was to depict Gambrinus, the mythological Flemish king of beers. Today the sketch hangs in the lobby of Fitger's Inn.

When the bottling house was complete, the Fitger's Complex stretched 340 feet along Superior Street from the east end of the bottle house to the west end of the millhouse (see pages 90 and 103 for photographs). Between them stood the original 1881 brewhouse and an empty space of thirty-five feet. In 1908 Lehle was called on to fill the gap with a brand-new $35,000 three-story office building he would blend among the other buildings with the same sandstone and bluestone finish. Lehle's final contribution to Fitger's decade of building and remodeling involved designing stables and a garage: trucks had started replacing wagons.

The office building contained a suite designed to be shared by Fitger and Anneke. It overlooked Lake Superior and was outfitted with a beautiful fireplace. Above its mantel hung a four-by-six-foot painting of a scene from Greek mythology titled *Diomedes Wounds Aphrodite* by Fitger's brother Arthur, who died in 1909 shortly after the office building was completed. At the time of Arthur Fitger's passing, Percy and Lydia Anneke were themselves mourning. Marcel Anneke, their twenty-three-year-old son, died in November 1908. He had suffered from respiratory problems all his life and passed while seeking relief in California.

PUTTING THE MALT INTO
DULUTH BREWING & MALTING (1900–1909)

Duluth Brewing & Malting matched Fitger's success. In 1901 DB&M made enough beer to require another storage facility. It would be the first of many buildings prominent Duluth architect J. J. Wangenstein would design for DB&M, including saloons and hotels in Duluth, Superior, and Iron Range towns. Like Northern, DB&M aggressively expanded its market using tied houses.

That year more DB&M ads appeared in local newspapers, including promos for DB&M's Moose Brand Beer, a repackaging of its malt-heavy standard beer. As the story goes, a large bull moose wandered through the brewery yard, causing a stir and inspiring Hoch to change the name. While the story might be true, the timing is likely off. The label for DB&M's original bottled beer in the 1890s featured an idealized etching of the brewing facility accompanied by the company's trademark: a moose's head emerging from a circle adorned with hops and wheat wreaths.

The moose soon became closely associated with the brewery and appeared on all of its products, whether or not it was Moose Brand Beer. And Moose Brand itself was available both as a strong porter and a brew of less than 2 percent alcohol, likely for the North Dakota market, labeled as Our Tame Moose. Some locals began calling DB&M the "Moose Brewery."

Construction of the long-anticipated malt house finally wrapped up in February 1902. It cost $100,000 and could produce 500,000 bushels a year, twice as much as the facility's original plans called for and much more than DB&M itself could use. The rest was sold to other brewers and makers of industrial alcohol, creating another income stream. DB&M shipped malt to accounts throughout the U.S. and England.

DB&M's brewing capacity had reached 150,000 barrels a year, and in 1904 the company bottled 1.1 million quarts of beer. The next year the brewery boasted that its payroll contained 125 names, including secretary Frank Hoch, Reiner's son. By then DB&M was marketing its wiener beer as Rex and also made a product called Vitosia Tonic, an extract of malt and hops described on the label as "a delicious strength-giving beverage for invalids and nursing mothers." New brewmaster John Lingelbach, a product of the Wahl-Henius Institute of Fermentology, had previously practiced his trade in Chicago and Milwaukee.

As the brewery expanded, so did its sales reach. Frank Trampish took charge of DB&M's business in Iron Range towns, acquiring property and building saloons and hotels that would be operated as tied houses, including Virginia's New England Hotel on Chestnut Street, operated by J. J. Sullivan.

In early April 1906 the *News Tribune* heralded the West End brewery's $45,000 expansion designed by Chicago

CROWNED BY SUCCESS EVERYWHERE!

Moose BRAND

"THE BEER THAT REIGNS SUPREME"

Duluth Brewing & Malting Co. Duluth, Minn. U.S.A.

A DETAIL FROM A POSTER ADVERTISING DULUTH BREWING & MALTING'S PRODUCTS, CA. 1900.
[P. CLURE COLLECTION]

A VARIETY OF DIE-CUT LABELS USED BY DULUTH BREWING & MALTING PRODUCTS BOTTLED BETWEEN 1900 AND 1906. THE TWO LABELS IN THE CENTER ABOVE SHOW THE EVOLUTION OF REX AS IT BECAME THE BREWERY'S MOST POPULAR PRE-PROHIBITION PRODUCT. OUR TAME MOOSE, VITOSIA, AND CHOW MALT WERE ALL MALT TONICS.

[K. MALZ COLLECTION]

DULUTH BREWING & MALT LABELS, CA. 1907–1914

ABOVE: A VARIETY OF LABELS (TOP ROW WITH NECK LABELS) USED BY DULUTH BREWING & MALTING FOR PRODUCTS BOTTLED BETWEEN 1907 AND 1914, WHEN THE FEDERAL FOOD AND DRUGS ACT REQUIRED SPECIAL LABELING. THE LAW WAS ENACTED "FOR PREVENTING THE MANUFACTURE, SALE, OR TRANSPORTATION OF ADULTERATED OR MISBRANDED OR POISONOUS OR DELETERIOUS FOODS, DRUGS, MEDICINES, AND LIQUORS, AND FOR REGULATING TRAFFIC THEREIN, AND FOR OTHER PURPOSES."

RIGHT: ON THE BACK LABEL FOR ITS VITOSIA MALT TONIC, THE BREWERY CLAIMED THAT THE BREW, WHICH CONTAINED ALBUMINATE OF IRON, CURED INSOMNIA, INDIGESTION, BRONCHITIS, COUGHS, AND COLDS AND SERVED AS A MARVELOUS APPETIZER.

[K. MALZ COLLECTION]

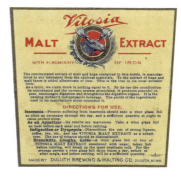

BREWERIES & UNIONS

By all accounts the breweries at the Head of the Lakes maintained a good relationship with their workers. West Superior Brewing Co. employees organized the region's first brewers' union in 1898, and by 1900 Northern and Klinkert were also union shops. Duluth brewers initially chose not to join, the *Duluth News Tribune* explained, because while "there is no objection on the part of the managers to have them organize...the men themselves do not seem greatly inclined to form an organization." Fitger's already paid better than union scale.

After Duluth brewers did unionize in 1900, they struck just twice. In 1901 they asked for a wage boost and a cut in hours from ten to nine a day. The breweries offered a more modest pay increase but no change in hours. When the union threatened to strike, the newspaper quipped, "The earnestness of the brewery employee who strikes cannot fairly be understood until you remember that he gives up free beer when he walks out." After two days on the picket line, workers accepted the brewers' offer. Two years later a week-long strike bought them the terms they asked for in 1903, and brewers also agreed to use only union-made malt.

Even as the market was dropping out beneath them as Duluth voted itself dry, Zenith City breweries continued to support their union employees. In February 1917 Duluth's breweries renewed contracts for at least two years with the 150 members of Duluth Brewery Workers' Union No. 133. The contracts were "favorable to the men" and one union man told newspapers, "There has always prevailed a good understanding between Duluth brewers and their employees."

This tradition continued after the repeal of Prohibition. When Victor Nelson purchased Northern Brewing in 1937, he promised to employ only union men and added a new message to the beer's label: "Union Made Beer." In August 1955 Northern entered into what the *Superior Evening Telegram* described as "the first guarantee wage plan" in the city's history. The brewery's new contract with Superior Brewery Workers Local No. 133 guaranteed employees 92 percent of their annual salary even if they didn't work enough hours to earn it. The agreement was an unlikely move for a brewery, which traditionally reduced production staff considerably during colder months as sales slowed down.

The brewer's union also made concessions, even agreeing to wage freezes in the late 1960s to help Fitger's, the last-surviving commercial brewery in the Twin Ports, stay open. The last union brewery workers lost their jobs in September 1972, when Fitger's closed.

A CARICATURE OF REINER HOCH DRAWN IN 1909.
[ZENITH CITY PRESS]

brewery architect Bernard Barthel, whose work include St. Paul's Schmidt Brewery. Wangenstein oversaw construction, which included a two-story addition to the wash house and another floor to a section of the brewhouse to make room for two large coil-system beer coolers. A new $15,000 grinding mill could process four hundred bushels of grain every ninety minutes, and so they also added a four-hundred-gallon copper kettle—said to be the second-largest brewing kettle in the U.S. at the time—ensuring the brewery could maintain its 150,000-barrel capacity. The expansion also included a $7,000 pasteurizing machine for the bottling works, a new grain dryer, and an ammonia-process ice machine.

The same article describing the expansion noted that the brewery now shipped 200,000 bushels of malt to eastern breweries every year. Mash—the grain residue left behind after the brewing process—was once sold to local dairymen as cattle feed, but each week DB&M was sending a train car of it to Milwaukee, where brokers sold and shipped it to Germany.

In 1907 DB&M constructed a tunnel under Helm Street to contain a pipeline connecting the brewhouse with a new bottling works, capable of putting 250 kegs worth of beer into bottles every day. The storage room held 130-barrel steel tanks lined with glass. Thanks to an 1890 exemption to the law governing the bottling of beer, the new bottling house's location across a "highway" allowed beer to be delivered from the brewhouse to the bottling works without the two buildings being considered "in communication" with each other.

But as the bottling works went up, a fire destroyed the facility's malt house and grain elevator. The loss was reported at $50,000. DB&M was rebuilding by November, incorporating the latest innovations in machinery. The malt house lost some of its castle-like features during the reconstruction.

A 1908 profile of the company that appeared in the *News Tribune* claimed the company made 100,000 barrels of beer in 1907 and employed over 200 people, 115 of them in Duluth alone. Others worked as salesmen or at one of the company's sixty branch houses "scattered throughout

the states of Wisconsin, Minnesota, Montana, and Kansas." Its bottled beer used imported Saazer hops while the hops for its draft beer came from Washington, Oregon, and New York—all brewed with "an inexhaustible supply of the purest and best water for brewing purposes anywhere on the globe." The malt they manufactured used barley grown along the Red River Valley in Minnesota and North Dakota.

Three months after the glowing *News Tribune* article, DB&M suffered a tragedy when its barn and stables caught fire. Newspapers reported eighteen horses and two mules were "roasted" in the blaze, and that barn boss Edward Graham survived only because his bulldog's howling had woken him up. Just two mules survived.

A Duluth Brewing & Malting advertising poster known as "The Voyeur," ca. 1900. [P. Clure Collection]

A BREWERY FOR THE PEOPLE...? (1906–1909)

As Fitger's and DB&M were improving production, expanding their markets, and fending off outside interests, in October 1906 the *News Tribune* reported that a new brewery was coming to the Zenith City, and its investors were looking at property in West Duluth. It was to be called People's Brewing Company.

Over the decades many have come to believe that the brewery was born of socialist ideas brought to Northeastern Minnesota by immigrants to "resist the evils of capitalism" represented by larger breweries that operated tied houses. The creation of People's Brewery, so goes the tale, involved a revolt of saloonkeepers against the likes of Fitger's, Duluth Brewing & Malting, Hamm's, and the other large breweries that owned many of the city's saloons and hotels. The city's

independent saloonkeepers would show them: they'd make their own beer to sell in their own saloons.

And perhaps that's just what promoter Fred C. Toelle wanted them to believe. Toelle, another German immigrant, was fifty-five when he visited Duluth in 1906. He had spent his life as a traveling salesman based in Detroit, Michigan, and had hit on a plan that had proved profitable. He came to the Zenith City looking for investors for a new brewery, trying to raise $300,000 at $100 a share. He bypassed the city's wealthy capitalists and targeted "liquor retailers"—aka saloonkeepers—to raise capital. He claimed to have done the same thing in seventeen other communities across the U.S.

Indeed, in 1900 the *Detroit Free Press* reported Toelle was promoting a new brewery, and that "many of the leading liquor dealers of the city will be among the stockholders." Toelle went on to establish at least seven breweries in 1905 and 1906 alone, including Capital City Brewing Co. of Indianapolis, Indiana; Falls City Brewery of Louisville, Kentucky; Franklin Brewing Company of Columbus, Ohio; Chicago Heights Brewing Co. of Chicago Heights, Illinois; Lake Brewing Co. of Houghton, Michigan; and Union Brewing Co. of New Orleans, Louisiana. Capital City's investors included 112 saloonkeepers, Fall City's over 200.

In 1905 he also established a People's Brewing Co. in Terre Haute, Indiana—and it wasn't the first. Between the 1880s and 1935 no less than a dozen other American breweries organized under the name People's. Toelle's method was to raise the capital and incorporate a brewery, accept payment for his organizational efforts, and then resign from the firm before it produced a drop of beer.

Duluth's People's Brewing Company officially organized on January 1, 1907, with a board of independent saloon owners, including Patrick Doran, co-owner of the Campbell & Doran Saloon at 205 West Superior Street; Frank G. Sandstedt, who owned a downtown saloon at 203 West Superior

Street; Thomas Doyle, whose saloon stood in West Duluth at 5519 Raleigh Street; Martin Smith, who owned both the Hotel Astoria at 102 East Superior Street and the Nicollet Hotel at 518–520 West Superior Street, in the heart of the city's Bowery; Michael J. Gleeson, who had a saloon in the notorious St. Croix district at 204 Lake Avenue South; Charles M. Forest, who ran another Bowery saloon with Alphonse Letourneau at 615 West Superior Street; and Charles F. W. Korth, who owned a saloon and a hotel on Gosnold Street (now Roosevelt Street) in West Duluth. Traveling salesman John B. Dunphy and Toelle himself rounded out the group. Doran would act as president, Sandstedt vice president, and Smith as secretary.

So the creation of People's wasn't a socialist revolt, it was a capitalistic investment opportunity. Proprietors of Duluth's independent saloons and hotels started their own brewery so they could get beer at a lower price and profit from both wholesale and retail sales. Fitger's, Duluth Brewing & Malting, and Northern Brewing had all been started by brewers partnering with capitalists. With People's, the saloonkeepers were the capitalists. They would have to hire a brewer.

In February the new brewing firm announced it had found a location between Forty-Second and Forty-Third Avenues West along Superior Street. They planned to build a $225,000 brewery, "modern in every concern," that could produce up to 75,000 barrels a year. It would be operational by October 1907.

TOP: THE PEOPLE'S BREWING COMPANY BREWERY UNDER CONSTRUCTION IN 1907.
[UMD MARTIN LIBRARY]

BOTTOM: THE BREWERY SHORTLY AFTER CONSTRUCTION WAS COMPLETED.
[DULUTH PUBLIC LIBRARY]

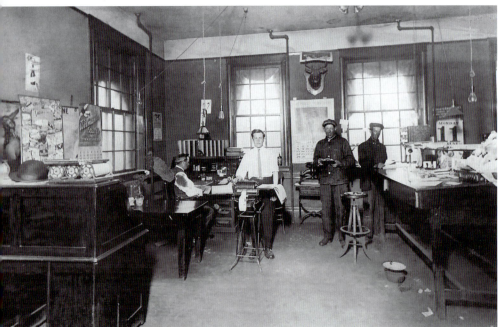

In March, however, Toelle had raised only $75,000. Apparently discouraged, he ran a notice in local newspapers stating that he had resigned and the brewery would not be built, asserting that Duluth did not "offer a sufficiently attractive field for such an enterprise." The news came as a surprise to People's board of directors, who responded immediately, assuring their stockholders that the brewery would be built. They had no idea what prompted Toelle's action, and clarified that he was brought to Duluth from Detroit "to promote the deal on a percentage basis." It appears that the Duluth project was among his last; by 1910 he was working in Detroit selling wholesale jewelry.

People's Brewing Co. officers and investors pressed on without Toelle, stating they could "build a brewery which will compare to any that Mr. Toelle has ever erected and that they can carry out the plans with better results and do so sooner than Toelle contemplated."

In June the *News Tribune* announced that Duluth's "Independent Brewing Company" would soon sign with a building contractor—apparently People's had reorganized after Toelle's exit, but the business itself would still be called People's. The company's officers reshuffled: Sandstedt was now president, Gleeson vice president, Smith treasurer, and Dunphy secretary. Construction would begin soon, and they hoped to be selling beer by May 1908.

TOP, FROM LEFT TO RIGHT: PEOPLE'S BREWING COMPANY ORIGINAL CORPORATE OFFICERS PRESIDENT FRANK SANDSTEDT, VICE PRESIDENT MICHAEL GLEESON, AND POSSIBLY EITHER TREASURER MARTIN SMITH OR SECERETARY JOHN B. DUNPHY IN THE BREWERY OFFICE, CA. 1908.

BOTTOM: ANOTHER VIEW OF THE OFFICE WITH FOUR PEOPLE'S EMPLOYEES AT WORK.
[UMD MARTIN LIBRARY]

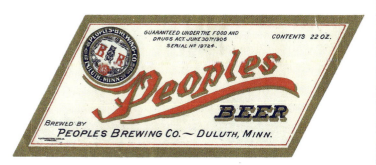

F. F. Bollinger of Pittsburgh broke ground on July 10. No architect is credited as drawing Duluth's People's Brewing Co. plant. Bollinger had already built several breweries in the east, and the design for its Westchester County Brewery in Mount Vernon, New York, is nearly identical to that of People's. When Bollinger broke ground in Duluth the firm was already at work on eight other breweries in the U.S.

The central building, which held the brewhouse, had a footprint of 160 by 125 feet and stood four stories high. Built of steel and concrete and faced with pressed brick and Bedford limestone from Indiana, the brewery cost $140,000. The company planned to produce 50,000 barrels of beer during its first year, although with its 175-barrel kettle the facility's capacity was twice that. Its 100-by-40-foot two-story bottling house cost $30,000, as did the 75-by-40-foot two-story stable that could house up to forty horses. The $18,000 office stood two stories tall. (The central building was also supposed to be outfitted with malting equipment capable of producing five hundred bushels a year, but there is no evidence it was ever built.)

Bollinger assured *News Tribune* readers that all equipment, from ice machines to boilers and the power plant, would be the "most up-to-date in Minnesota." To get the raw ingredients in and the beer out, the Northern Pacific Railroad extended a spur to serve the brewery. The board lured Ernest A. Koenig to Duluth to serve as brewmaster. Koenig had spent his first fifteen years in the business working as the brewmaster of Munich's Royal Bavarian Hofbräuhaus before

emigrating to the U.S. to attend Chicago's Wahl-Henius Institute of Fermentology. He then worked in San Francisco and Vallejo, California, and later in Peoria, Illinois. By the time he came to Duluth he had been brewing beer for thirty years.

Koenig had beer on hand for the annual stockholders meeting in early June, but it had not properly aged and wouldn't be ready for sale until July. The brewery already employed twenty men, and its sales agents busied themselves scouring the Iron Range to expand its market; its investors had already assured them a strong opening in Duluth.

They sure had a grand time at the grand opening on June 30. An open house scheduled for 3 P.M. to 5 P.M. lasted until nine in the evening to accommodate all two thousand curious beer drinkers who showed up to try the first batch of draft beer (the bottled beer—labeled simply "Peoples beer"—was still aging). Stockholders acted as a reception

TOP LEFT: THE FIRST LABEL FOR BOTTLED BEER BREWED BY PEOPLE'S BREWING COMPANY. [K. MALZ COLLECTION]

ABOVE: EMPLOYEES AND INVESTORS OF PEOPLE'S BREWING COMPANY IN FRONT OF THE BOTTLING HOUSE IN 1908. THIS PHOTO APPEARS ON THE OFFICE WALL IN THE PHOTO AT THE TOP OF PAGE 66. [C&R JOHNSON COLLECTION]

committee, a full orchestra played into the evening, and many a beer was downed in the wood-paneled taproom on the brewery's fourth floor, adjacent to the brew kettle and outfitted with plush leather furniture and a hand-carved bar. Local residents John Casey and Fred LePage enjoyed the beer a little too much and began to fight; both ended up in jail on drunk and disorderly charges.

CHANGE ON THE HORIZON

As the first decade of the twentieth century came to a close, four state-of-the-art breweries were operating on either side of St. Louis Bay. At the community's oldest brewery, the death of one of its oldest employees marked the changing times. Franz Heinrich, keeper of Fitger's Brewery Saloon, died in October 1909 of an unnamed stomach ailment. (Heinrich is pictured on page 108.)

He was fifty-five years old and had stood behind the bar for Fitger's since 1886, a year after he and his wife, Marie, first arrived in Duluth from Detroit via Germany. Heinrich,

known for his athleticism and good nature, was active in Duluth's Turnverein Society and the Sons of Hermann, a mutual aid society for German immigrants. He was called "one of the best-known German residents in Duluth" by the *News Tribune*, and more than fifty carriages participated in his funeral procession.

At Heinrich's funeral Duluth police officer John Link, the deceased's oldest friend, gave the eulogy. He had promised Heinrich he would do so twenty-five years before, and the bartender had made the same promise to the cop: they were both "free-thinkers, believing in neither church nor minister." Link praised Heinrich for his patriotism as both a German and an American:

> While so many forget their German home, that they are German offspring, and try to hide their nationality and lose the spirit of the Fatherland, adopting the customs of the new country and forgetting their language, Franz Heinrich was true—Franz Heinrich was ours. Not that he would for one minute forget his duty to the new adopted Fatherland, knowing the honor of being an American citizen. Still in his heart he loved Germany and never lost sight of an opportunity, in a spiritual way, to preach German culture, German ideals, German customs. And in his heart he was always true to the German language.

That type of dedication to the German Fatherland would be questioned just a few years later as World War I spread across Europe. Moreover, the temperance movement—fueled by the Anti-Saloon League—was pushing the nation toward the prohibition of alcohol. Beer, often advertised as a "non-intoxicant" and "health drink," would soon come under fire not just for its place in the saloons but also for its strong association with Germany, who would become the enemy. All four breweries at the Head of the Lakes had spent the previous decade creating facilities that could make high-quality beer for a long time, but as the future fell into focus, the horizon didn't look so bright.

TEMPERANCE
TURNS TO PROHIBITION

N A COLD FEBRUARY MONDAY IN 1910—the same day newspapers announced that the cities of Duluth and Superior would share the nickname "Twin Ports"—teamster Maurice McGinnis drove a Northern Brewery sledge across the frozen St. Louis River, hauling beer to Henry Ward's saloon near the site of the Minnesota Steel Plant, still under construction. The ice gave way, and the horses, wagon, driver, and beer all plunged into the river. McGinnis, a former Duluth alderman, managed to pull himself out of the frigid waters and "suffered no ill effects from his icy bath." The horses drowned. The *Duluth News Tribune* reported that the kegs were trapped under the ice and pondered the coming thaw: "In the spring, the time the poet says a young man's fancy lightly turns to thoughts of love, there are expected to be a large number of lovers of the amber fluid scattered along the St. Louis searching for the missing kegs."

It was a tough loss, but survivable. That year Northern, Superior's only brewery, was one of about 145 beer makers in the Badger state, which had lost nearly 14 percent of its breweries during the preceding ten years. The next nine would be worse, and by the end of the decade a new law would force Northern, its Duluth counterparts, and every other brewer in the nation to stop producing that amber fluid altogether. The temperance movement was gaining momentum, and beer had become a target. Due to its generally low alcohol content, beer had been considered a "temperate" drink. In fact Fitger's, whose bottled product contained 3.5 percent alcohol, advertised itself as a "temperance beer." Brewers across the nation advertised beer as a tonic for babies and nursing mothers. Whiskey had been the big target. The problem for beer makers was that saloons sold whiskey, and the nation's breweries owned or controlled most of the saloons (see "Breweries & the Saloon Business," page 50).

FITGER
BREWING COMPANY

DULUTH, MINN.

FITGER'S FORGES FORWARD

The same year Northern lost a load of beer beneath the ice, August Fitger attended the annual meeting of the United States Brewers' Association in Washington DC. When he returned to the Zenith City, Fitger told the *News Tribune* that "the consumption of beer through the country is increasing steadily and it is expected that the U.S. treasury will receive over $6,000,000 in [tax] revenue from this one source this year." Fitger went on to declare that all the "anti-saloon agitation of the past few years" was not accomplishing anything beneficial, despite claims that half of America lived in Prohibition districts.

Fitger was an active member of the U.S. Brewers' Association and had been paying attention to the temperance movement and the Anti-Saloon League for some time. In 1903 during a meeting of the Minnesota Liquor Dealers' Association, he gave a speech on "The Liquor Dealer's Position in the Community," in which he discussed the role saloon owners and brewers played in society. He declared the main objective of the association was "to oppose the sale of intoxicating liquors to minors, habitual drunkards and dissolute persons." To Fitger, prohibiting alcohol was impossible. "Beer, wine, and liquor will always be consumed," he said. The question was "to whom shall we entrust the selling?" He warned that "if you drive decent men out of the saloon business, the more you will drive unscrupulous men into it." Finally, he referred to his native Germany, where a community's prominent people were "the brewmaster, the burgomaster [aka burgermeister], and the preacher.... In the care of such a trio the morality of the people fared better than in most of our populous cities, with all their boasting demagogues, politicians, and pretentious steeples."

Seven years later, Minnesota liquor dealers and brewers had formed the Loyal Liberty Protective League. The group opposed proposed legislation that would allow the state's counties to decide individually if they want to prohibit the sale of alcohol. The league's objective was to "protect the business interests in the state of Minnesota by taking an active interest in selecting men for public office who will be most conducive to the prosperity of the entire state."

If Fitger was worried St. Louis County would soon go dry, he didn't show it. He and Beerhalter continued to make investments in the brewing facility. Beerhalter had married Martha Callie the previous January and moved into a house at 22 North Sixth Avenue East, paid for by the brewery. A son, John Beerhalter Jr., was born September 1910, a month after the arrival of a German chemist Fitger hired to set up an in-house laboratory to improve quality control.

Duluth brewing historian Coopen Johnson gives the chemist's name as von Sternberg and claims he was the "son of a baron," but research has not revealed his first name or ancestry. His name does not appear in Duluth directories, his stay in the Zenith City was brief, and while no one recorded his first name, Johnson credits him for "the largest and most successful investment Fitger and Anneke would ever undertake"—a field of sediment in California.

More specifically, a deposit of diatomaceous earth, made up of the fossilized remains of diatoms, a type of microalgae. The fossils form a soft sedimentary rock, which

becomes a fine white powder when crushed. It is used in metal polishes, toothpaste, cat litter, thermal insulation, and as a stabilizer in dynamite. More important to the brewery, diatomaceous earth also makes for a wonderful filter material. It was also called "kieselguhr," the same name as a company in Lampoc, California, that mined it. It was von Sternberg, Johnson says, who suggested to Fitger and Anneke they visit Lampoc: the Kieselguhr company was for sale.

The pair was impressed and spent $2 million to acquire the operation, both to mine and sell the diatomaceous earth and also to use it to improve their beer. Beerhalter is

FITGER'S DELIVERY TRUCK CA. 1911, WHEN A NEW COMBINATION STABLE AND GARAGE WAS BUILT TO HOUSE HORSES, WAGONS, AND TRUCKS. [FITGER'S COMPLEX]

In January 1910, the *Duluth News Tribune* and both Duluth and Superior's commercial clubs announced a contest asking entrants to come up with a new, shorter nickname for the Duluth-Superior region to replace "Head of the Lakes," which local boosters thought was more than a mouthful. Despite the state line between the cities, commerce on both sides of St. Louis Bay was so intertwined the two communities essentially acted as one, and the federal government already considered the bay one large port.

Hundreds of entries poured in, vying for the $10 gold piece offered as a prize. One entrant suggested "Siamese Twins" because "we cannot be separated." Ironically the prize for a shorter name went to the first of several people who suggested an even longer one: "The Twin Ports at the Head of the Lakes." Officials quickly shortened the new nickname to "Twin Ports."

By then 78,466 people resided in Duluth—an increase of about 25,500 from 1900. In ten years the Zenith City had boosted its population by nearly 50 percent. In Superior, the "Eye of the Northwest," the population had increased by 30 percent to 40,384, maintaining its status as the second-largest city in Wisconsin. Much of Duluth's expansion was aided by the development of the West Duluth communities adjacent to the U.S. Steel Company's new Minnesota Steel Plant, including Morgan Park, Gary, and New Duluth. The plant produced pig iron for the first time in 1915.

Duluth made a major change to its governance in 1912, voting out the old ward and boss system, in which its seven wards were each represented by two aldermen who served much like today's city councilors. In the old system, the mayor held much power and appointed city officials. Under the new system, five elected commissioners would take charge of different aspects of city government: public affairs, public works, public safety, public utilities, and finance. The mayor also served as commissioner of public affairs.

When America entered World War I in 1917, young men on both sides of the bay shipped out for training and then on to the trenches of France and Belgium; those that stayed home went to work. Iron-ore production and shipping stepped up for the war effort, and firms on both sides of the bay started building ships. The West Duluth communities of Riverside and Smithville were established as company towns for the McDougall-Duluth shipbuilding company.

The following year was particularly tough on the Twin Ports, as besides the war 1918 saw the Spanish Flu epidemic reach the Head of the Lakes. In October the Cloquet Fire—which stretched to the outer limits of Duluth—killed 453 people, injured or displaced 52,000 more, and consumed 250,000 acres—including thirty-eight communities. Both Duluth and Superior became refuge centers.

The war ended just before Prohibition began. While Duluth's western expansion had helped its population rise to 98,917, an increase of 26.1 percent, Superior's had dropped to 39,671, a 1.8 percent loss. That year company officials closed the Alger-Smith lumber mill, the last large mill from the years when Duluth and Superior sat at the center of the nation's lumber trade.

In June 1920 Duluth experienced perhaps the greatest human tragedy in its history when an angry mob stormed the city's police headquarters and lynched three young black men falsely accused of rape. The National Guard had to be brought in to keep the peace. A month later Duluth's new chief of police was arrested along with eleven others, charged with smuggling whiskey over the Canadian border (see page 104).

After the many trials involving both events ended, the Twin Ports navigated the next nine years with few major issues, as they sat on relatively solid financial ground. The Twin Ports remained a major shipping center, and the ore docks, grain elevators, and coal docks that lined the St. Louis River and Bay in both communities teemed with activity. Three major flour mills operated in Superior, and Duluth's Marshall-Wells had become the largest wholesale distributor of hardware on the planet. Despite this stability, Superior's population began a decline that would not stabilize until the 1940s.

Then came October 1929. As Duluth converted its famed aerial transfer bridge into an aerial lift bridge, the stock-market crash ushered in the Great Depression. It affected every industry, and by 1930 one-third of all Twin Ports residents had lost their jobs. The 1930 census reported that 101,463 people lived in Duluth, an increase of 2.6 percent and the height of its pre–baby boom population. Superior, meanwhile, had lost nearly 8.9 percent of its citizens, dropping to 36,133.

credited with creating the Fitger Kieselguhr Filter, a nickel-plated machine that used 254 sixteen-inch-long filter tubes, each three inches in diameter, to "correct the evils of pasteurization," by purifying beer without using steam. It made "draught beer in bottles" and prompted a name change.

In 1914 the brewery relabeled its Export Beer as Natural Beer. Fitger became increasingly involved with Kieselguhr, spending more time in California than Duluth. Kieselguhr began manufacturing and selling the filter to other breweries and wineries. Meanwhile, the brewery had continued to invest in equipment under Beerhalter. In 1911 architect Louis Lehle's final contribution to the Fitger's Complex went up, a combination stables and garage—Fitger's had recently purchased two trucks—that blended with his previous efforts. The company also installed state-of-the-art keg-cleaning equipment in the wash house.

The brewery also continued to expand sales territory and build more facilities outside Duluth, including a $22,000 office-and-apartment complex in Virginia, a $10,000 hotel in Warba, and a depot in Hibbing. When developers platted the town of Manganese on the Cuyuna Iron Range in 1911, Fitger's bought three lots for a hotel before a single resident moved to town. The next year the company purchased property in Cuyuna and built a saloon in Eveleth before turning toward sites in northwest Wisconsin, where it put up a saloon and restaurant in Iron River. In 1913 the brewery acquired the town of Washburn's brewery, opera house, and two saloons. By then Fitger's was making deliveries as far west as Montana and employed 225 men in Duluth alone, and August Fitger had been named a trustee of the U.S. Brewers' Association.

THE OTHER THREE THRIVE

While Fitger's improved equipment and thought ahead, the Twin Ports' other breweries focused on expanding sales. Duluth Brewing & Malting concentrated efforts to secure its trade on the Iron Range and in Duluth. In 1911 alone the brewery built a hotel in International Falls; purchased a

hotel in Bemidji, a saloon in Calumet, and an apartment/retail complex in Virginia; and planned a hotel in New Duluth to serve employees of the new Minnesota Steel Plant. According to Johnson, Fitger paid attention to DB&M's sales, recording in his personal diary that by 1910 the "Moose Brewery was selling 100,000 barrels of beer annually."

By 1911 DB&M was using two kettles to keep up with demand, one that could hold 150 barrels, the other 416—at the time, the second largest in the nation. The company's bottling equipment could fill eighty bottles a minute, and its malt house produced seven hundred bushels every day. The demand came from increased sales farther from home. A *News Tribune* article explained that Rex and Moose beer

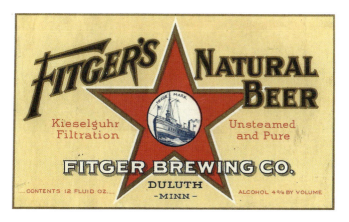

LEFT: A 1915 ADVERTISEMENT FOR THE FITGER KIESELGUHR FILTER

TOP: THE ORIGINAL LABEL FOR FITGER'S NATURAL BEER. [FITGER'S COMPLEX]

BOTTOM: A LABEL FOR FITGER'S NATURAL BEER MENTIONING THE KIESELGUHR FILTER PROCESS FROM 1914, THE YEAR IT WAS INTRODUCED. [K. MALZ COLLECTION]

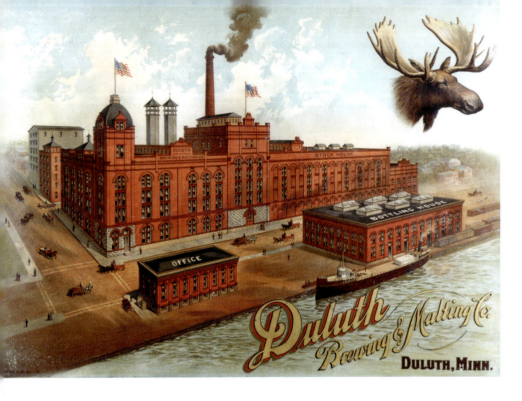

was sold in Wisconsin as far east and south as Eau Claire. In just Douglas County DB&M had accounts in Brule, Gordon, Nebagamon, Solon Springs, South Range, and of course Superior. Its Minnesota sales territory stretched from "International Falls on the extreme north border to the Iowa line on the south." The firm also had an agency in Mondak, Montana, that served accounts in a 150-mile radius.

In Marquette, however, Hoch and Charles Meeske's Upper Peninsula Brewing Company was feeling some political pressure. Germany's Kaiser Wilhelm was becoming increasingly militant—and unpopular. Upper Peninsula's flagship lager was called Drei Kaiser or "Three Kings," a nod to the brewery's castle-like appearance. But the name also suggested Germany's aggressive leader. So in 1913 Meeske changed the label to Castlebrew, advertising it as "the beer that made Marquette famous." But that wouldn't save the northern Michigan operation for long.

People's Brewery began the decade by paying dividends to its stockholders for the first time. By then John Dunphy, the brewery's secretary, had become its sales agent as well, distributing People's product out of a storeroom on Twenty-Third Avenue West. If Duluthians wanted beer delivered to their doors, they just had to call Zenith 927 and Dunphy would take their order for People's "famous bottled beer." The brewery's Thanksgiving advertisement claimed that drinking People's beer meant "new blood, better health, renewed strength and better digestion. It is the family beer that makes life worth living."

As the year closed, the *News Tribune* reported that sales of People's beer had increased, and that the brewery took that as a sign of "the general public going more for beer and less for liquor consumption." The plant increased production, and by March 1911 sales had greatly exceeded the previous year's. The brewery had expanded its business throughout the Iron Range and hoped to soon reach into Wisconsin in towns along the Minneapolis, St. Paul & Sault Ste. Marie Railroad, known as the Soo Line, which had recently built a depot to extend service to Duluth. At the brewery's annual stockholders meeting in June, secretary Theodor Frerker announced dividends of 10 percent. Shareholders presented president Frank Sandstedt with a diamond ring as a token of their appreciation of his work—they credit his efforts as the reason for the brewery's success. It now had a capacity to brew fifty thousand barrels a year.

Sadly, People's master brewer Ernest Koenig died on September 1; newspapers failed to mention what caused his death, only that he had been ill for about ten days prior to his demise. Assistant brewmaster Frank Luckow took over for Koenig. Luckow, a native of Germany and graduate of Chicago's Siebel's Brewing Academy (today's Siebel Institute of Technology), had joined People's in 1909 as a cellar man. He was just twenty-five and lived with Koenig and his wife when he first arrived in Duluth. He married Augusta Klepproth just months before Koenig's death. The brewery continued to prosper with Luckow manning the kettle.

In June 1912 the company—which now employed about fifty men with an annual payroll of $40,000—paid dividends for the third year in a row. Sandstedt was again reelected as president, Frerker secretary, and A. W. Anderson as treasurer. Vice President Michael Gleeson lost his position to M. J. Filiatrault, who owned a West Duluth funeral home. Gleeson remained as a shareholder and later returned to the board.

Two months later Anderson died of a "hemorrhage of the stomach" while visiting St. Paul, and in December Filiatrault resigned, replaced by Charles Forest. As with Koenig's death, these changes had no impact on sales. By the end of the year the brewery had announced substantial improvements that reduced costs and increased production. The company paid dividends again in 1913. That June a classified ad in the *News Tribune* posted by a stockholder offered nine shares of People's stock at $125 a share. The following year once again saw People's paying dividends to its investors.

The West Duluth brewery had become profitable despite heavy competition and a small market, limiting sales to Duluth and a few Iron Range towns. And they competed with more than Fitger's and DB&M: the Zenith City was home to agencies and depots for Pabst, Blatz (formerly Val. Blatz), Hamm's, Schlitz, Heileman, and Anheuser-Busch.

Across the bay in Superior, Northern Brewing thrived. In 1910 it again paid more in property tax than any other Superior company, a sign of its vast real estate holdings. That year the company announced plans for a new malt house, grain elevator, and bottling works. Contractors had the bottling facility under construction the following April after workers demolished and removed the old facility.

Northern continued to expand its real-estate holdings in Superior, building a two-story saloon designed by local

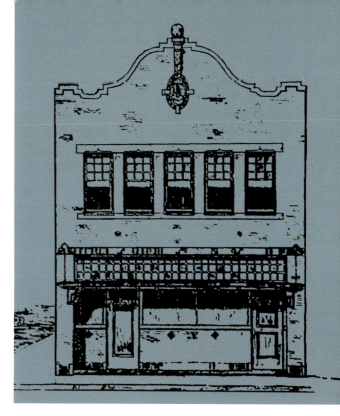

architect Frank E. Johnson at 1715 North Third Avenue in 1912 and operated by Charles Forsey when it first opened. Fittingly, today the building is home to the Cedar Lounge, which serves as the taproom for Superior's Earth Rider Brewing Company.

With its new fire proof bottling house, Northern now carried fifty employees on its payroll. Besides taxes, the brewery's payroll put $125,000 into the local economy. In late 1914 Erhardt reported the brewery had created another income stream, selling malt to accounts in South America who could not get the product from Europe because of the war. The first contract would bring in $27,000—worth more than $650,000 today. Despite this report, there is no evidence the malt house was ever built, just like in 1902.

Despite its position as Superior's home-town brewery and perhaps the city's largest holder of real estate, Northern struggled to compete. Its taxable corporate income reported in October 1914 was $27,738. In contrast, Blatz of Milwaukee sold $177,829 in Superior during the same period, La Crosse's John Gund Brewing Company $258,860, and the Fred Miller Brewery of Milwaukee $404,074. By law Minnesota breweries Fitger's, People's, and Hamm's could not own a saloon in Wisconsin. Duluth Brewing & Malting, originally incorporated in Michigan, sold $31,759 of beer in Douglas County.

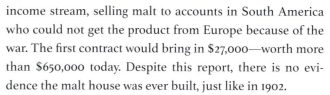

THE BUILDING SHOWN IN THE ARCHITECT'S SKETCH ABOVE WAS BUILT IN SUPERIOR BY THE NORTHERN BREWING CO. AS A TIED HOUSE IN 1912. TODAY IT IS ONCE AGAIN A TIED HOUSE, SERVING AS THE TAPROOM FOR EARTH RIDER BREWING CO.
[ZENITH CITY PRESS]

Liquor has played a role in the history of the western Lake Superior region from the time settlers first established Superior City in 1854. Walter Van Brunt, a pioneer himself, wrote that those who settled at the mouth of the St. Louis River were, "in the main, men of strong character; yet few were teetotalers, in all probability the total abstainer was the exception, in those days." One of them, Charles Lord, came to Superior to "take charge of the trading post and protect the Indians from the abuse of Spiritous liquors." Two years later Reverend James Barnett "held services in a building at Superior where [he] could hear the sound of the glasses in the saloon in the room below."

Five days after Reverend James Peet lamented in his diary on October 9, 1856, that the steamer *Lady Elgin* had arrived at Superior with "enough whiskey to keep the whole town drunk all winter," he and six others organized the Young Men's County Temperance Association. Peet moved his family across the bay to Oneota, where his fellow pioneers had already established the Oneota Temperance Society. When Jerome Merritt spoke before the society on July 4, 1859, Peet recorded sixty people had attended. Liquor could not be sold in Oneota Township, founded in 1856 by the Wheeler, Ely, and Merritt families, all Methodists; like Peet, Edmund Ely was also a minister, and Lucian Merritt would become one. The Oneota families owned the local trading post and did not allow liquor on its shelves.

Duluth historian Heidi Bakk-Hansen tells us that from its inception in 1873, the Women's Christian Temperance Union "enjoyed a following amongst the wives of Duluth's richest men." The Duluth Temperance Society, "devoted to opposition to the liquor traffic," incorporated in 1881 with $20,000 in capital stock. The money, worth about $485,000 today, was used to finance "lectures and other public awareness efforts within the city's immigrant neighborhoods." Between 1870 and 1919, when Prohibition became law, Duluth newspapers printed over six thousand articles and announcements regarding the temperance movement.

Duluth's perspective on temperance was complex. Bakk-Hansen describes those on either side of the issue during the years leading to Prohibition in terms of Protestantism versus Catholicism. The Drys were a combination of "wealthy Presbyterian ladies and imigrant Scandinavian Lutherans and Baptists who saw temperance as a solution to the plague of alcoholism amongst workingmen of the community." On the Wet side you could expect to find "German Lutherans of the 'high church' variety and Catholics... [who] considered beer to be the sustenance deserved for a hard six-days' work." And wine, of course, was essential to the Sacrament of Communion. Yet Reverend James McGolrick, the leader of Duluth's Catholics from 1887 to 1918, was described as "a most energetic temperance worker, having established many total abstinence societies."

The temperance movement's influence in Duluth is perhaps best reflected in the development of Lakeside, including Lester Park, which began in the mid-1880s.

When its founders—wealthy Methodists, Episcopalians, and Presbyterians—established the Village of Lakeside in 1889, they forbade the sale or manufacture of liquor within its borders. In 1891 state legislation turned the Village of Lakeside into the City of Lakeside. That same legislation anticipated Lakeside's 1893 annexation by Duluth and contained a provision that reflected its Protestant values: "The common council of the city of Duluth is hereby prohibited from ever granting any license to sell or dispose of any wines, spirituous or malt liquors within the limits of the territory hereby constituted as the city of Lakeside, after the same shall have been annexed to the said city of Duluth in accordance with the provisions of this act." The law stood in place until 2016.

The Anti-Saloon League organized the same year Duluth annexed Lakeside. The group targeted saloons as the source of most of the country's social ills and helped propel the temperance movement toward Prohibition. Duluth developed its own chapter, yet when Safety Commissioner William Hicken went on a crusade against saloons, blind pigs, and brothels in 1913, he was voted out of office.

In 1916 Duluthians—led by voters in districts representing Protestant strongholds Hunter's Park, the East End, and Lakeside—elected to go dry. Superior's Drys had won their battle a year before, lost it in 1916, and regained dryness in 1917. Prior to that, every election in Superior between 1900 and 1915 dealt primarily with laws governing the operation of saloons and candidates were most often described not as Republican or Democrat, but as Wet or Dry.

TEMPERANCE TIGHTENS THE MARKET

Northern had bigger worries than competition. Politics in Superior were becoming clearly divided among the "Wets" and "Drys." In 1911 Joseph S. Konkel ran for mayor of Superior as the "Anti-Brewery Candidate" and lost—but the next year he would begin a six-year run as Superior's chief executive. That year Superior handed out 164 liquor licenses, three more than state law allowed. The next year, under Konkel, the city pressured breweries to stop supporting "blind pigs," essentially any place that sold retail liquor without a license, and the Wisconsin legislature considered laws to end brewery saloons or lower the number of breweries in a city from one for every 250 people to one for every 1,000; if it had passed, the number of saloons in Superior would drop to forty.

In 1910 an agent from the Bureau of Indian Affairs began shutting down saloons in northern Minnesota in what was still sometimes referred to as Indian Territory. The 1854 Treaty of La Pointe specified that "no spiritous liquors were to be sold on any of the lands ceded to the government," a provision carried over in the 1855 Treaty of Washington, which ceded land west of St. Louis County and created the Leech Lake and Mille Lacs reservations. Under the treaty, brewers could make but not sell beer in all or parts of sixteen northern Minnesota counties, including a large swath of western St. Louis County (see figure on this page). Although Minnesota had since become a state, the federal government decided to enforce the treaty provisions. Fitger's and Duluth Brewing & Malting were heavily invested in many of the communities within the territory, which included Grand Rapids, Brainerd, Bemidji, and Moorhead. Overnight these operations became illegal.

That agent was William E. "Pussyfoot" Johnson, a former law-enforcement officer and journalist who became a highly controversial figure in the temperance movement, admitting to drinking liquor, bribing officials, and outright lying in his efforts to ban the manufacture and sale of alcohol in the U.S. The stealthy approach he had used to pursue suspects in the Oklahoma Territory, where he used a similar treaty to close saloons, had earned him his feline nickname. Johnson and his men forced the temporary closing, and in some instances bankruptcy, of saloons in towns across the region, including Nashwauk, Deer River, Bagley, Walker, Akeley, Grand Rapids, and others.

Judge C. A. Williams temporarily thwarted Johnson's effort, ruling in a suit brought by twelve Bemidji saloon owners that when Minnesota became a state in 1858 it "gained

the power of regulating the liquor traffic and repealed the anti-liquor clauses of the Indian land cessation treaties." When Johnson was rumored to be heading to Grand Rapids, the city's *Herald Review* wrote that residents should be on the look out for "blackmailing, wholesale perjury; the closing of some saloons; the influx of blind pigs innumerable; more drunken Indians; a heap of trouble; [and] no good results." They didn't have to worry: Johnson resigned in September 1911, and the matter of Indian Territory was forgotten—temporarily, at least.

The same year Pussyfoot Johnson roared through northern Minnesota saloons, East Grand Forks passed an ordinance outlawing tied houses, affecting thirty-seven of the city's forty-nine saloons and eliminating $18,000 in annual tax income for the municipality, nearly $450,000 today. The move came soon after a serious legislative effort to rid the state of tied houses. Republican representative John Johnson of Canby introduced a measure to "prevent liquor manufacturers or wholesalers from helping a retailer in securing a license or furnishing a building or fixtures for a saloon."

It failed, and Johnson accused the Brewery Trust of influencing the writing of the Republican state platform. Prominent Republican Chester Congdon, Duluth's most well-known and revered businessman, served in the Minnesota legislature that year. He and other northern lawmakers

Hotel Rex,
20th Ave. West and Superior St.,
Duluth, Minn.

A LITHOGRAPHIC POSTCARD
FOR THE HOTEL REX IN DULUTH'S
WEST END, CA. 1915. DULUTH
ARCHITECT JOHN J. WANGENSTEIN
DESIGNED THE REX AND MANY
OTHER DULUTH BREWING &
MALTING BUILDINGS, WHICH
OPERATED AS TIED HOUSES,
BETWEEN 1900 AND 1915.
TODAY IT IS CALLED THE HOTEL
ESMOND, DISTANCING ITSELF
FROM A NOTORIOUS PAST AS THE
SEAWAY HOTEL BY TAKING THE
NAME OF ANOTHER HISTORIC
DULUTH HOTEL THAT ONCE
SERVED THE WEST END (NOW
KNOWN AS LINCOLN PARK).
[ZENITH CITY PRESS]

voted against the measure. In turn, the Brewery Trust supported those lawmakers' concerns over tonnage-tax legislation regarding iron ore mined on the Iron Range—Congdon had made his fortune as head counsel of the Oliver Mining Company. The idea of a tonnage tax came up in Minnesota politics often between 1900 and 1921. Lawmakers wanted to tax the ore and collect it for the entire state; northern legislators like Congdon wanted no such things, as the Iron Range communities they represented, as well as Duluth, already collected tonnage tax.

Lieutenant Governor Sam Gordon, the 1912 Republican candidate for governor, vowed to get rid of brewery saloons. So did the city of Duluth, which contained the state-allowed maximum of 160 saloons or one for every 500 persons. Eliminating brewery saloons, and not reassigning the liquor licenses attached to them, would reduce that number dramatically. That year Congdon turned against his old allies. A Gordon supporter, he attacked brewers, calling them the "instigators of the tonnage tax bills" and telling newspapers that they "dominate the legislature and no bills are passed

detrimental to their interests. They have also blocked attempts to pass a reapportionment bill because of the fear that they will then be shorn of their political power."

Congdon explained that "in order to prevent the passage of the last tonnage tax bill, the northern Minnesota representative accepted any aid from any source, and this was the only alliance between the brewery and steel interests." Congdon said he supported Gordon "not because he is a great man, but because he will not fetch and carry for the brewers."

It is not clear if the Brewery Trust included any Duluth brewers. The *News Tribune* reported on a "secret session of midwest liquor men" held in Moorhead in September 1912. It mentioned that those in attendance came from breweries in St. Louis, Chicago, Milwaukee, and the Twin Cities but did not mention the Zenith City. If Fitger & Co. did belong, it would have made for some uncomfortable moments at Duluth's exclusive Kitchi Gammi Club, where Congdon, Fitger, and Anneke all held membership. Gordon lost the election, but remained active in Minnesota politics and temperance efforts.

Prohibitionists in both states kept pressure on the saloons and breweries the following year. When the so-called "brewery divorce" antibrewery saloon legislation of 1913 failed in Wisconsin, proponents blamed the "brewery interest," just as they had in Minnesota. On Minnesota's Iron Range, mining companies began banning liquor and beer from mining locations. Chisholm forced representatives of nine breweries, including all three Duluth concerns, to sign agreements vowing to never sell to blind pigs. The breweries signed similar agreements in Virginia and Hibbing.

Newly elected Hibbing mayor Victor Power went beyond that, passing an ordinance in April to stop further granting of licenses to properties owned or leased by breweries. Two months later the town passed an ordinance that would revoke licenses if it was discovered a

which weakened one of the brewing industry's chief arguments for keeping beer out of the temperance issue: beer sales were good for the national economy. Duluth's three breweries told newspapers in September 1914 that they handled $2 million in sales a year, paying $250,000 in taxes. They also contributed $100,000 a year to farmers purchasing barley and hops and had a combined payroll of $425,000 a year, over $10.3 million in today's economy. So when the federal government proposed increasing the beer tax that October to $1.50, Fitger embraced the idea, because it bolstered his argument to keep beer out of the prohibition argument.

As tension mounted in Europe during the summer of 1914, the papers turned to August Fitger to learn how the local German population would react. "I anticipate that possibly fifty Germans would leave Duluth and the ranges in the event of war," he told the *News Tribune*. "I know one young man who will return to the fatherland and there are probably two dozen in Duluth who would respond to any call Germany would make." That one young man was his

Top left: Label used for beer bottled by People's Brewing Co. from 1914 to 1919. [C&R Johnson Collection]

Bottom left: Northern Brewing Co. used this label on its bottled beer from 1914 to 1919. [J. Stein Collection]

Above: Employees of People's Brewing Co. and members of cofounder Michael Gleeson's family enjoy a picnic, ca. 1912. [E. Gleeson Collection]

brewery had a financial interest in the saloon and removed an ordinance preventing immigrants who had yet to obtain citizenship from obtaining a license so they would not be dependent on breweries to start a business.

Changes in federal income tax law introduced by the Sixteenth Amendment in 1913, left breweries more vulnerable to temperance sentiments. The federal government had been well served by taxes from beer sales and other excise taxes for over fifty years. The beer tax, one dollar per barrel, was first established to help the Union finance the Civil War. With money from income tax pouring into the federal coffers, the nation was becoming less dependent on beer sales,

ASHLAND BREWING COMPANY LABEL, CA. 1908.
[J. STEINER COLLECTION]

Ashland after opening a brewery in Taylors Falls, Minnesota, and that Becker also owned a brewery in Hurley, Wisconsin. Becker closed the Ashland Brewery in 1892.

An outfit named Muehler, Goeltz & Co. set up the Union Brewing Co. in Ashland in 1874 on Bay City Creek. Muehler was likely Erghott Muehler, a German immigrant who later became a saloonkeeper and then worked as a wheelwright. Conrad Goeltz, also a German immigrant, and his son Adam put the Goeltz in Muehler & Goeltz. While the brewery started with ambitious plans—the *Ashland Daily Press* reported its capacity at 12,500 barrels a year—the company lasted just two years.

Frederick W. Miller opened the Miller & Co. Brewery in 1888 between 107 and 123 Tenth Avenue East, which would have placed it along Bay City Creek at roughly the point where Lake Shore Drive (Highway 2) crosses

ASHLAND BREWING COMPANY LABEL, CA. 1908.
[J. STEINER COLLECTION]

Besides those breweries of Superior, other outfits made beer along the Wisconsin South Shore of Lake Superior in Washburn and Ashland before and briefly after Prohibition. The first brewery on Lake Superior's South Shore was likely in the township of Bay City, within the city limits of today's Ashland. Brewing historian Doug Hoverson, author of *The Drink that Made Wisconsin Famous*, recently found an 1881 report that declared, "The first brewery [in Ashland] was built in Bay City, but was discontinued after a short time." Hoverson notes that Bay City was vacated in 1860, so the brewery's activity had to be in the 1850s. Today Bay City Creek empties into Lake Superior between Tenth and Eleventh Avenues East in Ashland.

Ashland itself was home to three brewing operations prior to Prohibition. Frank Schottmueller opened his Ashland Brewery in 1872 at 900 East Second Street and in 1885 sold it to Philip Becker. Schottmueller, Hoverson reports, had come to

ASHLAND BREWING COMPANY, CA. 1888.
[ZENITH CITY PRESS]

the creek today. According to Hoverson, the outfit soon began advertising as the Ashland Brewing Co., a name it officially took on in 1901 when it reorganized with $100,00 in capital stock and Edward Bakken and Thomas B. Culver joined as vice president and secretary-treasurer, respectively. The brewery's labels included White Ribbon and Ashland Export and it also produced a pilsner and a malt extract called Mullenhauer's Tonic. The tonic was advertised as "a pure health giving malt tonic that tones up and invigorates the whole system." And despite its location along Bay City Creek, the *Duluth News Tribune* noted in 1905 that the brewery, capable of producing 24,000 barrels a year, used water drawn from an artesian well that reached 308 feet into the ground and had a "perpetual flow of 4,000 gallons an hour."

When Prohibition became law, Culver, who managed the brewery, converted its equipment to make condensed milk, and the *News Tribune* reported that in May

WASHBURN BREWING COMPANY, DATE UNKNOWN.
[J. STEINER COLLECTION]

WASHBURN BREWING COMPANY, DATE UNKNOWN.
[ZENITH CITY PRESS]

1919 the company changed its name to the Ashland Dairy Products Co. By the following April the facility was also manufacturing butter and ice cream as, according to newspapers, most of Ashland's fifty-eight former saloons had "converted to ice cream parlors." Unfortunately, by April 1922 Ashland Dairy Products was forced to lease the facility to another creamery due to "financial distress." Several investors tried to restart the brewery following Prohibition, but as Hoverson notes it never produced more than 440 barrels a year and closed in 1937.

It was an Ashland family that opened the Washburn Brewing Company in Washburn at the Southwest Corner of Third Avenue West and Fifth Street in 1890. According to Hoverson the Waegerles—John, Mary Madelaine, and George—ran the brewery until 1893, when that year's financial panic likely forced them to close. Another Ashlander, Charles Flynn, purchased the facility in 1896 and three years later, along with new investors, changed the name to the

Washburn Brewing Association. Hoverson explains that at this time the association may have entered an agreement with Schlitz to stop brewing.

PURE BREWING COMPANY
LABEL, CA. 1905.
[J. STEINER COLLECTION]

Ed Borgan's Pure Brewing Company began leasing the facility in 1904 and purchased it in 1908, very likely following Flynn's arrest for "assault with attempt to kill." At a saloon in Washburn's east end Flynn had gotten into a fight with Martin Larson and slashed his jugular vein, but Larson survived. The *News Tribune* reported that "Flynn was a prominent character in the city. In the early days of the city he was very wealthy.... At one time he was owner of a great deal of property.... During the last few years he has lost nearly all of his property and is now almost penniless."

Borgan kept the brewery operating until 1913, when he sold it to Fitger's along with Washburn's Opera House Block, Capitol Saloon, and Union Hall Saloon. In 1915 the city of Washburn voted to go dry. Soon thereafter newspapers reported that the brewery was being dismantled and its equipment shipped to Wisconsin's Arcadia Brewing Company. The Washburn brewery was demolished in 1941 to make room for a new Washburn High School.

The Dowling Building on Chestnut Street in Virginia, Minnesota, was built by Fitger's Brewing Co. as a saloon intended to serve as a tied house. The Piggot Building next to it was also built by Fitger's. [C&R Johnson Collection]

scientist, von Sternberg. Beerhalter later recorded that von Sternberg died in Germany when the poison-gas factory he worked at exploded.

Fitger kept up on news in Europe reading *Weser Zeitung*, a daily newspaper published by his brother Emil in Bremen. August Fitger received the weekly edition published for German expatriates. At first, Americans were divided over which side of the conflict to support. Fitger, a heavy contributor to the war relief funds, gave to both the Austro-German Red Cross fund started by Percy Anneke as-well-as the Graves Fund, a general relief fund started by Duluth pioneer Colonel C. H. Graves, digger of the Duluth ship canal, former Duluth mayor and Minnesota congressman, and the country's recently retired ambassador to Sweden. Duluth also established funds for Belgium, Poland, and England.

After a German U-boat sank the *Lusitania* in 1915, the entire nation embraced anti-German sentiment, which would reach its peak when the U.S. entered the war. And since beer was closely associated with Germany, and most American brewers were German immigrants, opposing beer would soon equate to patriotism.

In March 1915 Minnesota passed a law allowing counties to vote whether to ban the sale and manufacture of alcohol. This so-called Dry County Option, strongly opposed by the brewery interests, would be tested in nearly every Minnesota county over the next two years, and by 1917 only ten of those who brought the matter to a ballot would remain wet, and all of those were in the southern half of the state.

THE HEAD OF THE LAKES BEGINS TO DRY UP

A few months after the Dry County Option became law, federal agents stepped up efforts to enforce the ban on sales of liquor in so-called Indian Territory. The breweries could still make beer, but their market shrank considerably. The dwindling consumer base concerned Fitger, and in October 1915 he traveled to Washington D.C. with Hugh S. Fox, secretary of the U.S. Brewers' Association, to address the Bureau of Indian Affairs and state the brewers' opposition to enforcing the territorial ban in St. Louis County. Fitger argued that this selective prohibition would result in "lawlessness and uncontrolled activity of the bootlegger in Hibbing and Chisholm." His theory had support: Brainerd voted itself dry April 19, 1915, and the vote was followed by raids on establishments that continued to sell alcohol. The month before the new enforcement measure had forced the Brainerd Brewing Company to pour "seven train car loads" of beer down the drain. Newspapers reported that "during the process of emptying the vats, beer was at one time seven inches deep on the floors of the brewery.... Government agents guarded the stream of beer that flowed through the gutters."

Fitger's argument failed, but Fitger himself was elected the USBA's second vice president in October. He was proven right later that month when "Pussyfoot" Johnson returned to northern Minnesota to take part in police raids of saloons in Hibbing and Chisholm—even though he had no authority whatsoever. Just three months before he arrived in the Zenith City, the *New Republic*, a temperance publication Johnson produced in Westerville, Ohio, ran a scathing article on Hibbing, calling it the "worst-governed community in America." The day before Johnson showed up, Judge Page Morris declared the second Treaty of La Pointe constitutional and ordered saloons in Hibbing and Chisholm shuttered. Subsequent raids that December lead to many arrests for alcohol trafficking, and Indian Affairs agents photographed their activity and ran a photo essay of the raids in the *New Republic*.

Similar scenarios played out across the country. The next month Colorado went dry, and the Adolph Coors Brewing Company invested $1 million converting its brewery to manufacture malted milk. In Duluth, Fitger & Co. was already at work on ways to make marketable low- and nonalcoholic beverages. Beerhalter replaced chemist von Sternberg with Charles Ringler, whom he hoped could create low-alcohol beers his customers actually liked to drink. Together with Beerhalter, brewing researcher James Maury reports, Ringler developed Non-Alco, a malt-free "pure palatable beverage free from all drugs or alcohol," specifically for Iowa, which had banned the use of malt in near beer. The process for its manufacture was so unique it received a patent. Fitger's also produced Dakota Beer ("perfection guaranteed"), a near beer of less than 2 percent alcohol that complied with North Dakota's longstanding dry status. Another near beer, Golden Common Sense, contained less than 2 percent alcohol and was less intoxicating than "beers fostered and favored by Scandinavian temperance societies

and governments." As the laws changed, so would Fitgers.

People's made no apparent attempt to develop similar products, yet the West Duluth brewery remained profitable, paying dividends to its shareholders in both 1915 and 1916. Duluth Brewing & Malting, which had long been selling its low-alcohol Vitosia malt tonic, was also playing a waiting game. But Reiner Hoch was not as much worried about his Duluth brewery as he was his investment in Marquette. In early 1916 the Woman's Christian Temperance Union along with the Anti-Saloon League used the same argument that made northern Minnesota's Indian Territory dry to end liquor sales in Michigan's Upper Peninsula. The 1854 Treaty of La Pointe banning sales of alcohol on Indian lands in Minnesota also covered all previous agreements with the Lake Superior Ojibwe (also called Chippewa), including the 1842 Treaty of La Pointe that had made the U.P. part of the U.S.

Enforcing the treaty meant the sudden end to all saloons on the Upper Peninsula, which essentially comprised the entire market of Hoch and Meeske's Upper Peninsula Brewing Co. They shuttered the Marquette brewery (it did not reopen after Prohibition was repealed in 1933). Meeske, in the meantime, moved to Duluth and took Hoch's place as the company's president.

In Superior, Northern's owners spent $15,000 for an addition to the brewery in 1915, but newspaper accounts failed to mention how the brewery would use the new space. The investment may not have been wise. In April Superiorites voted on whether to make their community dry. While

WILLIAM E. "PUSSYFOOT" JOHNSON CALLED HIBBING, MINNESOTA, THE "WORST-GOVERNED COMMUNITY IN AMERICA."
[LIBRARY OF CONGRESS]

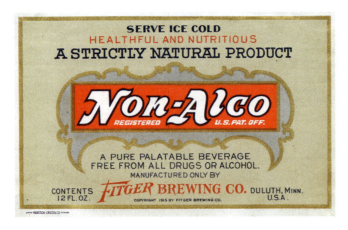

Prohibitionists lost, they were encouraged by progress. The *News Tribune* reported that when Superior voted on the same issue in 1909, 3,048 people voted to stay wet while 1,623 wished to go dry—a spread of 1,425 votes. The 1915 election resulted in 2,794 wet votes and 2,779 dry—a difference of only 15 votes. The following April, the Drys won by 33 votes.

Retail liquor sales in Superior came to a halt. Northern could still manufacture beer, but it couldn't sell any of it in its hometown, also its largest market. In July Northern introduced a nonalcoholic drink called Bingo they hoped to sell in Superior and other dry communities and set about retooling the brewery to manufacture the drink. There is no description of the beverage, but it more than likely was a near beer or cereal drink. Northern's secretary-treasurer and general manager L. A. Erhart saw the writing on the wall. After nineteen years he resigned from Northern, sold his house and other Superior business interests—including all stock in Northern—and moved back to Fond du Lac as the year came to an end. His replacement was Louis E. McKinnon, a Superior native who had moved to Fond du Lac to wed a local woman. He found a job with the Rueping family's malt operation in that city and eventually became the plant manager. In 1916 he returned to his hometown to assist Erhart and ended up replacing him.

Once Superior went dry, the pressure increased in Duluth. In June the city proposed "Ordinance B," which prohibited the "Purchase, Sale and Disposal of Intoxicating Liquors within the Limits of the City of Duluth." Duluth voters passed the ordinance on June 20, with 7,562 Dry votes and 7,211 Wet, a majority of 351 and a split of 51 to 49 percent. The law would go into affect July 1, 1917. Like Northern in Superior, Duluth's breweries could still make beer, but they couldn't sell it in Duluth. The year ended with the wedding of August and Clara Fitger's daughter Wilhelmina's marriage to

John Wallace McKenzie of Minneapolis. The couple exchanged nuptials at the Fitgers' home in Duluth, while the father of the bride could still legally offer beer to his guests.

EARLY PROHIBITION AT THE HEAD OF THE LAKES

The future of brewing couldn't have looked more bleak for brewery presidents Sandstedt, Meeske, and Fitger, who couldn't have been anticipating a bright future. While sales of their low- and non-alcoholic products helped, beer sales had already dropped dramatically for Fitger's in 1916. Johnson reports that Duluth's oldest brewery filled 25 percent fewer kegs than it had the previous year and had bottled less Natural Beer as well. If Fitger's took that kind of hit, the other Twin Ports breweries likely suffered similar losses, though People's remained profitable enough to pay stockholder dividends on 1916 sales. No matter what they paid their workers, Duluth's breweries soon required fewer and fewer employees as demand dropped while more and more of their sales territories went dry.

On June 30 Duluthians got soaked before the town went dry, lining up at all 148 saloons and hotels that held liquor licenses. The Spalding and St. Louis Hotels sold beer at fifteen cents a glass, and many of the Bowery bars offered shots of whiskey for a dime. Veteran police captain Anthony Fiskett told the *News Tribune* that he had toured Superior Street and "never have I seen the equal of the drinking tonight." (See "Bridges Between Wet & Dry" page 87.)

Meanwhile, across the bay, Superior prepared to reopen its saloons to Superiorites and Duluthians alike: the city voted to overturn its dry status less than a year after it was introduced. Saloonkeepers of some of Superior's former 168 drinking establishments fought to obtain a new license and hurried to prepare their former bars—converted to lunch counters, tea rooms, and "soft drink parlors" a year before—back into drinking establishments to serve Superiorites and the citizens of the soon-to-be saloonless Zenith City. While Superior saloons now served two cities, only 66 reopened as drinking establishments.

Within days Duluth and national breweries tried to take advantage of Superior's wet status. They could all now legally deliver beer to depots in Superior, and they assumed they could circumvent the Minnesota law by delivering beer technically sold in Superior to accounts in Duluth. On July 8 six wagon drivers from Fitger's, Duluth Brewing & Malting, and Pabst were arrested for delivering beer; the

THIS IMAGE OF PEOPLE'S BREWING CO. APPEARED IN THE 1916 PUBLICATION *THE BOOSTER BOOK: WEST DULUTH IN 1916* BY JOHN LOYAL MORRISION. MORRISON WAS A FIERCE PROPONENT OF PROHIBITION AND RAILED AGAINST THE EVILS OF DRINK AND POLITICAL CORRUPTION IN HIS NOTORIOUS *RIP-SAW* NEWSPAPER, PUBLISHED IN DULUTH FROM 1917 UNTIL MORRISON'S DEATH IN 1926.
[DULUTH PUBLIC LIBRARY]

GOING DOWN FOR THE LAST TIME

"SILVER JOE" WELCOMES BACK HIS OLD NIGHT-SCHOOL CHUM

OLD JOHN BARLEYCORN—SUPERIOR'S MOST POPULAR CITIZEN.

EDITORIAL CARTOONS THAT APPEARED IN THE *DULUTH NEWS TRIBUNE* (LEFT) AND THE *RIP-SAW* (RIGHT) COMMENTING ON ATTEMPTS BY DULUTH AND SUPERIOR TO GO DRY BEFORE PROHIBITION BECAME THE LAW OF THE LAND.
[ZENITH CITY PRESS]

Fitger driver was nabbed right next door to police headquarters. All eventually pleaded guilty and paid fines of $100.

In August the U.S. Senate passed the National Prohibition Act, which would ban the "manufacture, sale, or transportation of intoxicating liquors" throughout the entire country. But before it became law it had to be ratified, and for that it required the approval of thirty-six states.

Meanwhile, sales opportunities for Twin Ports brewers continued to decrease. By October St. Louis County and adjacent Carlton and Lake Counties voted to take the dry option, ending all beer sales on Minnesota's Iron Range. The economics of beer brewing had become even more complex when the U.S. entered the war in Europe that April. Later in the year the excise tax on a barrel of beer doubled from $1.50 to $3.00, and anti-German agitation had reached its pinnacle.

In early November the Duluth School Board announced that it had completed a process of "cleansing" all "objectionable laudatory passages for Germany, the kaiser, [and] the German flag" in books used throughout Duluth's school system. The school board, according to superintendent Dr. K. J. Hoke, had gone through forty-two textbooks and "eliminated every sentence that is in the least way laudatory to German ideals or rulers."

The action was spurred by an editorial in the *News Tribune* that appeared in September, arguing that books used for teaching the German language "should be entirely discarded." Four days after the school's announcement, librarian Frances Earhart told the paper that "pro-German propaganda has been ruled out of the Duluth Public Library." Then, on December 8, Duluth's school board not only voted unanimously to eliminate the teaching of both the German language and German political history beginning on January 1, it also passed a resolution "to require every teacher in the [Duluth] schools to sign a printed loyalty pledge which virtually makes every one a special government informer of suspected treason either in the schools or in the vicinity of them." Once signed, the pledges were to be framed and "hung in each hall office and assembly room in our public school buildings."

The following year August Fitger and Percy Anneke purchased $30,000 in Liberty Bonds, and Fitger's son Arnold

BRIDGES BETWEEN WET & DRY

As Prohibition approached, citizens of Superior and Duluth had fun circumventing local liquor laws. Each time a community went dry, area residents made a mad dash to stock up on booze and have "one last dance with John Barleycorn," a character of British folklore and the temperance movement's personification of beer and liquor.

When Superior first went dry, drinkers on both sides of the bay joined in the "turbulent hilarity" of June 30, 1916, the day before the law took effect. Superiorites "reinforced by 1,000 Duluthians" descended on the city's 163 saloons. Newspapers reported that "every saloon on Tower Avenue emitted laughter, jargon and song from the minute that nightfall settled until midnight."

In September the Duluth-Superior Street Railway Company reported that traffic on the Interstate Bridge had increased 10 percent. For thirsty Superiorites, Duluth's saloons were only a trolley car's ride away. The following April Duluth voted to go dry, with John Barleycorn's execution set for July 1. The previous evening, papers reported, police had found seventy-year-old Haakon Hendrikson in a "drunken stupor" at the foot of Garfield Avenue, the bridge's approach; one headline read "Pall Bearer at Last Sad Rites of John Barleycorn, Soused." Another story described more activities of June 30, 1917:

> Sportive Duluth hiccoughed a boisterous requiem over the fleeting spirit of John Barleycorn yesterday. The passing of the saloon to the ranks of outland business was accompanied with a gigantic drinking fest that started early in the morning and continued through the hour

set officially for the obsequies.... At twilight the downtown bars were lined four and five deep. In the cheaper saloons the patrons festooned the bars and the walls in a bleary picture.... At 9 o'clock it was impossible to get within 10 feet of a bar, and in most places entry could not be had.... In several old saloon landmarks, lines were formed, extending to the sidewalk, and the men served in turn. The white collared drinkers invaded the Bowery.... Gentleman and jack fraternized.... "Fifteen minutes more!" shouted a bartender on the Bowery. A renewed clinking of glasses sounded a deafening angelus and the bartenders perspired anew. With the end only minutes away the singing gave way to somber deportment that concerned itself chiefly with imbibing to the time limit. "John Barleycorn is dead—Long may it rain." "Let it pour." After the saloons closed at 10 P.M., the throng spilled onto Superior Street [some carrying] suitcases and surreptitious packages of liquor auctioned off at many saloons.... Liquor that couldn't be carried left in huge vans headed to Superior.

Why Superior? Because just as Duluth dried up, Superior went wet again, and booze figuratively sloshed back and forth across the bay as liquor traffic simply reversed direction. Once again, the day after the last night of drinking, the *Duluth News Tribune* wrote stories of those saying farewell to John Barleycorn. "He wasn't such a bad fellow," the newspaper quipped, "if you could leave him alone."

When Superior again banned liquor, Oliver, Wisconsin, just across the St. Louis River by way of the Oliver Bridge from New Duluth, became the nearest liquor outlet. Like Duluth's Morgan Park and Gary neighborhoods, Oliver (named for mining executive Henry Oliver) was home to Minnesota Steel Plant employees and their families. Of its thirty registered voters, twenty-one had voted wet.

Oliver quickly became the region's most popular community—and a problem for area law enforcement. Duluth mayor Clarence Magney and Safety Commissioner Bernard Silberstein met with senators and congressmen from both states urging them to close Oliver. They tried the Indian Territory argument that dried out much of northern Minnesota and Michigan's Upper Peninsula, but a judge ruled it did not to apply to Wisconsin. Finally, Minnesota senator F. B. Kellogg passed legislation to establish dry zones surrounding "mines, shipyards, munitions plants, and other war plants," forcing Oliver to go dry beginning June 30, 1919.

On June 29, droves of Twin Ports tipplers drove to Oliver to stock up. Each of Oliver's three liquor stores had raised their prices considerably as dryness approached. You couldn't blame the Eagle Liquor Store, as burglars had recently stolen stock valued at $2,900—more than $36,000 today. Eager shoppers clogged Commonwealth Avenue, and it reportedly took hours to cross the double-decker Oliver Bridge. On the Minnesota side, police in New Duluth awaited each car returning from Oliver, checking to see if they had sampled too much of their new purchases before driving home.

enlisted in the U.S. Army. Meanwhile the brewery's chemist, Charles Ringer, had given up on making beer in America—and apparently wanted nothing to do with war. He found a job as a brewmaster at Ontario's Port Arthur Beverage Company and crossed the border to practice his trade.

In Superior, the Drys fought back, and in July the city once again bid farewell to John Barleycorn. With both communities dry, Oliver, Wisconsin, became very popular. The village of Oliver is located immediately southeast of Superior and just across the St. Louis River from the

PART THREE: TEMPERANCE TURNS TO PROHIBITION (1910–1933) | 87

DULUTH—"HERE'S TO YOUR GOOD HEALTH."

An editorial cartoon by R. D. Handy of the *Duluth News Tribune* shows Duluth's namesake, Daniel Greysolon Sieur Du Lhut, sampling "Good Old Lake Superior Water" after the Zenith City voted to go dry.
[ZENITH CITY PRESS]

Duluth neighborhoods Gary and New Duluth. Like those two Duluth communities, tiny Oliver developed as a housing community for employees of U.S. Steel's Minnesota Steel Plant between New Duluth and Morgan Park, a U.S.S. company town.

To shut down Oliver's liquor trade, President Woodrow Wilson issued an order to ban liquor sales and manufacture within five miles of "any plant turning out government supplies"— and the Duluth plant was making steel for the war effort. People's Brewing Company soon found itself caught up in the controversy—its West Duluth location was very close to the five-mile radius. While People's was ultimately found to be outside the zone, it mattered little: a proclamation by President Woodrow Wilson banned the making of all malt beverages in order to store and save grain for the war effort. And even though the armistice ending the war was signed November 11, all brewers stopped making beer on December 1. Further, on November 18 Congress passed the temporary Wartime Prohibition Act, banning the sale of beverages with more than 1.28 percent alcohol. It would go into affect July 1, 1919.

The end of brewing caused some major shuffling at Fitgers. By then August Fitger was spending most of his time in California, overseeing operations at Kieselguhr

with his son Arnold, who had returned from the war unscathed. Arnold Fitger, who shared his father's sharp mind for business, would also establish several successful companies. Anneke's son Victor finished college and returned to Duluth that year and began working at the brewery but much of his career would be plagued by injury and illness. As the decade came to a close, Johnson reports, Percy Anneke traded his shares of Kieselguhr to August Fitger in exchange for enough of Fitger's brewery stock to become its major shareholder. As his company would stop making beer, Anneke's first action was to drop "Brewing" from the name Fitger Brewing Company. The move would turn out to be a shrewd investment for the Fitger family and a bit of a burden for the Annekes.

When brewing ended at midnight on November 30, Fitger's had already laid off an estimated fifty workers; more were expected to leave after everything that had been brewed was aged and bottled. People's president Frank Sandstedt told the *News Tribune* his brewery had "released three or four men, as the remainder are needed for bottling work. We have some stock on hand, but just how much I cannot say. When the bottling is finished the brewery will be closed." Neither Hoch nor Meeske spoke to the paper about layoffs at DB&M.

The new year didn't bring much hope to America's beer brewers. Nebraska became the thirty-sixth state to ratify the national Prohibition amendment on January 16, 1919, which was enough to ratify the amendment. Wisconsin ratified it the same day, and Minnesota the day after. Beginning January 16, 1920, saloons could no longer dispense any drink with more than .5 percent alcohol. Wilson's temporary ban on malt beverages kept Duluth breweries closed until Wartime Prohibition went into effect on July 1 and kept breweries from producing cereal beverages until national Prohibition went into effect the following January.

People's Brewing Company sold enough beer in 1918 to pay dividends to its investors one last time in March 1919, but it had been dealt a symbolic blow just months before with the death of one of its founders, Michael Gleeson. Gleeson, a native son of Tipperary, Ireland, came to Duluth in 1886 when he was twenty-three years old after spending time in Australia, Ontario, and Michigan. He spent a couple years as a teamster before taking a conductor job with Duluth's Street Railway Company in 1891. Between 1898 and 1901 he took on a series of jobs and moved briefly to Brainerd before returning to Duluth to open a drinking establishment at 204 Lake Avenue South in Duluth's notorious St. Croix District, home to saloons, brothels, and opium dens.

As he was helping to organize People's in 1908, he took a job as the proprietor of the Hotel Ormonde at 221–223 Lake Avenue South and worked there until 1917 when he became manager of the Metropole Hotel at 103 Lake Avenue South. It was at the Metropole on April 9 that Gleeson succumbed to bronchial pneumonia. The *News Tribune* wrote that "Mr. Gleeson was known the length and breadth of the city and Northern Minnesota as a genial, big-hearted man and was well thought of by all coming in contact with him. Openhearted, he was never known to have refused shelter or aid to an unfortunate person at any time. His hotel always had a bed for someone who needed it."

The newspaper did not report on what People's planned to do under Prohibition—if indeed Sandstedt and his fellow officers even had a plan. Since their investors and officers were chiefly saloon owners, and saloons were now out of business themselves, there wasn't much else for the company to do. Duluth Brewing & Malting, it seems, planned to take advantage of its malting facilities to make industrial alcohol. In August DB&M's Reiner Hoch and his son

Walter, the company secretary, changed a clause in its articles of incorporation to indicate it would remain a brewery but comply to new limits on alcohol content and expand its offerings: "The general nature of the business of this corporation will be the manufacture of malt and malt liquors and to manufacture and sell denatured alcohol."

Fitger's, already working on nonalcoholic drinks, would soon diversify to keep the company alive. The company's officials told Duluth newspapers they had no intention on making denatured alcohol, as it would require a remodeling of the brewing facility. They would continue to make their no- and low-alcohol drinks within the government restrictions on alcohol content and planned to reboil near beer they already had on hand that exceeded the limits: boiling beer vaporizes the alcohol, which is one way near beer was manufactured. On the other side of the bay, Northern was already producing its low-alcohol Bingo beverage, but it wouldn't take long until the operation in Superior came to a complete halt.

FITGER'S EMPLOYEES GATHER IN THE SECOND FLOOR OF THE OFFICE BUILDING, CA. 1920. AUGUST FITGER'S CHAUFFEUR RICHARD KOHTZ STANDS AT FAR RIGHT, NEXT TO BREWMASTER JOHN BEERHALTER SR. SECOND FROM LEFT IS CHARLIE "SPIKE" UNDEN, NEPHEW OF NICHOLAS DECKER, WHO TOOK OVER DULUTH'S ORIGINAL BREWERY IN 1865. CHARLIE UNDEN GREW UP IN THE BREWERY, MADE BEER THERE IN THE 1880S, HELPED BREWER MICHAEL FINK START A BREWERY ON THE IRON RANGE IN 1890, AND WENT TO WORK FOR FITGER'S IN THE 1890S, STAYING UNTIL HIS RETIREMENT IN 1938. [FITGER'S COMPLEX]

FITGER'S DIVERSIFIES (1920–1927)

Four days before Prohibition took effect on January 16, 1920, the oldest portion of the Fitger's Brewery—the 1881 Lake Superior Brewery building constructed by Mike Fink—stood engulfed in flames along Superior Street. Thanks to their thick stone veneers, the brewhouse and office on either side of the building were untouched by the flames. The former brewery's contents were likely worth more than the structure itself; it was used to store cases, barrels and advertising matter—all highly flammable. The *News Tribune* reported that "three hundred light barrels in one section of the building sent flames high above the four-story modern brewery which the old building adjoins. Firemen put six streams of water on the building from the roof and front windows."

The paper also reported that the old brewery was built in 1882 by August Fitger and quoted Fitger as saying, "I put those bricks in place with my own hands nearly 40 years ago." Fitger's statement may have been a bit of an exaggeration, as Fink had been producing beer within the

facility for months before he hired Fitger in the fall of 1882. It wasn't until October 1883, however, that Fink hired masons Meining & Yager to apply the building's brick veneer. So while Fitger could have helped put some bricks in the building, he certainly hadn't built the place by hand. Such details mattered little, as while a portion of his brewing complex lay smoldering, Fitger's youngest daughter Marion, twenty-three years old, died of tubercular meningitis in the family home a block away. In the wake of her death, Fitger pulled further away from Duluth, rarely visiting the Zenith City. By 1928 he and Clara had permanently moved to Beverly Hills, as had their daughter Wilhelmina and her husband John McKenzie, who had joined Fitger manufacturing filters made of fossilized earth.

Years earlier the brewery had made plans to replace the 1881 building with a grand structure complete with a rooftop garden. With the company's financial stability unclear as Prohibition began, the firm instead constructed a simple one-story building along Superior Street. Instead of basalt to match the other buildings, budget-minded masons faced it with brick salvaged from the fire. Further belt tightening included pay cuts. Those belonging to the brewers' union enjoyed protection, but office workers found their paychecks had shrunk. To soften the blow Victor Anneke treated them to a picnic at the Duluth Auto Club grounds at nearby Pike Lake. The next year every employee was invited, and the picnics became an annual event.

In order to navigate their new reality, on October 20, 1920, Fitger and Anneke amended the company's articles of incorporation to do business in "malt, sugar, molasses, corn,

cane and sugar vegetable products, chemicals, denatured alcohol, soft drinks, ice cream, soda fountain supplies, candies, cigars, [and] tobacco" and intended to "use a de-alcoholizing plant." The plan was simple: survive through diversification.

Exactly one year later Duluth candy maker James Pappas, along with John Chickers and M. L. Robinson, organized the Purity Candy Company, yet the company already existed, as back in April it had advertised for experienced chocolate dippers to apply at its downtown shop at 220 West Superior Street. In August a similar ad told applicants to report to 506–508 East Michigan Street—within the Fitger's Complex. The October incorporation papers were filed to save the company. Johnson reports that Fitger and Anneke became trustees of Purity Candy when Pappas and his friends faced bankruptcy. Once Purity fell into the hands of Fitger and Anneke, Pappas and Chickers became employees of the Fitger Co.—but they weren't happy with their salaries. Unpleasantness ensued, and when the dust settled the following year Victor Anneke had assumed presidency of Purity Candy and named longtime Fitger manager Jon A. Lamb its vice president. Pappas had opened his own

confectionary on Grand Avenue, and what became of Chickers remains unknown.

While Anneke and Lamb became better acquainted with candy, brewmaster John Beerhalter tried to do something about Non-Alco's lagging sales. With the new law, he had to keep the alcohol content of near beers, aka cereal beverages, below .5 percent. After releasing a cereal beverage labeled simply "Fitger's," he developed two new brews first advertised in February 1922: Dog's Head, described as a lager, and Pickwick. Fitger's even formed a separate company, the Pickwick Company, to manage sales of Pickwick and Dog's Head. Beerhalter was named its president, and Ludwig Hanson secretary-treasurer.

Pickwick was very likely first served publicly by Joe Wisocki at Fitger's former brewery saloon, which he began leasing in 1918. Fitger's had converted the saloon into a soft-drinks parlor when Duluth voted dry in 1917. The establishment's location and Wisocki's long-standing relationship with Fitger's made it the ideal testing grounds for Fitger's new beverages (see "The Brewery Saloon Becomes the Pickwick," page 108).

FITGER EMPLOYEES PHOTOGRAPHED BY NOTED DULUTH PHOTOGRAPHER HUGH MCKENZIE DURING THE 1924 FITGER'S COMPANY PICNIC AT THE DULUTH AUTO CLUB GROUNDS ALONG THE SHORE OF PIKE LAKE OUTSIDE OF DULUTH. THE TRADITION BEGAN IN 1920 AFTER VICTOR ANNEKE WAS FORCED TO LOWER THE SALARIES OF HIS OFFICE WORKERS DUE TO ECONOMIC STRAINS CAUSED BY PROHIBITION.
[C&R JOHNSON COLLECTION]

LABELS FOR CEREAL BEVERAGES OR "NEAR BEERS" BREWED BY THE FITGER CO. DURING PROHIBITION. PICKWICK WAS THE BREWERY'S MOST POPULAR PROHIBITION-ERA PRODUCT UNTIL THE ADVENT OF SILVER SPRAY. THE REX NAME WAS PURCHASED FROM DULUTH BREWING & MALTING WHEN IT CLOSED IN 1931.

[DOG'S HEAD, PICKWICK (LEFT), TOWN CLUB, AND REX: FITGER'S COMPLEX; LIBERTY BREW: NOEL BOELTER COLLECTION; CEREAL BEVERAGE AND "NEW" PICKWICK: K. MALZ COLLECTION]

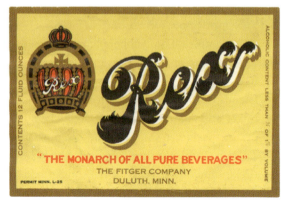

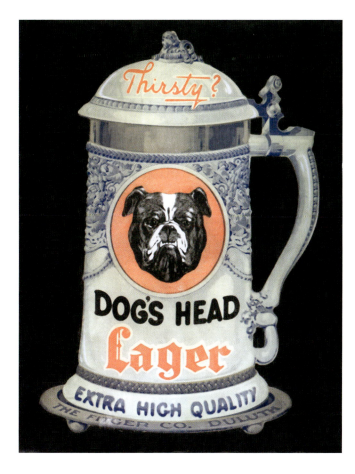

beverages Grape High Ball, Orange Fizz, Cherry Flip, Strawberry Ade, Lemon Soda, Cream Soda, Root Beer, Ginger Ale, and Apple Cider. The soft drinks sported bright yellow labels, and the apple cider's label assured consumers it was "pure and unfermented" and contained less than .5 percent alcohol. All the beverages were not only pasteurized but also filtered through "the famous Sweetland filter process," a renaming of the Kieselguhr filter.

The ad also boasted of Fitger's forty "distinctively individual" candy bars, cordial cherries, hard centers, bitter sweets, and assorted chocolates sold under the Greysolon and Fireside brands. Greysolon was a nod to Duluth namesake Daniel Greysolon Sieur du Lhut. The letter *F* of Fireside was stylized with the same font used to identify Fitger's Natural Beer.

The article also mentioned Fitger's sold its products across seven states through its distribution network of 20 sales reps, 10 agencies, and 115 jobbers (aka wholesalers). Johnson reports that the next year eighty-five people worked at Fitger & Co.'s Duluth facility and the Johnstown Company, which oversaw the company's real-estate holdings. The company pushed out 302 train-car loads of product in 1923, the same year it began distributing El Verso cigars.

Fitger's continued to expand its beverage, cigar, and candy offerings. Johnson explains that the cigar-jobbing division added El Producto, Garcia Grande, and others, including the Dan Patch, a regional smoke named for Minnesota's most famous racehorse, a celebrated harness racer who was never defeated. As the popularity of soda fountains increased, Fitger's added milk-based drinks to its beverage line, including an imitation chocolate milk shake and a Black Cow (chocolate-flavored root beer).

LEFT: ADVERTISEMENT FOR DOG'S HEAD LAGER, A NEAR BEER, CA. 1921.

BELOW: A DIE-CUT CARDBOARD TOY ADVERTISING FITGER'S DRINKS AND CANDIES, MADE SOMETIME IN THE 1920S. ITS FEET WERE ESSENTIALLY A WHEEL ATTACHED WITH A GROMMET SO IT COULD BE SPUN TO SIMULATE WALKING OR RUNNING. NOTE THAT THE GIRL IS SHOWN CARRYING THE SAME TOY.

[P. CLURE COLLECTION]

Later in the decade the company offered another near beer, Liberty Brew, touted as "Imported Saazer Hop Flavored." These beer-like products competed with more than just other near beers and malt tonics made by other breweries. Soft drinks had become popular—like Wisocki, many saloon owners had turned their bars into soda fountains. So Fitger's began manufacturing its own soft drinks in a variety of flavors.

In May the *News Tribune* published a special issue boosting local businesses, including the Fitger Company. An accompanying advertisement listed the company's offerings, not only Pickwick and Dog's Head but also carbonated

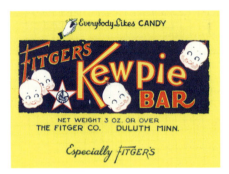

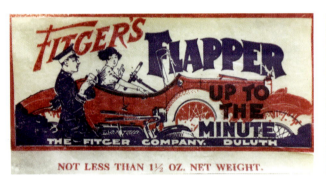

THESE LABELS ARE JUST A SAMPLE OF THE MANY VARIETIES OF CANDY BARS PRODUCED BY THE FITGER COMPANY DURING PROHIBITION. UNFORTUNATELY, MOST OF THE LABELS DO NOT DESCRIBE THE CANDY THEY WERE INTENDED TO PACKAGE. [LABELS ALONG THE TOP ROW ON THIS PAGE: FITGER'S COMPLEX; FITGER'S BARBECUE LABEL (FACING PAGE, CENTER ROW LEFT): C. OLSEN COLLECTION; ALL OTHER LABELS ON BOTH PAGES: C&R JOHNSON COLLECTION.]

Fitger's PING PONG
A DELICIOUS NUT ROLL

Fitger's SPARK PLUG
NET WEIGHT 1¼ OZ. OR MORE
THE FITGER COMPANY
DULUTH, MINN.

Fitger's MAPLE WALNUT
NET WEIGHT NOT LESS THAN 3 OZ.
THE FITGER CO,
DULUTH, MINN.

ASK FOR FITGER'S PADDY WHACK BAR
DULUTH, MINN.
THE FITGER COMPANY
NET WEIGHT 2 1-2 OZ. OR MORE
Fitger's BARBECUE
NET WEIGHT 2 1-2 OZ. OR MORE
THE FITGER COMPANY
DULUTH, MINN.

Fitger's SPANISH PEANUT BAR
NET WEIGHT 1 3-4 OZ. OR OVER
THE FITGER CO.   DULUTH.

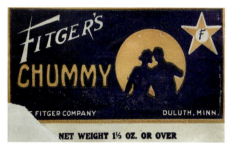

Fitger's CHUMMY
THE FITGER COMPANY   DULUTH, MINN.
NET WEIGHT 1½ OZ. OR OVER

Fitger's SKOOKUM
A BULLY GOOD BAR
NET WEIGHT 1½ OZ. OR OVER

Fitger's KING BEE NOUGAT
THE FITGER COMPANY
DULUTH, MINN.
NET WEIGHT 1½ OZ. OR OVER

Fitger's CHERRY DIPS
"MODIFIED CHERRIES IN CREAM"
NET WEIGHT 2 OZ. OR OVER
THE FITGER CO.
DULUTH, MINN.

Everybody Likes CANDY
Fitger's Big Boy
Especially Fitger's

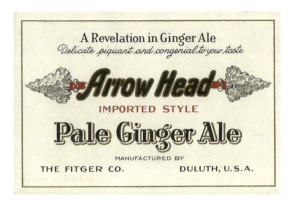

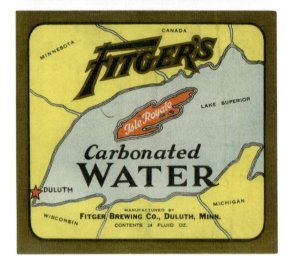

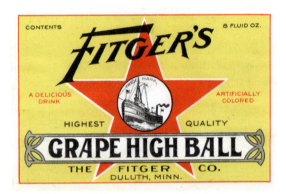

A SELECTION OF LABELS FOR SOFT DRINKS AND CARBONATED WATER BOTTLED BY THE FITGER COMPANY DURING PROHIBITION. THE SAME LABEL DESIGN FOR GRAPE HIGH BALL WAS USED FOR OTHER FLAVORED SODAS, INCLUDING ORANGE FIZZ, CHERRY FLIP, STRAWBERRY ADE, LEMON SODA, CREAM SODA, AND ROOT BEER. NOTE THAT THE NECK LABEL FOR FITGER'S CARBONATED WATER TOUTED ITS USE OF PURE LAKE SUPERIOR WATER, A THEME MOST DULUTH BREWERS WOULD USE TO MARKET THEIR BEERS AFTER PROHIBITION WAS REPEALED.

[LINDY JULEP, KITCHI GAMMI CARBONATED WATER, ISLE ROYALE GINGER ALE, GRAPE HIGH BALL, AND APPLE CIDER: FITGER'S COMPLEX; FITGER'S CARBONATED WATER: C. OLSEN COLLECTION; ARROWHEAD PALE GINGER ALE: K. MALZ COLLECTION]

Fitger's continued to develop dozens of its own candy creations, including Chocolate Hash, little more than cleverly packaged chocolate shavings (see page 196), evidence the company still needed to squeeze pennies to survive. During the 1920s the company produced such individually packaged candy bars as the King Bee Nougat, Cherry Dips ("modified cherries in cream"), Car-Mel-Nut, Spanish Peanut Bar, and its own Nut Goodie. Some candies were packaged with tantalizing names, but no description of the product, including the Kewpie Bar, Chummy, Spark Plug, Famous Hunch, Flapper, and Skookum, named for the Native American dolls popular at the time. At least Ping Pong, "a delicious nut roll," came with a description. And the sales pitch for Big Boy was simple: "Everybody likes candy." The former brewery also distributed national brands including Curtiss Candies (makers of Baby Ruth and Butterfinger), Mars Candies (Snickers, Milky Way), Wrigley's gum, and Smith Brothers cough drops.

While the company seemingly moved forward in the face of Prohibition, it suffered a major setback on the final day of 1923. Seventy-three-year-old Percy Anneke suffered a stroke that left him paralyzed. He moved to Monterey Park, California, and lived out his years in the care of his daughter, Margaret.

TOP: FITGER'S DRIVER MARTIN JORSTAD BEHIND THE WHEEL OF A FITGER'S DELIVERY TRUCK LOADED WITH PICKWICK NEAR BEER, CA. 1925.

BOTTOM: THE REAR OF THE FITGER COMPANY FACILITIES, CA. 1925. NOTE THE PAINTED SIGN FOR PICKWICK ON THE SIDE OF THE STOCK HOUSE.

[FITGER'S COMPLEX]

SWITCHING TO SODA (1920–1927)

The Twin Ports' other three breweries turned to soda as well—after all, they had the facilities to both make and bottle beverages. Duluth Brewing & Malting entered the Prohibition period on a dubious note. A story in the *News Tribune* of May 12, 1920, hints that the new company was perhaps overly eager to move out the old and make room for the new. A fire in the bottling house destroyed over $40,000 of "wrappings and paper stock...partially covered by insurance." The building was relatively undamaged, but the stock—likely labels for beer containing more than .5 percent alcohol—was completely consumed.

Hoch and Meeske changed DB&M's name to the Rex Company, and renamed the beverage division the Sobriety Company—brewmaster John Lingelbach had learned how to make soda. Lingelbach also produced two near beers containing less than .5 percent alcohol. One brand maintained the Rex name; the other was called Royal Brew and was advertised with the tagline "Fit for a King."

A third drink simply labeled Sobriety contained no alcohol. By August DB&M was advertising for employees. The following year the West End company first advertised its Lovit line of soda in a few basic but popular flavors: grape, orange, cherry, and a ginger ale it later labeled Minnesota Club. It advertised Lovit as "a better kind for a better class" and encouraged drinkers to "insist on being served with LOVIT."

Just as Lovit soda was becoming popular in Duluth, brewery founder Charles Meeske passed away after a year-long illness. The seventy-year-old Meeske had seen both the breweries he founded closed in five years' time. The *Daily Mining Journal* of Marquette, where he had spent most of his life, had nothing but praise for Meeske when it eulogized him the following day, stating in part:

> Mr. Meeske was a man of great geniality and disposition. He made friends easily and kept them once they were made. He was a German of the old school. The school that looked tolerantly on life and believed in being at peace with one another and their neighbors. He was kindly in his judgements and philosophical in his attitude. The prohibition involvement was viewed by him with a broad toleration, and though it wrecked considerably the fortune he had amassed he took it with notable calmness and restraint. He was a man keenly

interested in public projects and his benefactions, of which little was heard, were many.

Carl Meeske replaced his father as the firm's president, then took full control in 1922 when Reiner Hoch decided that the soda business wasn't his mug of beer. Three years earlier Hoch had divorced his wife, Mary, and moved out of the mansion he built a block away from the brewery in 1897. Perhaps the brewery was simply too close to his old home (see Reiner Hoch's Haunted House, page 168). Hoch left the brewing business and turned his attention to Gopher Real Estate, which he and Meeske owned, and invested in the Duluth division of the Acme Match Company.

At People's, Sandstedt remained in place as president, joined by William Carlson, T. G. Frerker, and M. J. Doyle. While brewmaster Frank Luckow stayed on, the company did not at first apply for a license to make near beer or malt beverages. It did change its name to the People's Bottling Company and is listed as such in Duluth directories throughout the 1920s. Research, however, uncovered no reports of dividends being paid during the 1920s, indicating the company reorganized its structure when it became a bottling company.

An undated newspaper article, likely from the early 1920s, provides what little information we have about the

LABELS FOR TWO OF THE NEAR BEERS PRODUCED BY THE PEOPLE'S BOTTLING COMPANY DURING PROHIBITION.
[K. MALZ COLLECTION]

$25.00 For a Name

The Northern Brewing Co., of this city, have reopened their plant, located on the corner of Catlin Avenue and Eighth street, after having been closed for the past three years, for the manufacture of high grade Cereal Beverages, Root Beer and other beverages.

These products are manufactured from the purest of materials and under the strictest sanitary conditions, thus ensuing to consumers the purest and most healthful of beverages.

Since perfecting our methods of manufacture, after months of experiment, these beverages have been submitted to experts for tests as to their purity, palatibility, and food and stimulative values and have been accorded such a great measure of commendation that we have decided that these strictly high class, first quality products are entitled to a distinctive name by which they may hereafter be known and advertised, and to secure such a name offer a prize of TWENTY-FIVE DOLLARS IN CASH.

Our Cereal Beverage

Is brewed from the choicest of materials, identical with those formerly used in the manufacture of beer; is aged with strictest care and precision, and is bottled under the most sanitary conditions, using only the most modern machinery and equipment.

It is a product pleasing to the palate, refreshing to the fatigued, and wholesome and invigorating to all who partake of it.

It is a home product for home consumption.

It is a recreation "For Old Times' Sake."

Its delightful sparkle, its agreeable inviting taste, with a small amount of alcohol (less than ½ of 1%), affords a wonderful beverage for the home and club, the party or the meal.

With its full flavor and delightful aroma it's difficult to tell the difference. Try it.

24 large or 36 small Bottles—$2.00.
(Cases and Bottles are never sold.)

Our Root Beer

A smoother, more satisfying beverage than our Root Beer we believe is hard to produce.

This Root Beer is composed of pure granulated cane sugar and water, to which is added the extracts of a number of roots and herbs of the highest quality and known for their high food and stimulative values, to which is added a certain quantity of carbonated water.

It is NEW, DIFFERENT, BETTER.

A Beverage which recommends itself to those who prefer something different.

Not only a soft drink but a food in liquid form, due to the large quantity of invert sugar contained therein.

WHOLESOME, DELICIOUS, INVIGORATING.

24 large or 36 small Bottles—$2.00.
(Cases and Bottles are never sold.)

CAN YOU NAME IT?

In order to secure a distinctive name for these beverages, as well as others we expect to produce in the future, we offer a prize of Twenty-Five Dollars, subject to the following conditions.

First—In order to qualify as a contestant, each person desiring to submit a name must purchase one case of either our Cereal Beverage or Root Beer at $2.00 per case, to be paid for on delivery. For each case purchased before December 1st, 1922, when the contest will end, the purchaser will be entitled to submit one name.

A coupon will be found in each case, on which the purchaser will write his or her name, and address, date of purchase, and the name submitted for consideration, and mail to us. Upon the close of this contest, December 1st, next, all names submitted will be placed in the hands of 3 competent judges who will select and rank the names submitted in the order of their value to distinctiveness, originality, and adaptibility as a beverage name.

These names will then be submitted to a leading Trade Mark Bureau who will determine as to which names are capable of being registered to cover a full line of beverages. The name so found to be best qualified will then be awarded the prize of $25.00, and the result published in the Superior Teegram as soon as decided.

Second—Try to make your name as catchy, and distinctive as possible so that it may have genuine attractiveness and value from an advertising standpoint in identifying our beverages to the consumer.

Do not submit a name which might be confused with any name now used to identify other beverages. Do not submit a name containing the name of any club or society, individual, firm, corporation or association; nor of any city or state or words which are merely geographical names.

Do not submit names which only describe the quality or character of our beverages, as these words as well as those heretofore mentioned are generally not considered as acceptable for registration.

A consolation prize of one case of either beverage will be given to each of the first ten persons whose names are selected by the judges but who do not win the cash prize.

GET IN THE GAME NOW!

Order as many cases of Root Beer or Cereal Beverage as you want now. Then select your names, one for every case you purchase, fill out your coupons, and mail to us.

LET'S GO!

NORTHERN BREWING CO.

Telephone Broad 2185.   —Phone Your Orders—   8th and Catlin Ave.

This ad for a contest to name Northern Brewing Company's new cereal beverage and root beer ran in the *Superior Evening Telegram* in November 1922. [ZENITH CITY PRESS]

Prohibition-era products, which included Golf Club, a ginger ale advertised as a "sure shot," a sparkling water sold as People's Choice, and a near beer called Safety Brew. Collectors have also found unlabeled bottles embossed with "People's Bottling Co., Duluth, Minn.," but no list of specific flavors could be found.

Across the bay Northern changed hands. The Rueping family sold the Superior brewery to a group of local men. Louis McKinnon stayed on as plant manager and John Kuehlthau remained brewmaster, and both were also likely chief among the local investors. Like his counterparts in Duluth, Kuehlthau learned to make soda, but the plant wouldn't reopen until November 1922, after it had retooled and obtained the proper licenses to produce cereal and carbonated beverages.

That same month the beverage maker, still called Northern Brewing Co., advertised a $25 prize to name its new cereal beverage and root beer. Northern touted its near beer as being "brewed from the choicest of materials identical to those formerly used in the manufacture of beer" and mentioned that "with its full flavor and delightful aroma, it's difficult to tell the difference." Northern promoted its root beer, made primarily of pure cane sugar, as "a food in liquid form." The contest came with a catch: participants had to buy a two-dollar case of one of the beverages to enter. To date research has not uncovered the winning names, or if anyone even entered the contest.

That near beer turned out to be much closer than near on July 29, 1924, when federal agents stopped Superior resident Robert Delahunt and found several kegs of strong beer in his car. The beer came from Northern. Near beer is made by making strong beer and boiling it to reduce the alcohol content, and someone at the brewery had filled kegs with strong beer that had not been converted to near beer. Federal agents searched the brewery after Delahunt's arrest

products People's produced during Prohibition. It also indicates the firm did eventually obtain a cereal-beverage permit: "The People's Brewing Company are [sic] manufacturers of near beer and a large assortment of carbonated drinks.... Fourteen people are employed at the plant. Products made are distributed throughout the Northwest." Breweriana collectors provide further clues to People's

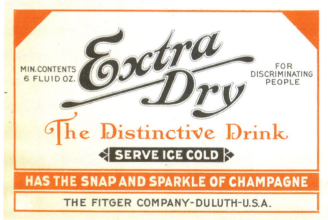

Top: A tin lithographic sign used to promote the Fitger Company's Silver Spray, ca. 1927.
[P. Clure Collection]

Bottom left: A label for Extra Dry, the predecessor to Silver Spray.

Bottom right: The first label used on bottles of Silver Spray.
[Fitger's Complex]

and found more strong beer in kegs. The Wisconsin Office for Prohibition Enforcement revoked the brewery's license to manufacture nonintoxicating beverages and convicted Delahunt of violating the Volstead Act, the law covering the enforcement of Prohibition. Delahunt sat in jail for a year, and Northern sat idle until Prohibition ended in 1933.

SILVER SPRAY KEEPS FITGER'S AFLOAT

Meanwhile, on the other side of the Interstate Bridge, Duluth's breweries managed to steer clear of legal violations. Following his father Percy's stroke, Victor Anneke was named president of the Fitger Company. August Fitger busied himself in California, looking after his various

THE BEST MIXER IN THE CROWD

FITGER'S PROMOTED SILVER SPRAY HEAVILY AND EVENTUALLY DISTRIBUTED THE DRINK IN THIRTY-THREE STATES. TOP LEFT: IMAGE USED ON SILVER SPRAY LETTERHEAD; TOP RIGHT: FITGER'S EMPLOYEES READY TO PARTICIPATE IN DULUTH'S WINTER FROLIC PARADE, CA. 1927; BOTTOM LEFT: THE FITGER COMPANY SALES TEAM WITH A TRADE-SHOW DISPLAY FOR SILVER SPRAY, 1929; BOTTOM RIGHT: THE RACIALLY INSENSITIVE COVER OF A BOOKLET FOR RECIPES USING SILVER SPRAY TO MAKE NOT ONLY DRINKS BUT ALSO JELLY, SHERBET, PARFAITS, AND BAKED HAM BASTED WITH SILVER SPRAY.

[WINTER FROLIC PHOTO: C&R JOHNSON COLLECTION; ALL OTHER IMAGES: P. CLURE COLLECTION]

investments including Kieselguhr, which he renamed the Celite Corporation. Victor Anneke relied on the skills and experience of John Beerhalter to help him guide the brewery through the beer-free 1920s.

In the summer of 1924 Beerhalter began purchasing a syrup extract from a small company in central Minnesota to make a beverage called "Extra Dry," advertised as having the "snap and sparkle of champagne." A 1930 *Duluth Herald* article mentioned that it tasted like white catawba grapes, still popular in nonalcoholic wine today. The arrangement was supposed to be exclusive, Johnson reports, but Fitger's discovered the extract's manufacturer was selling it throughout the state. Beerhalter replicated the formula and Fitger's began producing the product itself. He and Ludwig Hanson renamed the product "Silver Spray" and launched it on Independence Day, 1925.

Silver Spray enjoyed immediate success and eventually expanded Fitger Company sales across the country. Just

because Prohibition had outlawed the manufacture and sale of alcohol didn't mean Americans had stopped drinking. Those who didn't simply drink at home brought smuggled or homemade hooch with them to soda fountains, restaurants, hotels, and of course speakeasies, making it more palatable by mixing it with carbonated beverages. Some soft-drink parlors employed "pitcher pigs," unbreakable granite or metal pitchers filled with illicit alcohol. This allowed initiated customers to pay to have their sodas spiked. If police arrived, the soda jerk tipped the pitcher over and its contents disappeared down a drain. Duluth historian Heidi Bakk-Hansen reports that even before national Prohibition took effect, Duluth police had confiscated at least seven pitcher pigs.

Silver Spray targeted this very market: advertisements for the beverage stressed that it was "NOT a Ginger Ale," and ensured drinkers it was "The Best Mixer In The Crowd." In a 1965 interview, John Beerhalter Jr. joked that some people

INSIDE THE FITGER COMPANY BOTTLING HOUSE, CA. 1928, AS THE EQUIPMENT FILLS CASES OF SILVER SPRAY.
[FITGER'S COMPLEX]

At the stroke of midnight on January 17, 1920—the first day of national Prohibition—Duluth police dumped $30,000 worth of confiscated liquor "into the sewer of the garage repair shop under the Duluth police station." While the DPD tried to keep the event a secret—only Chief John Murphy, Mayor Clarence Magney, and other city officials knew of it—the newspaper reported that "a score of civilians, attracted from the odor...witnessed the 'ceremony.'"

The paper continued, "Whiskey, rum, beer and wine mixed on the concrete floor. Broken glass clogged the sewer." Safety Commissioner William Murnian joked with reporters that "if some of the gulls start climbing the aerial bridge today, don't be surprised, they've been drinking out of the Second Avenue sewer outlet."

Police had been collecting banned booze since 1917, when Duluth first went dry and hoarding began. Duluth historian Heidi Bakk-Hansen reports that by Christmas 1919, burglaries in the city's upscale East End had reached epidemic levels as thieves made off with stockpiles of illegal liquor. One unnamed man told reporters he had lost "25 cases of priceless liquor."

The wealthy had no problem accessing alcohol. Private clubs could keep any alcohol purchased prior to Prohibition. The Kitchi Gammi Club, whose members included August Fitger and Percy Anneke, installed small lockers behind its basement bar where members stored their personal stash, so that technically the club itself never possessed anything illegal. Club legends include a tunnel used to ferry liquor between the club's basement and the Lake Superior shore.

Bakk-Hansen explains that many other drop-off spots dotted the lake's North Shore, as bootleggers used a variety of methods to gets goods across the Canadian border. Unlit boats cruised the shoreline, toboggans glided across frozen rivers, and fast cars called "whiskey sixes" raced through the night at top speed.

The not-so-wealthy had to be more creative. Some risked arrest by setting up their own stills, and even housewives turned their kitchens into blind pigs. Others took advantage of legal exceptions that allowed for the medicinal or sacramental use of alcohol by asking physicians for prescriptions or even establishing "churches" that were little more than blind pigs. Others annually cooked up the two hundred gallons of wine or cider allowed by law. Duluth's Italians had long made their own wine, and even today vines can be found in the lower portion of what was once called Little Italy.

During the nation's first year of Prohibition, Duluth police were part of the problem. In July 1920, federal agents arrested Chief Murphy and ten others, including a former U.S. Marshal, for smuggling whiskey across the Canadian border. During the trial the evidence, ninety bottles of whiskey, disappeared from a vault in Duluth Police Headquarters. Murphy then testified that while on a fishing trip he had accidentally stumbled upon bottles of homemade beer, not hard liquor, confiscated it, and brought it to the station in Duluth. The next day his attorneys produced thirteen sacks of beer—allegedly taken from the police vault—to substantiate his testimony. On November 10 Murphy and his confederates were found not guilty.

Warren E. Pugh replaced Murphy. In early December Pugh participated in a raid of the "imposing residence" of Harry and Ann Papove in Lakeside. Pugh and his men found a very large still, three hundred gallons of corn mash, and twenty-seven gallons of moonshine ready for distribution—then "the largest still and greatest quantities of moonshine ever confiscated in a raid." The Papoves declared it was all for "personal use." Police also found thirteen gallons of homemade hooch at the home of a former police officer, and the National Guard Armory's custodian faced federal charges for making and selling moonshine.

And that was just 1920. For the next thirteen years, the pages of Duluth's newspapers were filled with stories of those caught trying to circumvent the Eighteenth Amendment. In March 1929 officials confiscated a 150-gallon still capable of "turning out moonshine at the rate of sixty gallons a day" and dumped 305 gallons of liquor down the drain in the basement of City Hall. The *Duluth Herald* made a similar bad joke to the one Commissioner Murnian had made nine years earlier, claiming the liquor was "stimulating the fish in Lake Superior."

How were things in Superior? Notorious Prohibition-era gangster Al Capone summed it up when he supposedly told a friend that "Superior is full of speakeasies and brothels...the law won't give you any trouble there."

went blind from drinking Silver Spray after mixing it with wood alcohol (see "Drinking During the Dry Spell," above).

Led by the efforts of Jon Lamb, Fitger's promoted Silver Spray like no product before it, especially in Minnesota and Wisconsin. According to Johnson, a seaplane hired by Fitger's flew over the Zenith City dropping fifteen thousand leaflets "extolling the goodness of the new beverage." Silver Spray sponsored local sports teams during Duluth's Winter Frolic, employees crawled inside huge "bottles" of Silver Spray and danced along the Superior Street parade route. The bottles also danced at St. Paul's Winter Carnival and Minneapolis's Aquatennial. The six-piece Silver Spray

Bubbles Orchestra performed at dances and events throughout the region. And when Victor Anneke decide to convert the one-story building that replaced the original brewery building in 1920 into a boxing training and exhibition facility, he named it the Silver Spray Gym.

Sales of Silver Spray eventually reached thirty-one states, and Fitger's set up distribution centers in Kansas City, Omaha, Tulsa, Dallas, Memphis, Toledo, Detroit, Chicago, Denver, Salt Lake City, Spokane, Seattle, Los Angeles, and San Francisco.

DEPRESSION LEADS TO REPEAL

Despite the success of Silver Spray, Victor Anneke had a fairly rough second half of the 1920s. His mother Lydia died in 1927 and his father Percy, paralyzed since 1924, died on April 26, 1928. That summer August Fitger announced that he had sold the Celite Corporation for almost $9 million—roughly $131 million today—and was officially retiring from the brewery business. Then came the October 1929 stock-market crash, ushering in the Great Depression.

The Fitger Co., at least, had diversified. Duluth Brewing & Malting and People's relied solely on near beer and carbonated beverages and faced stiff competition—Duluth already had plenty of soda bottlers before the former breweries entered the game. When Black Tuesday struck, Sandstedt, Frerker, and Doyle remained in charge of People's, and Frank Luckow continued to mix up the soft drinks. By January 1931 the company had fallen into receivership and had not payed taxes for the previous two years.

On January 30, 1931, the *Superior Evening Telegram* reported that People's Brewing Co. had been sold at public auction the previous day by order of the district court. The new

owners consisted of "a group of former stockholders" who bid $10,548 (worth about $173,000 in 2018). It was a good deal: the *News Tribune* reported that the buildings and equipment were valued at $46,000. The *Telegram* added that "the new owners plan to reorganize and begin the manufacturing of carbonated beverages at an early date." Those new owners/former stockholders included Secretary-Treasurer M. J. Doyle, Vice President Gust Anderson of Hibbing, and President Carl O. Hanson.

Hanson was no stranger to business. Born in Norway in 1886, he had immigrated to Duluth with his family and eventually became vice president of Duluth hardware wholesale giant Kelly-How-Thomson. He left the company in 1925 to launch the Hanson-Duluth Company, wholesale and retail dealers of auto supplies and radios—Hanson always had one eye on the future. Many others did as well. The Women's

LEFT: AUGUST FITGER'S BUSINESS PARTNER PERCY ANNEKE, CA. 1920, PRIOR TO THE STROKE THAT TOOK HIM AWAY FROM HIS BELOVED BUSINESS.

RIGHT: VICTOR ANNEKE, 1928. VICTOR FILLED HIS FATHER'S SUBSTANTIAL SHOES, HELPING TO STEER THE FITGER CO. THROUGH PROHIBITION AND ITS REPEAL.
[P. CLURE COLLECTION]

Organization for National Prohibition Reform (WONPR) led a movement to end the lawlessness created by the illegalization of liquor. With the Depression, America was also losing jobs at a rapid pace, and bringing back the beer and liquor industries would put people back to work. Hanson, who owned a few shares of People's stock, became convinced the return of beer was not far off. So he sold his company and formed the group that bought People's. As the *Telegram* noted, the "men who purchased the plant are of the belief that the manufacture of real beer is not far distant." Even under Carlson the company struggled until Prohibition ended.

Over at Duluth Brewing & Malting, Carl Meeske wrestled with more than the failing economy. Brewmaster John Lingelbach had died on March 11, 1929, seven months before the crash. Just over a year later, on March 27, 1930, a notation in the Fitger Company log read "Carl Meeske calls RE taking over the Rex Co.—he offers all kegs, cases, bottles, trucks, fixtures, labels, crowns, trade marks, good will, etc. for $6,500 plus actual cost on cartons of extracts, etc., bring the total to about $7,000" or roughly $104,000 in 2018. The next day the log read "We accept Meeske offer. Will take over Rex 4/15."

Morale must have been pretty low at Duluth Brewing & Malting, because it couldn't even make it to the closing date. On April 12, a Saturday, Meeske called Fitger's to explain that "all his men are quitting this evening and want us to take the business over right away." Meeske, Schmid, Beerhalter, Victor Anneke, and Fitger's vice president Tom Miller met at

ten the next morning. By the afternoon they had sent a press release to local newspapers, which announced that Fitger's "would continue the manufacturing of Minnesota Club Ginger Ale, Lovit Beverages and Rex and Royal brew cereal beverage," and that the purchase would mean that Fitger's would add fifteen to twenty more names to its payroll, most of them former Rex Co. employees, and eighty-five people already worked for the company. While DB&M's buildings and real-estate holdings were not included in the deal, Fitger's got something Meeske would one day regret, including: the rights to DB&M's former flagship beer brands, Rex and Moose. Just prior to the acquisition, Fitger's had introduced several more sodas including Isle Royale Ginger Ale, Lindy Julep (a lime drink named for Minnesota's Charles Lindbergh), and Kitchi Gammi—pasteurized, carbonated water from Lake Superior. In 1930 Fitger's produced sixty thousand bottles of soda every day.

It also added another near beer called Town Club. Advertisements for the malt beverage promised it was not just hop flavored, like Liberty Brew, but actually made with "Imported Saazer Hops"—Fitger's really wanted to send the message that Town Club was as near to beer as near beer could get. A *Herald* report mentioned that by April 1930 the new brew was "attracting favorable attention throughout the Northwest" and that the Duluth firm had recently sent an entire train-car load to New York.

Silver Spray remained the most successful Prohibition product Fitger's ever produced. The same 1930 *Herald* article touting Town Club mentioned that Silver Spray was such a success, countless imitators had attempted to replicate the Fitger formula but all had "fallen into obscurity." Fitger's maintained at least fifteen Silver Spray distribution centers across the country, and had recently opened accounts in Texas, Louisiana, and Arkansas. A year earlier the company did $1,250,000 in business, worth over $18 million today.

Prohibition's repeal couldn't come fast enough for Anneke and Beerhalter. In September 1931 they decided to focus on beverages, selling their underperforming candy division to Duluth's Barnes Candy and the cigar-distribution business to Duluth grocery wholesaler Rust-Parker-Martin. It still wasn't enough to avoid the necessity of layoffs, and the staff was reduced dramatically. Beerhalter would later tell researchers that despite all its efforts, Fitger's lost money during every year the Eighteenth Amendment was the law of the land.

With the ladies of the WONPR fanning the winds of change, the Wets took control of Congress in 1930, and in 1932 Americans elected Franklin D. Roosevelt president. On February 20, 1933, Congress passed the Twenty-First Amendment, repealing Prohibition, but it would take until December to be ratified. The Cullen-Harrison Act, also known as the "Beer Act," legalized the sale of beverages with an alcohol content of 3.2 percent. It reached Roosevelt's desk on March 21, 1933, and he signed it without hesitation. Beginning at 12:01 A.M. on April 6, 1933, American breweries could start selling beer again, even if it was 3.2 beer.

Three of the Twin Ports' four former beer breweries began getting ready for beer before Roosevelt even signed the act, but Fitger's alone stood ready to deliver on April 6. The brewery had been gearing up since early March and was prepared to bottle 3.2 beer under the Natural Beer label. Because Fitger's had never stopped making near beer, all the brewing machinery remained in good operating condition, making retooling easy—and the brewery already had wort, allowing time to age the beer properly before the big day. A federal agent locked the gate to Fitger's yard at 6 P.M. on April 5 to make sure nobody tried to break in prior to midnight. Empty trucks lined up two abreast along Superior Street between Fifth and Seventh Avenues East. Additional trucks sat inside the brewery yard waiting to be loaded.

Johnson reports that, "The beer parade started promptly at midnight. Police Sergeant Elmer Stovern fired a pistol as the starting signal and Scott Cash, an inspector for the Federal Bureau of Industrial Alcohol, unlocked the gates to the brewery. A German 'Oompah' band immediately struck up 'Happy Days are Here Again.'" Brewery workers loaded 147 trucks after midnight; the first, driven by Tim Belland, headed off to Two Harbors. On that first day Fitger's sold 19,000 cases and 1,260 kegs of beer. August Fitger later noted that in one night, the federal government "collected $80,000 in excise taxes from Fitger's!" Like his story about building the 1881 brewery, his estimate stretched the facts. It was

CELLAR BOSS CHARLES ZENTNER (STANDING) AND FRANK FRONCKOWIAK TRY SOME OF THE FIRST BATCH OF 3.2 BEER AFTER PRESIDENT FRANKLIN ROOSEVELT SIGNED THE SO-CALLED "BEER BILL," WHICH MARKED THE BEGINNING OF THE END OF PROHIBITION. FITGER'S WAS THE FIRST TWIN PORTS BREWERY TO GET BACK TO BREWING BEER.
[FITGER'S COMPLEX]

THE BREWERY SALOON BECOMES THE PICKWICK

Michael Fink's 1881 Lake Superior Brewery housed a taproom/bierstube called simply the Brewery Saloon. It was likely first operated by John Tischer, who in 1882 applied for a license to operate a billiard table on the premises. German immigrant Franz Heinrich (see page 68) became saloonkeeper in 1886, a year after August Fitger and Percy Anneke purchased the brewery.

In 1894 Fitger and Anneke expanded and remodeled the saloon, hiring artists Feodor von Luerzer and John Fery to paint murals in its large Dutch Room. Fery's landscapes adorned one side and von Luerzer's playful scenes the other. Von Luerzer depicted elves brewing beer, drunken monks, and Fitger's boyhood home in Delmenhorst, Germany. An 1895 sportsman's guide called the saloon a *Bier-Stube* and described it eloquently:

> The walls...are decorated with artistic frescoes representing the manufacture of beer under the direction of grotesque little gnomes, from the growth of grain to the finished product in the keg. There is a mammoth fireplace, the shelf over which is adorned with a valuable collection of mugs of famous design, antlers, ancient armor and other curiosities. The old oaken table and spindle leg chairs, leaded windows and paneled wainscot give an air of antiquity to the room, easily convincing one that he has transported across the seas and dropped into the feudal age of the German Empire.

FITGER'S BREWERY SALOON IN THE 1890S (TOP) WITH LONGTIME SALOONKEEPER FRANZ HEINRICH SITTING FRONT AND CENTER, AND IN 1907 (BOTTOM).
[C&R JOHNSON COLLECTION]

When Heinrich died in 1909, his assistant, Polish immigrant Joe Wisocki, took over as saloonkeeper. In 1914 Fitger's hired architect Anthony Puck to design a new saloon building which they constructed immediately west of the brewery at 508 East Superior Street. Workers moved the 1894 murals to the new building to adorn the walls of its Dutch Room, and Fery painted a few more. The original Brewery Saloon closed December 31, 1914, and the new facility opened the next day. The *Duluth Herald* covered the transition:

> Many hochs [cheers] and farewells were exchanged late last night at the famous old saloon in the Fitger Brewery addition that for many years has been a unique resort. The hochs were in celebration of the death of 1914 and the advent of 1915, and because it was the last night in the old place, a number of old patrons sang appropriate songs. Today the new saloon nearby was opened. All of the pictures in the old place were removed to the new one and at eleven P.M. the key was turned into the lock.

After Duluth went dry on July 1, 1917, the brewery converted the saloon into a soft-drink parlor and then leased the building to Wisocki. In 1921 Fitger's introduced a near beer named Pickwick, likely first served publicly by Wisocki at the former Brewery Saloon, which many Duluthians now called "Joe's." Shortly thereafter, the legend goes, patrons began saying they were "going to Joe's to have a Pickwick," which they soon shortened to "I'm going to the Pickwick." So Wisocki renamed the establishment the Pickwick.

If the name changed in 1921, Wisocki didn't mention it to the publisher's of Duluth's city directory. The business appears as Joe Wisocki Saloon or Soda Fountain in directories until 1925, when it was first listed as the Dutch Room restaurant. Between 1928 and 1935 it is registered as "Joe Wisocki's Restaurant." Advertisements for the Dutch Room pictured the eatery's front door, over which hung a sign for Pickwick. Ads published in 1933, however, indeed refer to it as the Pickwick. Beer returned to the Twin Ports at 12:01 A.M. on April 6, 1933. The previous day's newspapers contained an ad featuring a photo of Wisocki holding a mug of beer. It read in part, "See Joe at 12:01! At one-minute-after-twelve o'clock Friday morn, Joe will serve up the good 3.2 Fitger beer in the Old Dutch Room of the Pickwick Tavern! Join the merriest crowds in town!" Some accounts state that at least nine thousand people were part of that merry crowd.

The next day the *News Tribune* explained how Joe Wisocki and his loyal patrons commemorated the event: "Wisocki... drew his last glass of near beer at 11:59 1/2 P.M., and then threw it into the fireplace. Promptly with the first stroke of the clock at midnight, he drew the first glass of legal beer drawn in Duluth since June 30, 1917." (It wasn't the last glass of Pickwick ever poured; advertisements in the next day's newspapers mentioned Joe still had plenty of the near beer on hand.)

It wasn't until 1938 that Duluth directories first list the tavern as "The Pickwick." The Wisocki family purchased the building in 1945, just before Joe retired and handed the reins to son Joe Junior. Joe Wisocki died in 1954, but the restaurant stayed with his family until 2010. The Pickwick continues to serve Duluth today, and much of it looks the same as it did when it first opened as Fitger's Brewery Saloon in 1915.

A POSTCARD ADVERTISING JOE'S PICKWICK SALOON, CA. 1935.
[ZENITH CITY PRESS]

AN ADVERTISEMENT FOR THE DUTCH ROOM, CA. 1925.
[C&R JOHSON COLLECTION]

DULUTHIANS CELEBRATE THE RETURN OF BEER AT THE PICKWICK, APRIL 6, 1933.
[C&R JOHNSON COLLECTION]

closer to $8,000, or about $140,000 today—a healthy sum that still illustrates Fitger's point: the brewing industry was good for the economy.

The following evening Victor Anneke hosted a celebration inside the brewery's boardroom—August Fitger, while still chairman of the board, no longer spoke for the company. Anneke gave a speech, which was broadcast throughout the region on WEBC Radio. It began:

Tonight marks an historic moment in the progress of Duluth and the nation. After fifteen years of enforced idleness, a great industry goes back to work again. Thousands of men are being put on new payrolls. Millions of dollars are being spent in this renewed activity. Tonight, as I said, is historic in our national life, for tonight marks more than the legalization of beer… [and] the end of the stranglehold which the foes of true temperance have long had upon our laws, and which they have sought, by every means, to enforce upon an unwilling public. Tonight should be remembered, it seems to me, because it was tonight that the right to true temperance, moderation, and good fellowship has been reborn in this country of ours, and the uncontrolled, intemperate drinking of harmful concoctions behind closed doors has been struck a death blow. Good fellowship belongs in the home, the club, or the legitimate hotel and café. Let's put it there once more and keep it there.

By the time Anneke had left the air, Twin Ports residents had been drinking Fitger's beer for much of the day. Beer was back, but the nation would still be under Prohibition until the Twenty-First Amendment was ratified—and even then Duluth would remain dry, as its own 1917 decision to ban alcohol sales superseded the national law.

RETOOLING, REBRANDING, AND REDUCTION

PROHIBITION TOOK A HEAVY TOLL ON THE NATION'S BREWING INDUSTRY, and Minnesota paid its share. Brewing historian Charles Dick found that nearly half of Minnesota's breweries did not reopen following repeal. Remarkably, all three of Duluth's breweries returned, joining twenty-two others across the state, including the three largest, St. Paul's Hamm Brewing Company, the Minneapolis Brewing Company (makers of Grain Belt), and Gluek's, also in the Mill City. In Wisconsin, about 115 brewers stopped making beer in 1919; over 90 returned to brewing in 1933—including Superior's Northern Brewing Company. Blue Label was back on shelves by October 1933 with a new ingredient: pure Lake Superior water. Because its water had become brackish, Northern had to stop drawing from its artesian well for brewing and began using water from the Superior Water, Light & Power Company's system, which drew water from an intake pipe that jutted into the lake from Minnesota Point.

NORTHERN REORGANIZES—TWICE (1933-1940)

J. S. Cochrane returned to his former job as Nothern's engineer and fired up the boilers on March 22, 1933, for his new boss, Rudolph Peterson. Peterson, a former Tower Avenue saloon operator, reorganized the brewery in 1932. John Stariha served as vice president, former manager Louis McKinnon returned as secretary-treasurer, and McKinnon's son Frank signed on as a driver. Northern did not announce the name of its brewmaster.

At the same time a new Wisconsin law driven by tavern owners forced liquor stores to stock beer at room temperature, which in turn required breweries to pasteurize bottled beer to ensure longer shelf life. When the law changed Northern followed a national trend by bottling some of its beer without pasteurization—it had to be kept cold and was advertised by many breweries as "draft beer in a bottle." Some breweries called their unpasteurized bottled beer "keg beer" or "picnic beer."

When legal strong beer and booze returned to the Twin Ports in January 1934, the community was struggling along with the rest of the country, hopeful the new president's New Deal would dig them out of the Great Depression. The repeal of Prohibition was the first step to put people back to work.

The 1938 Duluth mayoral election symbolically marked the shift in the region's history. Thirty-one-year-old Rudy Berghult upset beloved five-term mayor Samuel F. Snively to become the youngest mayor in Duluth's history and the first Duluth mayor born in the Zenith City. The following year workers dismantled Duluth's famous Seventh Avenue West Incline Railway and constructed Enger Tower in memory of a generous pioneer. As the decade closed, the populations of both communities had stabilized. Duluth's decreased for the first time since 1875, but only by .4 percent to 101,065. Superior dropped just 2.8 percent to 35,136.

Then war came, and the Twin Ports again sent its sons to battle and went to work. As Iron Range mines pulled ore from the earth as fast as they could, ore docks set records loading boats with iron ore that made the steel that built bombs and tanks and ships, some right here in the Twin Ports. Shipbuilding facilities on both sides of St. Louis Bay employed over ten thousand men and women, averaging ten ships a month while producing a fleet of 230 vessels. Superior's Butler Shipyards beat them all, producing seven cargo carriers, twelve frigates, and thirteen coastal freighters.

The postwar baby boom helped Duluth bounce back, its population reaching 104,511 in 1950. Superior remained stagnant as a .5 percent gain brought the Wisconsin city to 35,325 souls. But by then the rust was beginning to show on both sides of the St. Louis. The same factors that bruised the community's breweries took a toll on other local industries. The growing highway system reduced train and shipping traffic in the Twin Ports, and soon giant warehouses in both cities stood vacant. Marginal businesses failed, and even successful operations fell prey to larger companies who bought up competitors and closed down factories to consolidate production. Meanwhile, fluctuating iron-ore demand kept the region unstable and invasive species all but eliminated commercial fishing. Similar scenarios played out in other industrialized communities established along the Great Lakes. The Head of the Lakes was becoming the buckle of the Rust Belt.

In 1956 Duluth dropped its commission system and adopted the mayor/city council approach in use today. Both sides of the bay were filled with hope when the St. Lawrence Seaway opened in 1959, allowing oceangoing vessels to reach the Great Lakes which, hopefully, would drive more commerce through the harbor. But it wouldn't end the decline of manufacturing.

Duluth's population reached 106,884 in 1960, its all-time peak. Superior, however, had declined 5 percent to 33,563, forcing it to close some public schools. In Duluth, urban renewal eliminated the city's Bowery—and

dozens of historic buildings along with it. The expansion of I-35 cost Duluth entire neighborhoods including Lower Oneota west of the ore docks and Slabtown centered at the base of Twenty-Seventh Avenue West, home to Duluth Brewing & Malting.

As Northern Brewery shuttered its doors in 1968, the city that surrounded it was in the midst of losing another 4 percent of its population, which dropped to 32,237 before the decade was out. By the time Fitger's bottled its last beer in 1972, Duluth had been losing over 500 people a year for twelve years and the population dropped to less than 100,500. Both communities continued to struggle. While Superior dropped over 8 percent in the 1980s, it has since stabilized at roughly 27,000 citizens. From 1970 to 1990 both cities lost 15 percent of their populations. In the early 1980s Skoglund Outdoor Advertising put up a billboard reading "Will the last one leaving Duluth please turn out the light?" The joke hit too close to home for many in the proud community to appreciate. After a strong public response the billboard was removed the same day it went up.

Thanks in part to its embrace of tourism and its position as a regional medical center, the local economy began improving at the end of the 1980s. Brewing returned to the Twin Ports in 1994, and since then the Twin Ports' populations have stabilized to roughly 27,000 in Superior and 86,000 in Duluth.

Walter Glockner took over as brewmaster and superintendent in February 1935. Glockner, a native of Sayda, Germany, had learned his craft working at his father's brewery and malt house before graduating the Master Brewers program at Munich's Technical University. He worked as a brewmaster in Europe and South America before coming to the U.S.

Soon after Glockner got to brewing, Northern hit a snag with its packaging. While it had long called its premier beer Blue Label, Premier-Pabst—makers of Pabst Blue Ribbon—objected to the potential consumer confusion created with Northern's use of the name and the image of a ribbon or scroll used on labels. Not only had Pabst trademarked Blue Ribbon and the use of blue ribbons on labels since 1898, but

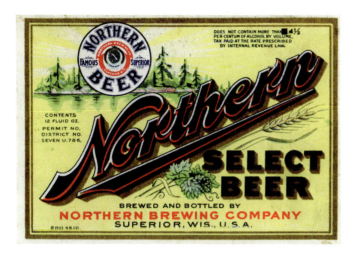

in 1920 the company had also trademarked the name Blue Label for its malt extract. Yet Northern's use of Blue Label on strong beer predated Pabst's malt extract.

The solution was a compromise: Northern would stop using images of a blue ribbon on packaging. If it wanted to continue calling its beer Blue Label, the label itself could not be blue. The words Blue Label could be printed in blue ink, but they could not be set in the same typeface used on Premier-Pabst products. Premier-Pabst even agreed to reimburse Northern for the cost of having new printing plates made for its revised labels. At this same time Northern also produced Northern Select Beer—and used a yellow label to advertise it.

While Northern was settling its conflict with Premier-Pabst, Rudolph Peterson died suddenly at the brewery. George Ehmann left the Kingsbury Brewing Co. of Sheboygan, Wisconsin, to manage Northern that December, and soon thereafter George Volkert replaced Glockner. Volkert had brewed for the Joseph Wolf Brewing in Stillwater, Minnesota, prior to Prohibition. Joseph Wolf had not reopened.

LABELS USED BY NORTHERN BREWING CO. BETWEEN 1933 AND 1938. A LAWSUIT BROUGHT ON BY THE BREWERS OF PABST BLUE RIBBON PUT AN END TO NORTHERN'S BLUE LABEL BEER. [J. STEINER COLLECTION]

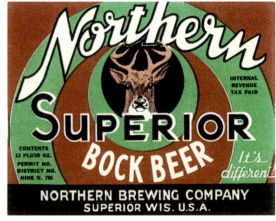

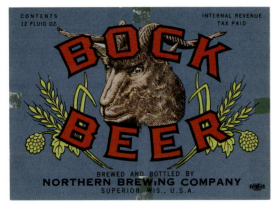

A SELECTION OF LABELS USED BY NORTHERN BREWING CO. BETWEEN 1938 AND 1950. NOTE THE BLUE NORTHERN SELECT LABELS; THE LOWER LABEL INCLUDES THE PHRASE "UNION MADE BEER" AND A UNION "BUG" OR LOGO, INDICATING IT WAS MADE AFTER VICTOR NELSON BECAME THE BREWERY'S OWNER IN 1938. THE BOCK BEER LABEL (BOTTOM LEFT) WAS USED BY MANY BREWERIES; THE PRINTER SIMPLY CHANGED THE BREWERY NAME.

[TOP LEFT, CENTER: J. LEMKE COLLECTION; CENTER LEFT: P. CLURE COLLECTION; BOTTOM LEFT AND CENTER: C. OLSEN COLLECTION; ALL OTHERS: J. STEINER COLLECTION.]

As 1937 ended the *Superior Evening Telegram* touted Ehmann and Volkner's success. Sales had jumped thanks to the introduction of Northern Superior beer, which also came in a bock. The label featured the head of a buck deer, as Ehmann explained: "The buck deer is the symbol of Upper Wisconsin, and our beer is not brewed for Chicago or Minneapolis, but for upper Wisconsin taste and preference." A winter beer called Xmas Brew also helped sales that year.

Ehmann also predicted that Northern's Blue Label, which Volkner had "changed and improved," would further increase overall sales. The article closed with the names of all twenty-seven Northern employees, who the company boasted received "the highest brewery wages at the Head of the Lakes" and most other Wisconsin cities.

Perhaps the wages were a bit too high, for the rosy picture the newspaper painted in December 1937 quickly faded. Northern declared insolvency in June 1938—but the brewing didn't stop for long. In August Victor Nelson, Oscar Johnson, and John Frischler purchased the brewery from trustees. Nelson, the company president, was a well-known Superior road contractor.

Nelson took out a full-page ad in the *Telegram* for a "contract" between himself and the people of Superior promising that Northern would keep brewing beer in Superior, employ only Union men "who live and spend their money in Superior," use only the finest ingredients and Lake

Superior water, ensure its new Northern Pale beer was available throughout the region, do all it could to "bring more business and tourists to the Great Northwest," and follow all laws to eliminate "anti-social conditions" associated with drunkenness. Thirty-three employees witnessed Nelson sign the agreement, including nearly everyone listed the previous December. Ehmann stayed on as manager, but brewmaster Volkner was gone. Nelson invested in the brewery, including a new bottling plant and other improvements totaling $40,000. Under his guidance, the brewery's business stabilized. Ehmann also stopped making Blue Label beer, but the label for Northern Select would now be blue and carry the message "Union Made Beer."

Choice," which was likely meant to appeal to those who had served in World War I and implied that the beer was as strong as it had been prior to Prohibition. Breweries across the nation produced beers labeled with similarly patriotic names.

In 1938 People's replaced Choice with Stag Beer, an extra-pale pilsner that featured a deer on the label. It was initially advertised as "The Monarch of Beers," then "The Sportsman's Beer." At about the same time People's also began brewing a short-lived pilsner named Carleton Club and made seasonal beers, including a bock and a winter beer. In 1937 Hanson contracted for People's to become the region's 7-Up distributor and later added Royal Crown Cola to the product line.

DULUTH'S WESTERN BREWERIES
FIND THEIR FEET (1933-1940)

While Northern struggled to restart following Prohibition, across the Interstate Bridge Carl Hanson's finely tuned business skills had People's up and running—and delivering beer—by July 1933. Hanson had put twenty-five men on the People's payroll back on January 15. The brewery received its permit in early March, and by mid-May Frank Luckow's crew had six thousand barrels aging in tanks adjacent to the bottling house, where workers had installed a $10,000 bottling and washing machine and a new labeling machine.

The following year People's labels advertised its beer as People's Choice, first used in the 1920s for its brand of sparkling water and reused for an "old style" beer. The label featured an image of the Great Lakes and the taglines "Duluth to the sea—see Duluth" and "Made with crystal clear Lake Superior Water." It was also available as an unpasteurized bottled picnic/keg beer. During the 1930s People's also bottled Buddy Beer, advertised as "The Veteran's

TOP: PEOPLE'S BREWING COMPANY IN 1933.
[UMD MARTIN LIBRARY]

RIGHT: A TIN SIGN ADVERTISING PEOPLE'S BEER AS "THE PEOPLE'S CHOICE," CA. 1934.
[P. CLURE COLLECTION]

PEOPLE'S BREWING CO. PRODUCT LABELS 1933–1938

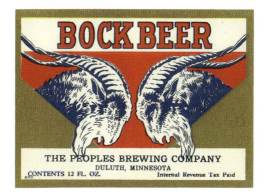

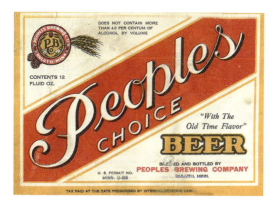

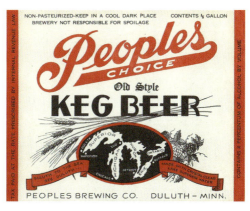

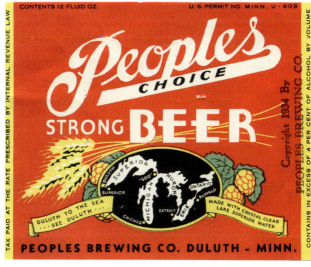

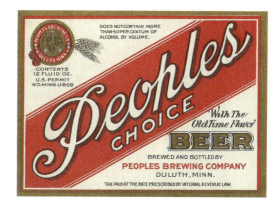

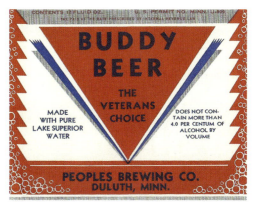

THE BOCK BEER LABEL (TOP LEFT) WAS USED BY MANY BREWERIES AT THE TIME, PERSONALIZED BY THE PRINTER FOR EACH BREWERY. BUDDY BEER WAS TARGETED AT THOSE WHO MISSED THE BEER THAT WAS BREWED PRIOR TO PROHIBITION. PEOPLE'S BECAME DULUTH'S 7-UP DISTRIBUTOR IN 1938. NOTE THAT THE 7-UP LABEL STATES THAT THE PRODUCT CONTAINS LITHIA, AKA LITHIUM CITRATE, LONG USED IN PYSCHIATRIC MEDICINES TO FIGHT DEPRESSION. JUST AS COCA-COLA ORIGINALLY CONTAINED COCAINE, LITHIUM PUT THE "UP" IN 7-UP FROM ITS INTRODUCTION IN 1929 UNTIL 1948.

[PEOPLE'S CHOICE WITH NECK LABEL (CENTER): C. OLSEN COLLECTION; ALL OTHERS: K. MALZ COLLECTION]

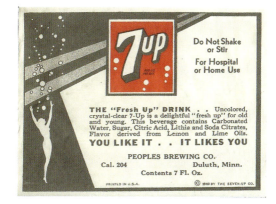

THIS PAGE
TOP: EMPLOYEES AND VEHICLES OUTSIDE PEOPLE'S, CA. 1938, AFTER IT INTRODUCED STAG BEER AND BECAME DULUTH'S 7-UP DISTRIBUTOR. THE BREW KETTLE (LEFT) AND AGING VATS (RIGHT) IN 1936.

FACING PAGE
TOP LEFT AND RIGHT: AN UNIDENTIFIED EMPLOYEE WORKS THE PEOPLE'S BOTTLING LINE, 1937. BOTTOM LEFT: THE RACKING ROOM, 1936; BOTTOM RIGHT: THE LOADING DOCK, 1935.

[UMD MARTIN LIBRARY]

PEOPLE'S CHOICE BECAME STAG IN THE LATE 1930S, ABOUT THE TIME CARLETON CLUB WAS INTRODUCED.

[STAG LABEL (CENTER RIGHT): J. LEMKE COLLECTION; PEOPLE'S CHOICE (TOP LEFT) AND STAG (BOTTOM RIGHT): K. MALZ COLLECTION; ALL OTHERS: C. OLSEN COLLECTION]

The addition of 7-Up fell between two significant losses. Frank Sandstedt, People's president from its inception until well into Prohibition, retired in 1932 at sixty-six. He died on May 25, 1934, after a brief illness. In early 1940 Frank Luckow—brewmaster since 1911 decided to call it quits at fifty-six. He likely had health issues as he died, like Sandstedt, just two years after leaving the brewery.

East of People's in the heart of Duluth's West End, Duluth Brewing & Malting struggled to get back to brewing. Reiner Hoch had died in May 1930. When the Beer Bill passed in 1933, Carl Meeske purchased Hoch's remaining shares in the brewery and Gopher Real Estate from his heirs and reorganized the brewing company under its original name. He then scrambled to resurrect the old brewery with a new team operating new equipment. To raise capital he sold stock to over one hundred investors.

Meeske put carbonated-beverage expert Gus Severson, a thirty-year veteran of the original DB&M, in charge of the bottling works. Meeske then hired L. G. Hiebel as his sales and advertising manager, and made Fred Voss the plant's chief engineer. Officers and board members included Vice President A. E. Boswell, Treasurer Carl M. Boswell, and Secretary F. J. Schulthels, all investors from northern Michigan. Assistant Secretary D. S. Holmes lived in Duluth.

Meeske tapped Henry Schmid as his brewmaster and head maltster. A forty-four-year veteran of the brewing industry, Schmid had spent Prohibition making beer in Monterey, Mexico, for Cervecería. Prior to that he had brewed for Anheuser-Busch and Inland Brewing & Malting Co. of Spokane, Washington. Schmid's brewing crew included twenty-three-year-old Bob Ostern, who took a job in the cellars, the lowest rung on the company ladder, on February 8, 1934. Ostern would later tell researchers the position meant the world to him. In 1998 he remembered telling

Duluth Brewing & Malting's advertising campaign for its new beer asked drinkers to tell their bartenders to "Make Mine Karlsbräu," as seen on the side of a train car (above) and a tin sign (left). [P. Clure Collection]

Following Prohibition, Duluth passed stringent liquor laws. Many were common-sense regulations. Beer could be sold as early as seven in the morning, and bars closed at midnight. Liquor could not be mixed nor consumed in an automobile. The legal drinking age, twenty-one, complied with state law. Sales were limited to established "liquor districts."

Others didn't make much sense. While restaurants and hotel counters could sell liquor, it could not be served at stand-up bars; saloons with existing bars had to install fixed stools. Nightclubs and cabarets could not serve liquor. No booze was allowed where anyone danced, screened a film, or played football or baseball. Liquor stores could not sell tobacco or soft drinks. Bartenders asked for provisions that allowed only men to drink at bars; women could drink in a booth, which must be opened at one side. Live music was allowed, but only if performed by union musicians. And, to protect union bartending jobs, women could not "go behind bars where liquor is primarily dispensed."

In 1941 the city council allowed dancing, music, and "other forms of entertainment" at on-sale establishments, but never on Sundays. And no more live music, only tunes played on radios. The decision to allow dancing was reversed less than two months later, at the same time the city council responded to a request from the local musicians' union to *allow* live music in taverns by revising the liquor ordinance to specifically *prohibit* live music from all establishments that sold liquor.

The live-music issue was followed by a debate over jukeboxes, as opponents argued that music could lead to dancing, which would irreversibly corrupt young people. The city council wanted to allow jukeboxes so that saloons would make more money and the city could then raise the cost of liquor licenses. When the council passed an ordinance allowing the mechanical music machines with a 3–2 vote, a delegation of "approximately 100 persons crowded the city hall council chambers" armed with a protest signed by representatives of thirty-one Duluth churches. The council caved, banning jukeboxes on January 24, 1944. The ordinance was later repealed.

In 1954 Duluth established a Liquor Board to advise the city council. In 1963 Municipal Judge Thomas J. Bujold ruled that Duluth's 1933 law forbidding women from drinking at bars was unconstitutional. In 1973 the council voted to "permit dancing on Sundays in hotels, clubs and restaurants qualifying as food-serving establishments licensed for Sunday liquor sales." It also allowed restaurants to serve drinks over their bars on Sunday, as long as food made up 40 percent of total sales.

The 1934 provision with the most impact created "liquor districts" to restrict liquor licenses to specific commercial zones. The largest was along Superior Street from Thirty-Third Avenue West to Fourteenth Avenue East and included Rice's Point and the St. Croix District (today's Canal Park Business District). Five smaller districts were established in West Duluth. You could not buy liquor in any other neighborhood—and certainly not in Lakeside/

Lester Park, where an 1891 state law banned liquor sales. When the University of Minnesota Duluth relocated its campus in the 1950s, another district was added: liquor sales were banned within a one-mile radius of the college's Kirby Student Center because most students were not of legal drinking age.

Beginning in the late 1950s Duluth's Gateway Urban Renewal Project eliminated the Bowery—essentially Fourth Avenue West to Mesaba Avenue along Michigan and Superior Streets—by demolishing nearly every building within it. The city then began the long process of redistricting to prevent another Bowery from developing. But attempts to spread liquor sales throughout the city faced persistent resistance from community and religious leaders. In September 1973 the city council finally passed an ordinance that opened all of Duluth's commercial districts to liquor sales, "except," as the *Duluth News Tribune* reported, "for the statutory sacred cows of the Lakeside and UMD areas."

The UMD issue was resolved a year later, after the drinking age was lowered to eighteen. After several attempts to open sales in Lakeside and Lester Park, a November 2015 referendum vote showed that 67 percent of all Duluthians and 53 percent of Lakeside/Lester Park residents wanted the ban repealed. In 2016 state legislators repealed the ban in Duluth's easternmost neighborhoods along with the prohibition of Sunday sales at liquor stores. Since that time only one liquor license has been requested and granted in Lakeside, none in Lester Park.

himself, "If I can get a job there, I'll have a real job." In time Ostern had more than a job; eventually he ran the entire company.

Carl Meeske told newspapers he spent $300,000 updating the 1896 brewery, bringing the plant's brewing capacity to 125,000 barrels a year with the help of a 450-barrel brew

kettle the *Duluth Herald* called "the largest in the Northwest." It contained fifteen thousand pounds of copper.

None of that beer would carry the names of the original DB&M's flagship brands, Moose and Rex. Fitger's had purchased the rights to them when DB&M folded in 1930. So Meeske sponsored a contest to find a name for its

Bohemian-style pilsner beer, and the winner took an inside track by incorporating Carl Meeske's name: Karlsbräu, aka Carl's Brew. It would become very popular, and the brewery also bottled holiday, bock, and an unpasteurized keg beer under the Karlsbräu name.

Meeske was able to bring back one of his father's former beers, Castle-Brew, the pre-Prohibition beer known as Drei Kaisers until World War I. The labels still included an image of the Upper Peninsula Brewery and boasted that the beverage inside was "approved for its quality since 1878," the year Reiner Hoch and Charles Meeske first started making beer together. The brand lasted just a few years, a sign that tastes were changing. In the 1930s DB&M also began bottling soft drinks, including Salisbury brand carbonated water.

While DB&M initially focused sales to Duluth and northern Minnesota, it eventually reached a wider market. The West End brewery employed seventy-five people in the summer, fifty during colder months. Perhaps DB&M's great asset was its malt house. The brewery was one of just ten

in the nation, including St. Paul's Hamm Brewing Co., that made its own malt. The other 590 had to buy it from someone else, and many bought it from DB&M.

A 1938 story in the *Herald* described the entire malt-making process, from choosing the best barley, steeping it for six days until it sprouts, heat-drying the sprouted grain, and finally "knocking off" the sprouts. The sprouts, now a byproduct, were shipped to dairies as feed. The dried barley was now malt, its starches changed by the process to create dextrose, the sugar that, with the help of yeast, becomes alcohol in the brewing process. The malt house at the DB&M complex processed six hundred bushels of barley every day. That year, the paper reported, the malt house ran twenty-four hours a day every day of the week. The brewery estimated it would spend

Top: A Karlsbräu sign for Duluth's Green Parrot Tavern, located on West First Street between Lake Avenue and First Avenue West.

Left: A glass sign for DB&M's Gold Shield Beer, ca. 1939. **[P. Clure Collection]**

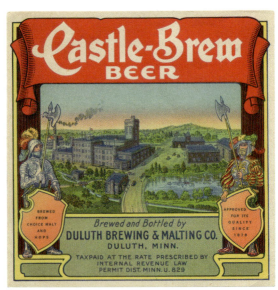

THE CASTLE-BREW LABEL FEATURED AN IMAGE OF THE UPPER PENINSULA BREWING CO. IN MARQUETTE, MICHIGAN, FOUNDED BY DB&M FOUNDERS REINER HOCH AND CHARLES MEESKE.

[C. OLSEN COLLECTION]

THE SWITZER-HOFF LABEL (BOTTOM CENTER) CARRIES THE PERMIT NUMBER FOR DULITH BREWING & MALTING, INDICATING THAT THE DULUTH BREWERY BOTTLED THE BEER WHICH WAS THEN DELIVERED TO STORES IN IOWA BY RITZ DISTRIBUTING OF DES MOINES.

[K. MALZ COLLECTION]

KARLSBRÄU WAS NAMED FOR DB&M PRESIDENT CARL MEESKE. "KEG BEER" OR "PICNIC BEER" WAS UNPASTUERIZED BEER IN A BOTTLE AND HAD TO BE KEPT COLD.

[KARLSBRÄU KEG BEER LABELS: C. OLSEN COLLECTION; ALL OTHERS P. CLURE COLLECTION]

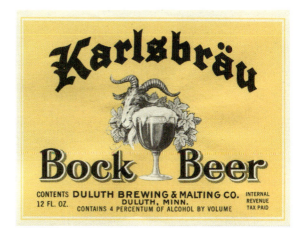

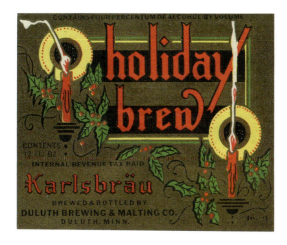

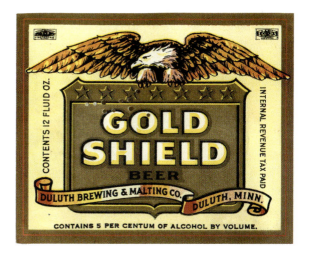

TOP LEFT AND RIGHT: MOST BREWERIES IN AMERICA MADE SEASONAL BEERS TO ENCOURAGE SALES, INCLUDING BOCKS IN THE SPRING AND "HOLIDAY" OR "WINTER" BEERS DURING THE COLDER MONTHS.

BEGINNING IN 1933, AMERICAN BEER BREWERS WERE REQUIRED TO INCLUDE THE PHRASE "TAX PAID AT THE RATE PRESCRIBED BY INTERNAL REVENUE LAW" ON EACH LABEL AND CAN. STARTING IN 1938, THE PHRASE WAS SHORTENED TO "INTERNAL REVENUE TAX PAID." THE REQUIREMENT WAS ELIMINATED IN 1950.

[ALL LABELS: C. OLSEN COLLECTION]

GOLD SHIELD WAS DULUTH BREWING & MALTING'S "PATRIOTIC BEER," A TREND DURING THE 1930S THAT INCLUDED PEOPLE'S "BUDDY BEER" AND FITGER'S "VETERAN'S CHOICE."

$250,000 on barley that year (nearly $4.5 million in 2018 dollars). By then brewmaster Schmid and his crew had introduced a patriotic brand of its own, a pilsner called Gold Shield whose label featured an iconic eagle.

As the decade came to a close, Schmid and his crew adjusted the recipe for Castle-Brew. Brewhouse employee Bob Ostern remembered that the new beer was lighter, as "young people and women liked it better and it was cheaper too." Beginning in 1940 DB&M began packaging it as Royal Bohemian. A billboard campaign introduced the new brand to regional drinkers, promising "a new beer sensation" and "quality above all" and declared the beer was "something to look forward to."

That year Schmid had the honor of giving away the bride at a wedding that united Duluth's two largest breweries, at least symbolically: his daughter Marie married John Beerhalter Jr., son of longtime Fitger's brewmaster John Beerhalter.

FITGER'S FACES MORE CHANGES (1933–1940)

John Beerhalter Jr.'s 1940 marriage to Marie Schmid capped off seven very transitional years at Fitger's. The brewery was firing on all cylinders in April 1933, the first in the Twin Ports to deliver beer as Prohibition underwent repeal, and Beerhalter Jr. had joined the brewhouse staff. Confident that brewing would return, during Prohibition Beerhalter Jr. had apprenticed at F. Goetz Brewing Company of St. Joseph, Missouri, making Goetz Pale, called "the most famous near beer ever brewed." Maury reports the younger Beerhalter intended to find a job in Canada or Mexico until repeal altered his plan.

The summer after the brewery shipped that first post-Prohibition beer, Fitger president Victor Anneke, his wife, Elsa, and one of their sons were injured in a car accident. All, as well as their chauffeur, were hospitalized. It took Victor Anneke, who already suffered

providing for Duluth's St. Luke's and St. Mary's Hospitals, Los Angeles's Lincoln Hospital, and a hospital in Charlottenburg, Germany. He also left Victor Anneke some stock and made similar provisions for Beerhalter Sr., longtime employee Walter Johnson, brewery attorney P. C. Schmidt, and Richard Kothz, Fitger's personal chauffeur in Duluth until Fitger moved to California.

While he mourned Fitger, Beerhalter Sr. busied himself reconfiguring the brewery. Workers dismantled the Silver Spray Gym—back in the beer business, the brewery needed the space. Beer took over the bottling house, so soft-drink production moved to the garage on Michigan Street. It became known

from injuries received in a 1917 motorcycle accident, until the following summer to recover.

Charles Krause, Anneke's father-in-law, helped John Beerhalter Sr. manage the brewery in Victor's absence. Krause was sixty-seven years old, the recently retired secretary-treasurer of Missouri Belting in St. Louis, manufacturers of belts used in industrial machinery. Outside of his son-in-law, Krause's only connection to the brewing industry was his friend Adolphus Busch, founder of Anheuser-Busch, who died in 1913. It wasn't the first time Anneke had called on Krause to handle a tough job; as Prohibition set in, Krause visited Duluth to inform employees they had lost their jobs.

October 1933 saw the death of August Fitger, a few days shy of his seventy-ninth birthday. His will was generous to hospitals,

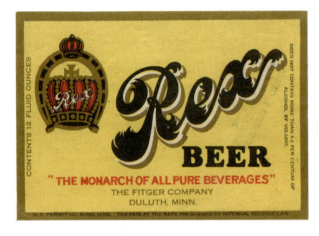

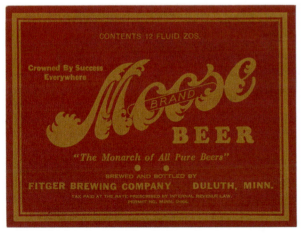

as the Pop Shop. The stable, which saw its last horse in 1932, became the garage. Beerhalter Sr. also hired a new German-born chemist, Johannes "Johnny" Hey, who first came to Duluth in the 1920s to work in the Minnesota Steel Plant.

Since Joe Wisocki was not about to give up his lease on the Pickwick—originally Fitger's Brewery Saloon—the brewery had no place to serve its own beer. Coopen Johnson reports that the company remedied this by converting a room in the office basement into the brewery's taproom. It held about fifty people and was used for meetings, employee celebrations, and other gatherings. The brewery later rented the taproom for $10 a night, including a bartender and unlimited beer. According to Johnson, the practice ended in the 1960s after college students exploited the policy. (The taproom location is now a retail space within the Fitger's Complex.)

By the time Anneke made it back to the brewery, business was thriving. The brewery had repackaged its product

FITGER'S BEGAN USING THE PHRASE "NATURALLY BREWED, NATURALLY BETTER" (TOP CENTER) TO ADVERTISE ITS NATURAL BEER IN THE 1930S.

[BOCK AND NATURAL BEER (TOP CENTER): C. OLSEN COLLECTION; KEG, GREEN LABEL, AND NATURAL LABEL (BOTTOM CENTER): FITGER'S COMPLEX]

THE GREEN LABEL (CENTER) WAS IN USE VERY BRIEFLY, AS BEER THAT WAS NOT PROPERLY AGED DID NOT TASTE GOOD AND WAS CALLED "GREEN BEER."

TOP RIGHT: LEGION BEER WAS FITGER'S ATTEMPT TO ATTRACT DRINKERS WHO PREFERRED THE BEER BREWED PRIOR TO PROHIBITION. BOTTOM RIGHT: FITGER'S USED A GENERIC LABEL FOR ITS HOLIDAY BEER.

[LEGION: K. MALZ COLLECTION; HOLIDAY: FITGER'S COMPLEX]

"men, FREE PRIZES – of Fitger's he-man's beer!"

Get in the Contest

8 Free Prizes every week... free where—register its weight—let the dealer send in your application. GRAND prizes at the end of three months. Get in Fitger's weekly Fishing Contest. Catch one of the four biggest fish in the Northland and get 3 cases of Fitger's Beer FREE every week! No complicated entrance requirement. Simply show your fish to a Fitger dealer anywhere. Enter your biggest bass, pike, muskie or northern pike. Contest sponsored by Minnesota Tourist Bureau. Listen to Fitger's Northland Radio Chain broadcast every Friday night at 9:30 over WCCO, WEBC, WMFG, WHLB. Listen to this swell fishing review and variety show besides.

Fitger's is a real man's beer, and how!... Not a "sweet" beer...no sir. Packed full of tang and sparkle, with a real head of foam and malty, as real beer drinkers want it.

We make Fitger's especially for your taste up here in this country. And the formula for Fitger's got its start in another place where men are men and beer drinkers are two-fisted—in Augsburg, Germany. Ask our brewmaster about that. He came from Germany himself and he knows!

He-man's beer? You'll tell the world... but watch the ladies go for it, too! Try a bottle today at your regular tavern ... take some home to the "Missus".

NOT A SWEET BEER

Fitger's Beer is made like Bavarian-type beers. Not sweet, but malty, sparkling ... with a fresh, clean, tangy after-taste!

Fitger's
natural – brewed

ABOVE: A NEWSPAPER AD FOR FITGER'S NATURAL BEER, AKA FITGER'S "HE-MAN'S BEER." [C&R JOHNSON COLLECTION]

RIGHT: MANY OF FITGER'S ADVERTISEMENTS INCLUDED THE PHRASE "SINCE 1881," THE YEAR MIKE FINK BUILT THE LAKE SUPERIOR BREWERY, NOT 1882 WHEN AUGUST FITGER BEGAN MAKING BEER IN DULUTH OR 1885 WHEN HE AND PERCY ANNEKE TOOK FULL OWNERSHIP AND THE BREWERY BECAME KNOWN AS THE A. FITGER & COMPANY LAKE SUPERIOR BREWERY. [P. CLURE COLLECTION]

health declined. Krause, meanwhile, was pushing seventy. According to Johnson, Anneke called his childhood friend Arnold Fitger and asked him to take charge of the Duluth operation. Fitger was already busy running several companies, including the Refactories Corp., the Horseshoe Cattle Co., the Fitger California Company (an investment group),

CONTINOUS HIGH QUALITY SINCE 1881

Fitger's NATURAL BEER
"Brewed in Duluth"

Naturally Brewed...   Naturally Aged...

Naturally Better!

—Insist on Fitger's Fine Beverages—
SCOT SODA—GINGER ALE—LIME RICKEY—CLUB SODA—CARBONATED WATER

as Fitger's Natural Beer, advertising it as "naturally better!" It was available bottled in both 3.2 and strong versions and, briefly, a dark version. Like Duluth's other brewers, Fitger's also bottled an unpasteurized picnic beer, a bock in the springtime, a holiday beer in the winter, and Legion, which (like People's Buddy Beer) was marketed to veterans.

Anneke and Beerhalter Sr. continued the Fitger's tradition of keeping up with innovations by becoming the first Twin Ports brewery, and one of the first in the nation, to package its beer in cans. The brewery first announced Fitger's Natural Beer in cap-sealed cone-top cans in a full-page newspaper ad in November 1935. On the twelfth, the first cases went to the Pickwick and Two Harbors distributor Tim Belland. Johnson credits Belland with urging Anneke to make the move to cans. While sales figures for that first year aren't available, Johnson reports that in 1936 the brewery shipped 417 train-car loads, its all-time record. (See page 195 for a photo of the cans.)

It is more likely Belland urged Krause to can beer. Anneke never fully recovered from the accident and despite spending much time in Texas soaking in mineral spas, his and Kelco Co., which processed kelp to extract chemicals used in a variety of industrial applications.

While Arnold Fitger visited Duluth as often as he could, for the most part he operated the brewery, in his words, by "remote control" from California. He also put his faith in brewmaster Beerhalter Sr., giving him full control of the brewing operation and telling him to "go full speed ahead."

"From one generation to another, goes Fitger's secret for honest beer enjoyment"

Here's John Beerhalter, Fitger's famous Master-Brewer, talking to son John about a batch of Nordlager Beer cooking in the giant kettle. And no pot or pan in your kitchen is scoured any brighter than this big kettle, showing the barrel of care that goes into every bottle of Fitger's Nordlager Beer.

The Fitger Folks

THE reason you'll always go on getting that fine, flavory, enjoyable beer from Fitger's year after year, is because brewing grand beer is a family tradition at Fitger's. John Beerhalter's skill has made our beer what it is for 35 years, and son John is his father all over again when it comes to having a knack for making beer with that genuine Old-Country flavor. Their secret for processing malt is what makes our beer so keen and refreshing. And the slow honest way we let our beer age, gives it the malty, Old-Country flavor you're likely to miss in a sweet beer. So enjoy beer at its best. Order a case of Fitger's Nordlager Beer from your dealer right now.

Listen to Fitger's Sportsman's Special radio feature. Music, laughs, fishing tips. Friday nights at 8:30 P.M. on WCCO, Minneapolis; WEBC, Duluth; WMFG, Hibbing; WHLB, Virginia.

Brewed the honest way

FITGER BREWING CO., DULUTH, MINN.

Fitger wrote to Beerhalter Sr. and the other company officers every day, and Beerhalter Sr. also spent time working directly with Fitger in California. During Arnold Fitger's first year the brewery expanded sales and distribution to the southern half of the state and hired Chicago's Burnett Agency to handle advertising. The firm targeted beer drinkers in northern Wisconsin, Minnesota, and the Dakotas who fancied themselves rugged sportsmen using hunting and fishing motifs and advertising Natural as "Fitger's he-man's beer" made for "real beer drinkers."

"Real beer" likely referred to many other post-Prohibition beers, which were much lighter. Tastes had changed. Under Prohibition, mixing bathtub gin so it was palatable increased the popularity of cocktails. More women consumed alcohol and were allowed in drinking establishments for the first time, and many of them enjoyed beer—lighter beer. The advertisements didn't forget that half of the population: Natural was also for "Ladies who like things RIGHT, too." One ad featured a woman identified as Sallie Marsh

LEFT: ADVERTISEMENTS FOR FITGER'S NORDLAGER BEER FEATURED JOHN BEERHALTER SENIOR AND JUNIOR EITHER HUNTING, FISHING, OR TESTING BEER.

ABOVE: A NEON SIGN ADVERTISING FITGER'S "NATURALLY BETTER!" NATURAL BEER OUTSIDE OF ESKELI'S TAVERN AT 108 EAST FIRST STREET, DULUTH, CA. 1930S.
[P. CLURE COLLECTION]

CONTENTS 12 FL. OZ.

Fitger's
PREMIUM PALE BEER
FITGER BREWING COMPANY, DULUTH, MINN.

INTERNAL REVENUE TAX PAID

CONTENTS TWELVE FLUID OUNCES ★ FITGER BREWING COMPANY. DULUTH. MINNESOTA

Fitger's
Nordlager
BOCK
STRONG BEER

★ INTERNAL REVENUE TAX PAID ★

CONTENTS THREE FOURTHS QUART ★ FITGER BREWING COMPANY. DULUTH. MINNESOTA

Fitger's
Nordlager
natural brewed
BEER

★ INTERNAL REVENUE TAX PAID ★

CONTENTS 12 FL. OZ.

Fitger's
PREMIUM PALE BEER
FITGER BREWING COMPANY, DULUTH, MINN.

CONTAINS 4.9 PER CENTUM OF ALCOHOL BY VOLUME

INTERNAL REVENUE TAX PAID

★ FITGER BREWING COMPANY. DULUTH. MINNESOTA ★ INTERNAL REVENUE TAX PAID

Fitger's
Nordlager
natural brewed
PICNIC BEER
STRONG

CONTENTS ½ GALLON • MUST BE KEPT IN A COLD DARK PLACE **NOT PASTEURIZED** BREWERY NOT RESPONSIBLE FOR SPOILAGE

CONTAINS 4.9 PER CENTUM OF ALCOHOL BY VOLUME

CONTENTS ONE FULL QUART (32 FL. OUNCES)

Fitger's
Nordlager
natural brewed
BEER

INTERNAL REVENUE TAX PAID ★ DULUTH. MINNESOTA

★ FITGER BREWING COMPANY ★ DULUTH

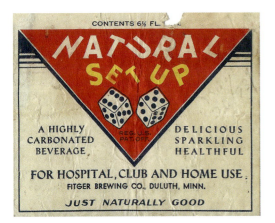

CONTENTS 6¼ FL.

**NATURAL
SET UP**

REG. U.S. PAT. OFF

A HIGHLY
CARBONATED
BEVERAGE

DELICIOUS
SPARKLING
HEALTHFUL

FOR HOSPITAL, CLUB AND HOME USE
FITGER BREWING CO., DULUTH, MINN.

JUST NATURALLY GOOD

FITGER'S PALE BEER WAS INTRODUCED IN THE LATE 1930S AND ITS NAME WAS SOON CHANGED TO NORDLAGER. NATURAL SET UP WAS A NONALCOHOLIC DRINK TARGETED AT THOSE LOOKING FOR A "HEALTHFUL" SOFT DRINK AND MAY HAVE BEEN SIMILAR TO 7-UP, WHICH ALSO TOUTED ITS USE IN HOSPITALS.

[PALE BEER, NATURAL SET UP: K. MALZ COLLECTION; NORDLAGER BOCK: P. CLURE COLLECTION; NORDLAGER PICNIC: C. OLSEN COLLECTION; NORDLAGER QUART: J. LEMKE COLLECTION]

who testified that she didn't mind the "he-man" label and that Natural was "one beer I can really go for myself."

Beerhalter Sr. went after another customer base by introducing Nordlager in 1937. The new beer cost one-third as much as Natural, a price-point product designed to reach a less-affluent market. Burnett took an aggressive approach to promote the beer in Duluth, including a skywriting campaign. Both Natural and Nordlager, Johnson reports, were advertised on the weekly *Fitger's Sportsman Special Variety Show*, a radio show broadcast by stations in Minneapolis, Virginia, Hibbing, and Duluth. Minneapolis's WCCO reached into Iowa and Wisconsin, new sales territory for Fitger's. The radio show offered fishing and hunting tips, skits, and music and promoted Fitger's-sponsored contests with prizes of hunting and fishing gear. Some of the programming Fitger's featured would be recognized as racist today. On Friday

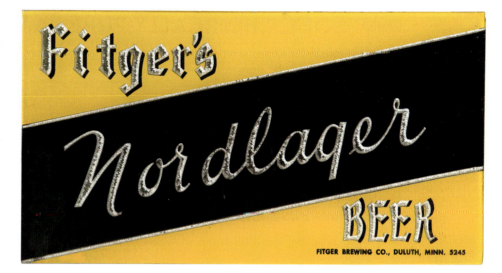

nights the show featured national entertainers Pick and Pat who, like Amos and Andy, portrayed caricatures of African Americans. Advertisements depicted the pair in blackface.

Unfortunately, Anneke's health did not improve. He spent much of 1937 in and out of St. Mary's Hospital, where he died on October 20. His wife, Elsa, spent her remaining years a widow, but often found herself in the public eye. A virtuoso pianist, between the 1920s and 1950s she performed as an acclaimed soloist with the St. Louis Symphony Orchestra, the Minneapolis Symphony Orchestra, the Chicago Symphony Orchestra, and, naturally, the Duluth Symphony Orchestra. She died in 1995 just eleven months shy of her one hundredth birthday.

Fitger's also said goodbye to Charlie "Spike" Unden, who retired on April 25 after, newspapers said, "61 years' service" at Fitgers. That would have placed his starting date in 1876, nine years before Fitger's existed, but the exaggeration was fitting. Unden's brewing roots reached back to his early childhood in the 1860s, growing up in the midst of his uncle Nicholas Decker's brewery. Spike Unden arguably knew more about the early history of beer brewing in Duluth than anyone ever has.

ABOVE: A TIN SIGN FOR NORDLAGER BEER, CA. 1939.

LEFT: (FROM LEFT) FITGER'S OFFICERS ARNOLD FITGER, JOHN BEERHALTER SR., AND WALTER JOHNSON WITH SALES MANAGER FRED HITCHCOCK DURING A 1938 SALES CONFERENCE AT DULUTH'S SPALDING HOTEL.
[P. CLURE COLLECTION]

Beer is made of many things, more so today than ever thanks to the craft brewing movement—hops and grains and yeast of course and sometimes fruit or coffee or even hot peppers. But no matter what else a brewer puts in it, when the brewing's over, beer is 95 percent water, making the quality of that water, particularly its mineral content, extremely important to the brewing process. It can even define regional beers.

Case in point: Donald Dierckins was a practical brewer at St. Paul's Theo. Hamm & Co. Brewery for over twenty-five years beginning in the mid-1950s. Olympia Brewing Co. purchased the brewery in 1975 and began making Olympia there alongside Hamm's. Dierckins and other loyal Hamm's drinkers were happy to drink Olympia brewed in St. Paul if they couldn't have a Hamm's "because of the water," which was drawn from the same artesian well. The same thing happened when Stroh Brewing Co. bought out Olympia in 1983. After Stroh's shuttered the facility in 1995, many loyal Hamm's drinkers switched to Schmidt, also brewed with water drawn from an artesian well in St. Paul.

Water from Lake Superior came to define the beer brewed in the Twin Ports, but that wasn't always the case. When Gottlieb Busch and Louis Kiichli started making beer at the Head of the Lakes in 1859, they built their breweries along streams. Busch famously set up shop on what came to be called Brewery Creek in Duluth, a "pure mountain stream on the North Shore of Lake Superior." Kiichli drew water from the "big slough," later called Faxon Creek, which fed into the bay just north of today's Barker Island. Other pioneer breweries drew water from Superior's Nemadji River and Duluth's Buckingham Creek.

It wasn't until November 1869, when Gustav Kiene established his short-lived brewery on Minnesota Point, that beer was first made with Lake Superior water (he called the beer Lake Superior Ale). Twelve years later, Mike Fink moved out of Duluth's first brewery and built a new facility on the shore of Lake Superior and began drawing water from the lake. The move proved prudent: as Duluth's population boomed in the 1880s, the hillside above the brewery became heavily populated, and residents used Brewery Creek as a sewer. From the early 1880s until 1900, Duluth experienced a number of typhoid epidemics.

There's no telling just how pure Lake Superior water was when August Fitger and Percy Anneke purchased Fink's brewery in 1885—Brewery Creek emptied into the lake just a block or two north of the facility. Breweries established in the 1890s did not sit along the shore. Superior's Klinkert, which evolved into Northern, used water from an artesian well, as did Duluth Brewing & Malting. Two years after DB&M was established, Mayor Henry "Typhoid" Truelson led the city to construct the Lakewood Pump House just north of Duluth's border and establish a public water works that delivered treated Lake Superior water throughout most of the Zenith City. People's Brewery, established in 1907, used water straight from the city tap. Following Prohibition, DB&M stopped using its well and switched to city water. So did Northern, tapping into the public works, which drew water from an intake pipe on Minnesota Point that, like the one in Lakewood, reached far into the lake. Today's brewers use these same water sources.

It was in the 1930s that Twin Ports breweries first began promoting their beer as containing Lake Superior water. Shortly after Prohibition ended, People's began advertising its People's Choice Beer as "Brewed with Crystal Clear, Chemically Pure Lake Superior Water." When Fitger's introduced Rex Imperial Dry in 1946 the label claimed it was made with "Pure Lake Superior Water." Later Fitger promotions would tout the brewery's products as having been "Brewed with matchless Lake Superior water." Advertisements for Northern's Vic's Special reminded beer drinkers it was "Brewed with Famous Superior Water Which Makes Fine Superior Beer."

It wasn't just marketing hype: the brewers themselves strongly believed in Lake Superior water. One veteran Fitger's employee wrote in 1938 that "one of the most important substances [in Fitger's beer] is good old Lake Superior water." In 1956 DB&M president Carl Meeske told the *Duluth News Tribune* what made Lake Superior water special: "The water's extremely soft, almost like rain water, and that's an important factor in brewing good beer. Hard water tends to make beer flat. If water's hard, breweries have to give it special softening treatment." And those treatments use chemicals—hence that good ol', *chemically pure* Lake Superior water.

Following Victor Anneke's death, Arnold Fitger bought Anneke's shares of Fitger's, gaining controlling interest in the brewery. As chairman of the board, Fitger remained in California and continued to send directives to Duluth on a daily basis. One of them named Beerhalter Sr. the company's president—the first time ever someone with a name other than Fitger or Anneke held the title. After thirty-six years of service, he'd earned it.

With Arnold Fitger's support, Beerhalter Sr. continued to improve plant operations and experiment with new styles of beer. The pre-Prohibition model of breweries building and owning saloons and hotels operated as tied houses did

not work under post-Prohibition liquor laws, so the company sold off real-estate holdings to pay for upgrades. Beerhalter Sr. purchased a pasteurizer and improved the packaging process with a new bottling machine, washer, and soaker. According to Johnson, once the upgrades were in place Fitger's could fill, seal, and label two hundred bottles a minute.

Many of those bottles carried new labels, including the short-lived Premium Pale Beer, which sold for less than two years. In 1939 Beerhalter Sr. repackaged Fitger's Natural as Rex, one of the brands it acquired from DB&M in 1930. They'd tried the tactic before, attempting to bring back both DB&M's Rex and Moose labels, but the heavy beer did not catch on with younger drinkers. The new brand came with a new tagline "Naturally Brewed, Naturally Better."

As the 1930s came to a close, all twenty-five of Minnesota's breweries that refired their kettles in 1933 were still making beer. Hamm's in St. Paul remained the giant, with a capacity of over 800,000 barrels a year, followed by Minneapolis Brewing Company at 500,000 barrels. Gluek's, St. Paul's Schmidt, and Fitger's tied for third at 200,000 barrels. DB&M, at 100,000 barrels, came in seventh, and People's 25,000-barrel capacity put it on par with four others near the bottom of the list. Six of them would be gone within ten years. For the next twenty years Minnesota's beer production would steadily increase as the number of breweries steadily decreased—a nationwide trend. In Wisconsin seventy-four of the eighty-seven breweries brewing in 1934 were still operating in 1940, nearly a 15 percent decrease. But in Superior, Northern stood strong under new management.

An oversized "bottle" of Nordlager beer adorned the front end of the Fitger's float entered in the 1938 VFW Parade in Superior.
[P. CLURE COLLECTION]

ANOTHER WAR & ITS AFTERMATH (1941–1950)

When America entered World War II in December 1941, breweries across the country felt the impact in different ways. Even before the U.S. declared war on Germany and Japan, a Defense Tax raised the tax on a barrel of beer from $5 to $6. War affected the cost and availability of everything from grain and hops to metal for cans, glass for bottles, and paper for labels. Malt was rationed and train cars scarce. And workers left breweries to join the service.

Many of the nation's smaller regional breweries suffered, but others thrived by obtaining contracts to make beer for the troops. Those few breweries that had their own malt houses, including Duluth Brewing & Malting, produced distiller's malt used to create industrial alcohol, much needed for the war effort in part to manufacture smokeless gun powder. DB&M received a government contract in 1943, and soon its payroll increased 33 percent. For the next three years DB&M shipped a train-car load of distiller's malt to plants across the country every three days. None went to other breweries, but DB&M made enough traditional malt to keep producing its own beer.

Meanwhile, Royal Bohemian had become extremely popular. Advertisements in 1943 called the brew "The Aristocrat of Beer" and reminded drinkers to buy extra war bonds. DB&M also took a page from Fitger's playbook

DULUTH BREWING & MALTING'S ROYAL BREW (TOP CENTER) BECAME ROYAL BOHEMIAN IN THE EARLY 1940S. LABELS ON THIS PAGE ARE A GREAT EXAMPLE OF HOW THE SAME LABEL WAS CUSTOMIZED FOR BEERS OF VARYING QUANTITY OR ALCOHOL CONTENT PACKAGED UNDER THE SAME NAME. DEDICATED COLLECTORS EVEN TAKE NOTE OF THE DIFFERENT FONTS USED FROM PRINTING TO PRINTING. [ROYAL BREW: P. CLURE COLLECTION; 12 OZ. BOTTOM RIGHT: J. LEMKE COLLECTION; ALL OTHERS C. OLSEN COLLECTION]

FACING PAGE
TOP LEFT: MALT DRUMS; BOTTOM LEFT:
KILN ROOM OF THE MALT HOUSE; TOP AND
BOTTOM RIGHT: VIEWS OF THE ENGINE ROOM.

THIS PAGE
TOP LEFT: BREW KETTLE; TOP RIGHT: WASH
HOUSE; BOTTOM RIGHT: RACKING ROOM.
[P. CLURE COLLECTION]

and sponsored its own radio show, *Royal Bohemian Melodies*, which aired on Duluth's WDSM Radio four evenings a week. Russell Gravelle, who worked for the brewery as an accountant from 1937 to 1966, recalled in 1998 that despite wartime restrictions, DB&M shipped a record twenty-seven carloads of Royal Bohemian in 1944. By then the brewery had opened accounts throughout Minnesota and in Wisconsin, Michigan, and North and South Dakota. In 1945, women joined the bottling line.

The brewery celebrated its fiftieth anniversary with a full-page advertisement in the January 1946, edition of the *Duluth News Tribune*. The ad highlighted what was unique about the brewery: not only did it make its own malt, but it also grew its own hops on a farm in Corvallis, Oregon, while very few American breweries did either. That way DB&M could make a "fully controlled product from start to finish," the key to Royal Bohemian's taste and popularity. The beer remained popular for the rest of the decade.

Without a malt house of its own, the Fitger Brewing Company tightened its belt like most other American breweries by using alternative grain and reusing whatever it could, down to the bottle cap. Advertising campaigns were curbed, and the radio show ended. The company also went through another round of farewells and changes at the top. Six months after the U.S. entered the war, June 27, 1942, Arnold Fitger died in Beverly Hills after a long unspecified illness. He was fifty-one years old.

The Fitger family estate took ownership of the brewery and kept John Beerhalter Sr. in place as president and manager. By then the brewery was a Beerhalter family affair, with Beerhalter Sr. at the top and sons John Jr. in the brewhouse, Erwin in charge of the Pop Shop, and J. Richard managing sales. In early 1944, Johnson reports,

a stroke struck Beerhalter Sr., forcing him to relearn how to walk and talk. While he returned to work months later, his restricted abilities limited his time at the brewery. John Jr. took over as brewmaster.

Following the war, Fitger's returned to brewing beer with "the finest ingredients." It once again updated its equipment to ensure purity: new glass-lined fermenters, stainless-steel wort coolers and clarifying machines, a "Sterilamp" that used ultraviolet light to kill bacteria, and a new bottling machine that ensured that Fitger's beer was "absolutely untouched by

ABOVE: DULUTH PHOTOGRAPHER PERRY GALLAGHER JR. TOOK THIS PHOTO OF FITGER'S EMPLOYEES GATHERED FOR A PARTY DULUTH'S SPALDING HOTEL, 1940.

LEFT: A FITGER'S DELIVERY TRUCK FROM THE 1940S, CUSTOMIZED TO PROMOTE NORDLAGER BEER.
[P. CLURE COLLECTION]

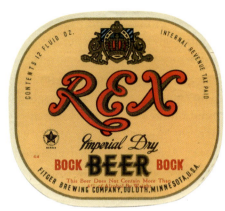

AFTER A FALSE START IN THE EARLY 1930S, FITGER'S WAS ABLE TO TURN THE FORMER DULUTH BREWING & MALTING FLAGSHIP BRAND REX INTO ITS OWN PREMIER BEER IN 1939 AS A REBRANDING OF FITGER'S NATURAL BEER, [MIDDLE ROW LEFT: J. LEMKE COLLECTION; MIDDLE ROW CENTER: FITGER'S COMPLEX; ALL OTHERS: C. OLSEN COLLECTION]

human hands." The beer, now called Rex Imperial Dry, was brewed with "Pure Lake Superior Water." Elsewhere, the brewery advertised Rex as "The World's Finest Beer" and "The Beer that Meets the Flavor-favor Everywhere." At the Pop Shop, Erwin Beerhalter's crew filled bottles of Squirt, a national grapefruit-flavored soda first introduced in 1939. Fitger's was now its regional distributor.

John Beerhalter Sr. struggled following his stroke. In 1948 the Fitger board named him chairman and John Jr. president and general manager. Symbolically, the change from father to son was marked by a change in the racking room, as old wooden kegs gave way to, lightweight aluminum kegs. Fitger's unofficial historian Coopen Johnson filled them when he first went to work at Fitger's in July 1948.

Brewing Company in Baker City, Oregon. In order to reach the next level he attended Chicago's Siebel Institute.

After graduating Hartel took the brewmaster's job at the Elgin Eagle Brewing Company in Elgin, Illinois, then spent Prohibition on a farm in western North Dakota. He bounced between breweries immediately after Prohibition, first to the Eberly Brewing Co. in Jackson, Michigan, then the Arcadia Brewing Co. of Arcadia, Wisconsin, and next Portage, Wisconsin's Eulberg Brewery. Each time he became frustrated with his bosses, who didn't always recognize the necessity of quality ingredients. He finally landed at Peter Bub Brewery in Winona, Minnesota, then Minnesota's eighth largest brewery. There Hartel created All American Beer, an all-malt brew that became a

In Superior, Northern Brewing's Victor Nelson struggled not only with wartime shortages, but with keeping a reliable brewmaster on the payroll as well. He finally found Joe Hartel in 1943. A native of Regensberg, Bavaria, Hartel came to the U.S. in 1909 when he was twenty-two years old. He already had six years of brewery work under his belt, having gone to work in his hometown brewery at sixteen. Hartel first landed in Spokane, Washington, then took a job in British Columbia before signing on with the American

hit. Unfortunately, Peter Bub's marketing department hadn't done its homework. Nebraska's Columbia Brewing had been selling a beer called All American since 1933, and soon Hartel's new beer was pulled from shelves.

Hartel took charge of Northern's entire operation and soon developed a reputation for brewing quality beer. For the next eighteen years he would keep Northern Beer a strong and popular regional brew. He demanded hard work and a spotless, sanitary operation and rewarded his crew by demanding Nelson give his brewers $100 bonuses at Christmas. He was also a modern brewer and understood the science of making beer. While Northern never hired a chemist of its own, Hartel would often call on Johnny Hey, Fitger's chemist, for advice.

To speed up the brewing process, Hartel would open the brewery's windows in the dead of winter so the wort would cool faster. Ice coated the floors, and his son Dick, who worked alongside his father for two decades, twice developed pneumonia.

Hartel also indulged his new boss. After the war Hartel packaged some of the flagship Northern Pale into shorty

bottles with a screen-printed label that read "Vic's Special." The brewery also moved from wooden kegs to aluminum kegs, an occasion Hartel marked by giving the entire staff Northern Beer neck ties. Cap-sealed cone-top cans of Northern hit stores in the summer of 1948 carrying the tagline "We made it good, you made it famous." Northern advertised the occasion with a poem:

> In the bottle it gained its fame.
>
> In the can it's still the same.
>
> Be it "Northern" or "Vic's" bottled or canned,
>
> It is always a "Truly Superior" brand.
>
> "We made it good, you made it famous."
>
> A better beer you cannot name us.
>
> Drink it with Pleasure, drink it with Zest.
>
> The ingredients in it are certainly the best.
>
> So when you want beer be sure you demand
>
> "Northern." It's now both bottled and canned.

ABOVE: BESIDES DB&M (SEE PAGE 136), TWO HARBORS DISTRIBUTOR LARS M. SVEE ALSO SOLD BEER FOR SUPERIOR'S NORTHERN BREWING CO. [P. CLURE COLLECTION]

LEFT: THE LABEL USED ON NORTHERN'S BOTTLED BEER IN THE 1940S. [J. LEMKE COLLECTION]

A TIN THERMOMETER (ABOVE)
AND A PRINT OF A PAINTING BY
CHARLES M. RUSSEL (RIGHT),
BOTH USED TO PROMOTE PEOPLE'S
REGAL SUPREME BEER IN THE
LATE 1940S.

[P. CLURE COLLECTION]

By then Northern was producing 25,000 barrels of beer each year, the peak of its production and the same capacity as People's in West Duluth, which was undergoing changes as well. Longtime People's brewmaster Frank Luckow, who retired in 1940, died in March 1942. His son Robert remained on the People's payroll, but did not take over brewing. Another son, Ralph, took a job with DB&M.

Hanson replaced Luckow with twenty-seven-year-old Howard Ruff. The brewery then launched a new advertising campaign for Stag. Oddly enough, the ads contained the phrase "Since the Gay 90's," even though the brewery was established in 1907. The ad also asked Stag drinkers if they had "tried it lately" and noticed its "new improved super quality." The ad explained that Super-Stag beer, "the all grain beer," was "the creation of skill and experience of five generations, and a century in the brewing industry of the family of Howard Ruff, our new brewmaster." Ruff's great-grandfather Caspar first opened a brewery in Quincy, Illinois, in 1842.

Ruff proved to be a solid brewmaster and introduced a new beer to the People's line dubbed Ruff's Olde English Stout, not a traditional stout but rather a malt liquor with an alcohol content of 6 percent. Despite his pedigree and the popularity of Olde English, Ruff lasted just three years. He eventually landed in Oshkosh, Wisconsin, where he became the longtime brewmaster of that city's People's Brewing Company. He died on the job in February 1972, and eight months later the brewery closed forever. Before he left Duluth, however, Ruff made one lasting contribution

to the People's story by introducing the brewery's flagship pilsner: Regal Supreme.

People's first marketed Regal Supreme as a "friendly" beer, with labels urging drinkers to "Say Hello with Regal Supreme" and ads promising that "its high quality makes lasting friends." (It was also "taste teasing and Palate Pleasing.") To further promote the brand, People's sponsored the *Haymaker's Ball* on KDAL Radio every Saturday night and the "heartwarming, melodic programming" of sentimental Scottish crooner Rance Valentine's *Yesterday's* program Tuesday's on WEBC Radio. With the new product, Duluth's three breweries each offered a beer whose label referenced a kingly word that began with an *R*: People's Regal Supreme, DB&M's Royal Bohemian, and Fitger's Rex Imperial Dry.

Hanson replaced Ruff with thirty-five-year-old Ted Wollesen, who had served as Fitger's assistant brewmaster from 1940 until 1943, when he left to take a job driving truck for

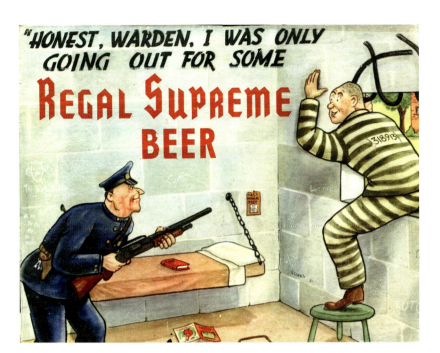

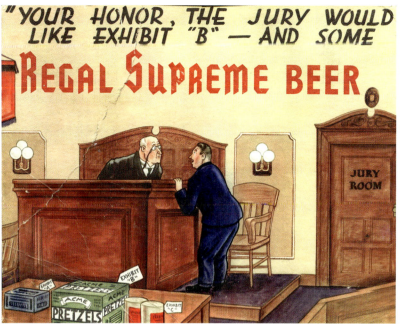

Superior's Globe Shipyards. Records show he spent significant time in Germany in the mid-1930s, likely to attend brewing school. He signed on as People's brewmaster in 1945.

Two years after Wollesen took over brewing, Ruff's Olde English Stout was repackaged as Olde English 600 to reference its strength. With strong sales of both Olde English and Regal Supreme, Wollesen and Hanson decided to expand. New equipment included a pasteurizer that allowed the brewery to fill four hundred cases of beer in an hour. The forty-ton machine required "one of the largest hauling jobs ever made into Duluth." Carl Hanson told newspapers the brewery was "sorry we have been unable to satisfy our customers' demands for Regal Supreme beer." A print ad explaining the upgrades read:

> So many of you have discovered the golden goodness of REGAL SUPREME beer that we've begun a vast expansion program to meet the demand. During 1947 a new bottling line has been installed in addition to many other

pieces of new equipment; and storage and fermentation facilities are being added daily...steps which will soon DOUBLE our capacity. Yes...we've changed the picture quite a bit this year, but 1948 will see many more changes...all designed for just one purpose: to brew the BEST beer possible.

The notice failed to mention canning equipment—People's started packaging Regal Supreme in cone-tops about the same time as the other improvements were made. Not only was Hanson's brewery booming, but things were looking up for his 7-Up franchise as well. In January 1948 the *Herald* announced that Hanson had purchased the former Precision Products Co. facilities at 212 North Fortieth Avenue West as the new home of its 7-Up bottling plant, was opening 7-Up plants in Virginia and Brainerd, and was planning for a Superior facility. As the 1940s came to a close the People's machine seemed to be firing on all cylinders, but less than seven years later its engines would grind to a halt.

People's Brewing Company used these cartoon posters to promote Regal Supreme beer in the 1940s.
[P. Clure Collection]

THE LABEL FOR RUFF'S OLDE ENGLISH STOUT, NAMED FOR PEOPLE'S BREWMASTER HOWARD RUFF, WAS USED FOR A SHORT PERIOD BEFORE THE BEER'S NAME WAS CHANGED TO OLDE ENGLISH 600, MAKING IT EXTREMELY RARE. SIMILARLY, THE REGAL SUPREME LABEL AT TOP RIGHT, WHICH LIKE THE RUFF'S LABEL HAS SEEN BETTER DAYS, WAS USED FOR A VERY BRIEF TIME IN THIS CASE BECAUSE IT CARRIED THE SLOGAN "THE CHAMPAGNE OF BEERS," USED BY THE MILLER BREWING COMPANY. THE CENTER LABEL SHOWS THAT PEOPLE'S CHANGED THE SLOGAN TO "THE CHAMPION OF BEERS."

[CENTER LEFT: J. LEMKE COLLECTION; KREEMI-BRU: K. MALZ COLLECTION; ALL OTHERS C. OLSEN COLLECTION]

ADVERTISING EXPANSION & BREWERY CONTRACTION (1950–1960)

The brewing industry changed dramatically after World War II. As with many other industries, the development of the nation's highway system added convenience for shipping, and the advent of the refrigerated semitrailer meant that breweries could greatly expand their markets—those that could afford it, anyway. Larger regional breweries, which could also produce beer much less expensively, began squeezing out community brewers. The advertising game also favored the big boys, as the bigger a brewery became, the more it could afford to spend on advertising. Hoverson notes that from 1948 to 1958, the average profit of America's breweries dropped from 7 percent to 1 percent, an incredibly tight margin. The small breweries took another big hit when the federal government raised tax on beer to $9 a barrel.

Some large breweries became national giants. Beer from Milwaukee's Pabst and Miller, St. Louis's Anheuser-Busch, and Colorado's Coors reached more and more cities farther and farther away from their home cities. Minnesota's own Hamm's got in on the act, and by 1956 the St. Paul brewer was the fifth largest in the nation and would eventually own breweries from Los Angeles to Baltimore.

Across the nation this combination of increased competition and tight operating budgets led to the closing of many small regional breweries. Others merged, cosolidating production in an attempt to survive. Many gave up and sold to larger breweries, who then used the acquired facilities to meet the ever-increasing demand for their product. Hoverson points out that 466 breweries operated in the U.S. in 1948; ten years later there were just 240, a drop of 48.5 percent. Minnesota started the 1950s with nineteen breweries. Six would be gone by the end of the decade. In Wisconsin, breweries dropped from about seventy-five in 1940 to roughly forty-five

in 1950, a 36.5 percent loss. It would lose another 36 percent over the next ten years, with just thirty remaining in 1960.

The Twin Ports was certainly not immune to this trend, and by the midpoint of the decade some were suggesting that, to survive, Duluth's three breweries should merge and focus sales on the "Three Rs"—People's Regal Supreme, Duluth Brewing & Malting's Royal Bohemian, and Fitger's Rex Imperial Dry. Carl Hanson of People's even had promotional signs printed and distributed to Duluth taverns urging drinkers to select one of the city's Three Rs. He later explained that while the taverns remained loyal to Duluth brands, liquor stores did not. And soon one of the Rs would be gone as Fitger's stopped using the name Rex (as well as Nordlager) altogether and began marketing its flagship product as simply "Fitger's Beer." Instead of merging, the breweries increased advertising.

THE FRONT OF THE FITGER'S FACILITY LOOKING EAST ON SUPERIOR STREET, 1950S. NOTE THE ICEHOUSE, THE BUILDING AT RIGHT WITH THE PEAKED ROOF, WHICH WAS BUILT IN 1881 BY MIKE FINK BEFORE AUGUST FITGER EVER VISITED DULUTH. DULUTH VAN & STORAGE, FAR RIGHT, WAS BUILT BETWEEN THE ICEHOUSE AND THE PICKWICK IN 1933. BOTH WERE DEMOLISHED IN THE 1960S TO MAKE ROOM FOR A PARKING LOT AND AN ADDITION TO THE PICKWICK.
[P. CLURE COLLECTION]

DRINKING ON THE JOB

That brewery employees drink beer on the job is hardly a trade secret. Some drinking is essential—as with any good cook, you have to taste what you are making. And in the nineteenth century, when typhoid was rampant and potable water scarce, beer was often essential to keeping a workforce going. At one time many fire departments, including Duluth's, required firefighters to drink beer with meals rather than the local water so they would not get sick. The brewing process boils out impurities.

In 1902 the *Duluth News Tribune* reported on consumption at Duluth's breweries. The article came in response to a study by the Brewer's Benevolent Bureau of New York that claimed that "most of the men [employed at breweries] are big and strong and...nearly all can lift more than 400 pounds. Workmen who average more than twenty-five glasses of beer a day are in better health than any other class of men."

The study reported that some Gotham City brewery workers consumed up to seventy-five glasses of their product every working day, but the average was "less than forty." The newspaper said that Duluth's brewers "laugh at the story." Most Duluth brewery workers sampled no more than six beers a day. In 1939 Fitger's Bottling Department foreman certified that in March a total of thirty men worked the equivalent of 403 days and consumed 1,209 twelve-ounce bottles of beer or fifty cases—three beers per shift.

The average nine-hour workday at Fitger's included three "stops" for beer, "when seldom more than two glasses of beer are consumed" by each worker. This accounting did not include another beer or two at lunch or supper. Duluth Brewing & Malting kept a similar schedule and set up a bar "on the main floor where beer is served to the employees."

Duluth brewing historian Coopen Johnson wrote employees called beer breaks at Fitger's "beer time," and enjoyed the beer in the "beer hole," or employees break room. By the time Johnson went to work for Fitger's in 1948, the large number of employees required scheduling separate beer breaks, and so "brewhouse and the wash-house employees had their beer break earlier than the bottle house." Employees that worked in other departments could choose whichever break they wished—and some, Johnson implied, chose both.

Fitger's beer hole was located relatively close to the railroad spur that served the brewery. In the 1980s Duluthian Lee Ann Guerndt, whose father worked at Fitger's, recalled stories she'd been told as a child: "The beer hole was where everyone, including businessmen off the street, could get their beer tapped right out of the cellar. It was so cold, in order to drink it, they had to dip their steins in boiling water." Johnson verifies that a tub of hot water was on hand to "warm up tankards." Over the years trainmen figured out how to time their arrival at Fitger's with beer time and often brought along sausage to share with brewery workers, offering a little wurst in exchange for Fitger's best. They cooked the sausage in the tankard-warming tub. Beer time at Fitger's, Johnson writes, stopped in the 1950s. The tradition ended nationwide in the 1960s.

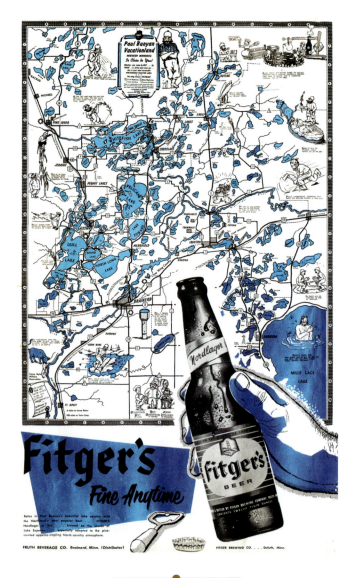

WELCOME TO "FITGERLAND"

As the community's largest brewery, Fitger's had more advertising dollars to spend than the others, and it showed. Taverns throughout the region advertised Fitger's beer using a variety of signs, including clocks and novelties such as calendars, ash trays, lighters, bottle openers, playing cards, and thermometers. The brewery even produced a cardboard lamp in the shape of Split Rock Lighthouse, an iconic landmark of the Lake Superior North Shore. Fitger's also incorporated the lighthouse on its labels.

Perhaps recognizing it couldn't compete nationally, Fitger's focused on establishing its product as *the* northern Minnesota beer. Beginning in the 1950s, advertisement taglines for Fitger's included "The Best of the Great Midwest," "The Call of the North," "The Flavor of the Great North Shore," and "Brewed on the Shore of Lake Superior." The brewery's familiar phrase "Naturally Brewed, Naturally Better" became "Locally Brewed, Naturally Better." Duluth newspaper ads and six-pack wraps mentioned Fitger's was "Brewed for the Folks Who Live Right Here," and billboards scattered throughout the region declared "This is Fitgerland."

Billboards and print ads also emphasized Fitger's as a rugged outdoorsman's beer, just as print ads had in the 1930s. They featured scenes of canoe country, waterfowl taking flight, fly-fishing along North Shore streams, and even Highway 61—all of which further reinforced the North Woods theme. Another tagline sought a wider market, reminding drinkers "Everyone Here Likes Fitger's Beer."

And just as Fitger's had embraced radio advertising in the 1930s, it took to television in 1955 by sponsoring the *Ten O'Clock Report* featuring Earl Henton on Monday, Wednesday, and Friday evenings on KDAL Channel 3. It made sense: throughout the country, more people were drinking at home than in taverns. As DB&M's Carl Meeske pointed out a year after Duluth's first TV station went on the air, sales in liquor stores outpaced sales in taverns for one reason: "television—people stay home."

ABOVE: DULUTH WEATHERMAN JACK MCKENNA (LEFT) AND SPORTSCASTER DOUG DUNCAN OF WDIO-TV PAUSE FOR A STILL PHOTO DURING THE TAPING OF A COMMERCIAL FOR FITGER'S BEER IN 1967.
[C&R JOHNSON COLLECTION]

LEFT: A CARDBOARD SIGN ADVERTISING FITGER'S BEER AND REFERRING TO "FITGERLAND," AKA NORTHERN MINNESOTA.
[P. CLURE COLLECTION]

year he spent $85,000 on a new pasteurization unit. The *Herald* said the new machine, which could fill and pasteurize 240 bottles or 300 cans of beer every minute, would increase the brewery's capacity from three thousand to four thousand cases a day. The new machine, designed to fit within the existing bottle house, occupied nine hundred square feet. Workers had to cut a large hole in the building to install it. Beerhalter Jr. told newspapers the new machine meant that Fitger's staff would grow from seventy-four to ninety-three people, and Fitger's beer would now come packaged in flattop cans.

To increase sales to match its new capacity, the brewery introduced a less-expensive beer, said to have tasted very similar to regular Fitger's but darker in color. The brewery named the new brew Twins Lager for the Twin Ports and advertised it as "twice as refreshing!" The name took on more significance in 1960 when the Minnesota Twins became Major League Baseball's newest team.

By the time it advertised on television, Fitger's had gone through more changes at the top. In 1951 tightening profit margins made the Fitger family uncomfortable, and they entertained an offer to sell the brewery to outside interests. In Duluth, John Beerhalter Sr., longtime Fitger secretary-treasurer Walter Johnson, and accountant Bert Jeronimus pooled their money and purchased the brewery for $500,000, roughly $4.8 million today. Coopen Johnson reports the deal took two years to finalize, and in the end Beerhalter Sr. controlled 59 percent of the company. Walter Johnson became vice president and Jeronimus secretary-treasurer.

John Beerhalter Jr. had been elected president of the Minnesota Brewers Association months before his father died on July 7, 1955. Like his father, Beerhalter Jr. knew the importance of keeping the brewery up-to-date. The next

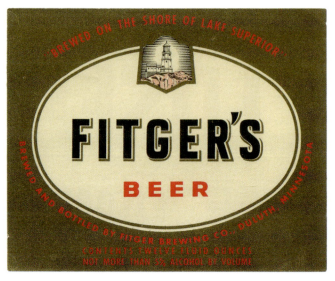

MAKE A DATE WITH 58!

For Duluth Brewing & Malting, the 1950s began with the return of Bob Ostern, who had left to attend Chicago's Siebel Institute. Ostern had acted as brewmaster Henry Schmid's right hand since the 1930s, and although he was now a certified master brewer, that's just the way Schmid wanted to keep it. Years later Ostern would tell researchers that he essentially did most of the work while Schmid got the lion's share of the credit. Schmid made sure everyone knew who was number one—Ostern remembered his cigar-chewing boss did not like his authority questioned.

One of the first things Ostern did when he returned was change Royal Bohemian's recipe, pushing its alcohol content to 5.7 percent. Unlike today's craft beers, at the time most of

the nation's strong beer rarely contained more than 4 percent alcohol, and those that did—like People's Olde English 600, were often considered malt liquor. They named the new beer Royal 57.

At a meeting with local food vendors, participants joked people would soon call DB&M's new brew the "Ketchup Beer," because the name reminded them of Heinz 57. Ostern feared the name would result in a lawsuit from the condiment giant, so he wrote to Heinz. As he had guessed, they asked him to change it. After just six months, DB&M stopped shipping Royal 57. Ostern recalled that all the existing packaging, promotional materials, and even neon signs for Royal 57 were then hauled away and buried in a landfill.

Ostern then pushed the beer's alcohol content to 5.8 percent and renamed it Royal 58. On December 20, 1951, DB&M used a full-page ad in local newspapers to announce the name change. It included a new slogan, "Make a Date

ABOVE: SVEE DISTRIBUTING'S DB&M TRUCK, ADVERTISING ROYAL 58 IN THE 1950S.

LEFT: A TIN SIGN WITH A THERMOMETER FEATURING THE ROYAL 58 SLOGAN "MAKE A DATE WITH 58."
[P. CLURE COLECTION]

with 58!" While its high alcohol content caused some to call it the "headache beer," Royal 58 was a hit.

The following year, however, DB&M made a surprise move closing its malt house, reportedly to save money. The malt house had helped the brewery survive most of Prohibition and thrive during World War II, but since the war, larger regional malting operations had sprung up to serve the ever-growing national breweries. The Duluth brewery likely didn't use and sell enough malt to justify the cost of operating the facility.

Although smaller, DB&M marketed almost as aggressively as Fitger's. Besides making a date with 58, signs suggested one should "Treat Yourself Royally" by having a Royal 58. Karlsbräu was marketed as an "Old Time Beer" and advertisements asked beer drinkers if they remembered the "good old days" or suggested that they tell their bartenders to "Make Mine Karlsbräu."

Following Fitger's lead, DB&M also issued a number of signs and novelties of all stripes— even lampshades. And they also pursued customers with scenes of the great outdoors.

LEFT: A NOVELTY ADVERTISING PIECE FEATURING A BOTTLE OF ROYAL BOHEMIAN. NOTE THAT THE NECK LABEL IS FOR ROYAL 58. NECK LABELS IDENTIFIED BOTH ROYAL 57 AND ROYAL 58 WHILE THE BREWERY USED UP ITS ROYAL BOHEMIAN LABELS. THE BREWERY NEVER PRINTED A LABEL FOR ROYAL 57.
[P. CLURE COLLECTION]

ABOVE TOP: LABEL FOR ROYAL BOHEMIAN PRINTED IN 1950 PRIOR TO THE RELEASE OF ROYAL 57 AND ROYAL 58; BOTTOM: THE LABEL FOR ROYAL 58.
[C. OLSEN COLLECTION]

Like John Beerhalter Sr., DB&M president Carl Meeske also enjoyed hunting and fishing. For much of his life Meeske wore a prosthetic left hand after he lost the original in a hunting accident. Working with the sportsman theme DB&M's sales staff employed everything from puns (Royal 58 provided fishermen with "reel pleasure") to

operations, yet just two years later he accepted an offer from the Lucky Lager Brewing Co. and moved to San Francisco to become its brewmaster. Carl Meeske stepped out of the office and into the brewhouse to take charge of brewing. Likely suffering from medical issues, and perhaps also recognizing that he wasn't the brewer Ostern had become, Meeske asked his former brewmaster to return to Duluth in the summer of 1957. Ostern was barely back to the DB&M's famous kettle when Meeske died on October 2, just three days shy of his sixty-fifth birthday.

Meeske's estate, including the brewery and Gopher Real Estate, went to his wife, Myrtle, and his elderly sister, Ella. Ostern, now the company president, reported to Myrtle and Ella Meeske monthly but, as he later told researchers, they had few concerns about the brewery. The realty company and Carl's other investments kept them quite comfortable. According to Ostern, when he took over the brewery, DB&M owed stockholders over $90,000 and Duluthians drank more Hamm's than Royal 58.

three-dimensional cardboard signs that looked like taxidermically mounted walleyed pike, largemouth bass, and brook trout.

One campaign rolled out in the late 1940s featured J. F. Kernan's sportsman-themed paintings (see page 136). Kernan's work, extremely popular from the 1920s until his death in 1958, consisted of "nostalgic and often humorous illustrations celebrat[ing] the simple comforts of home, family, and outdoor recreation." Kernan paintings, which resembled those of Norman Rockwell, graced the cover of the *Saturday Evening Post* twenty-six times. Other breweries also used Kernan's work to promote their beer, including Cincinnati's Burger Brewing Company.

Henry Schmid, DB&M's brewmaster since 1934, passed away on January 14, 1954, shortly after retiring. Bob Ostern finally had full control of DB&M's brewing

THE SMALLER BREWERIES STRUGGLE

While DB&M and Fitger's advertised throughout the region, the Twin Ports' two smallest breweries spent their marketing dollars much closer to home. After only five years of cone-top cans, Northern switched to flat tops in 1953. The cans exclaimed "It's Superior" and an oval above the name contained an image of three pine trees, symbolizing the North Woods of Wisconsin. Vic's Select remained in its signature stubby bottle with the screen-printed label that declared the beer inside was "Brewed with Famous Superior Water Which Makes Fine Superior Beer" and asked beer drinkers to "PIC-ME."

A much smaller advertising budget meant that Northern produced far-fewer promotional items than Fitger's and DB&M. It offered taverns signs and clocks and the usual bottle openers, ashtrays, and playing cards and even a cribbage board, as well as some unlikely items bearing the brewery's name, including a meat tenderizer. Despite the small budget the brewery made a big statement in its hometown by installing a billboard featuring a large clock along Highway 53 at the Nemadji River, reminding residents it was always time for a Northern.

Top Right: Northern brewmaster Joe Hartel and his wife, Emily, enjoy a beer at a party in 1954.

LEFT: A NORTHERN BREWING MEAT TENDERIZER, A VERY INTERESTING CHOICE FOR ADVERTISING A BREWERY.

TOP RIGHT: NORTHERN BREWMASTER JOE HARTEL AND HIS WIFE, EMILY, ENJOY A BEER AT A PARTY IN 1954.

BOTTOM RIGHT: JOE HARTEL (RIGHT) AND HIS SON DICK NEXT TO NORTHERN BREWERY'S FILTER SYSTEM, CA. 1955.

[P. CLURE COLLECTION]

Seventy-five-year-old Northern president Victor Nelson decided it was time to retire in February 1956. He sold the brewery to liquor distributor Northwest Liquor Co. of Stevens Point, Wisconsin, owned by Peter Slomann. Slomann named Robert E. Rooney Northern's new president. Rooney knew the brewery and its market well, as he was already president of Northern Liquor, a subsidiary of Northwest Liquors, based in Superior. One of the first things Rooney did for the brewery was to give Joe Hartel the green light to increase the quality of his flagship beer. Hartel's strategy was to improve the ingredients. A full-page ad in the *Telegram* announced that the brewery had begun to use imported Bavarian hops that would make Northern the beer "with the

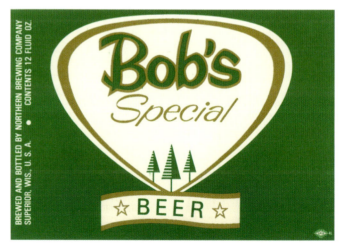

new taste thrill." In an accompanying article Hartel stated, "At Northern brewery, we use only the finest malt and hops...and beer here is aged just the way it was many years ago...naturally, without added chemicals."

By the time Hartel's first batch of Bavarian-hopped beer aged long enough to reach shelves, Victor Nelson had died, and soon Vic's Special was replaced by Bob's Beer, named for Rooney. The next year, Hartel improved the beer again by replacing the facility's old asbestos filter system with one that, like Fitger's Kieselguhr Filter, used diatomaceous earth.

Over in West Duluth, People's also relied on a small advertising budget and like Northern focused its energy promoting Regal Supreme as a hometown beer. By 1950, the beer had a new spokesman: seventeenth-century French

soldier and explorer Daniel Greysolon Sieur du Lhut, the Zenith City's namesake.

Labels and signs for Regal Supreme depicted du Lhut as a swashbuckling musketeer, and his face adorned cans and labels, although they got his name wrong, referring to du Lhut either as "Sieur Du Luth" or "Sieur Duluth." The sales staff even developed a print campaign telling du Lhut's life story in fifteen separate ads reminiscent of the then-popular syndicated newspaper feature *Ripley's Believe It Or Not!* Each ad asked "Do you know these facts about Sieur Du Luth?," but while the copy indeed contained many facts, it also contained plenty of fiction.

People's also tried on a few taglines of its own. Early labels carried the phrase "The Champagne of Beers," extremely similar to Miller High Life's "The Champagne of

A PAINTING OF PEOPLE'S BREWING CO. FACILITIES MADE IN 1950 OR 1951 BY ARTHUR FLEMMING. FLEMMING DID A SERIES OF PAINTINGS DEPICTING WEST DULUTH LANDMARK MANUFACTURERS AND THE ARROWHEAD BRIDGE, WHICH CONNECTED WEST DULUTH AND SUPERIOR FROM 1927 UNTIL 1985. THE PAINTINGS WERE COMMISSIONED BY THE OWNER OF THE KOM-ON-INN IN WEST DULUTH AND ARE STILL ON DISPLAY AT THE TAVERN TODAY. [ZENITH CITY PRESS]

Bottled Beer" (Miller dropped "bottled" in 1969). Another advertising phrase asked drinkers to "Say hello with Regal Supreme," and a wall clock called People's flagship brew "Duluth's Finest Beer."

People's was the only Twin Ports brewery that did not use a North Woods or sportsman theme in its advertising. Instead, in the late 1940s People's used Charles M. Russell's Western-themed paintings to promote Regal Supreme, including images of Native Americans on a buffalo hunt or acting as scouts for the U.S. Calvary (see page 146). Perhaps this was because Westerns were popular movies at the time.

Despite its efforts People's simply could not compete against the strong regional and national competition it faced. Its Olde English 600 did find its ways into stores in the Pacific Northwest and, surprisingly, Puerto Rico, but the cost of shipping likely made such distribution unprofitable.

Ted Wollesen, brewmaster since 1945, left the brewery in 1954. Hanson selected Robert Luckow, son of longtime People's brewmaster Frank Luckow, to take Wollesen's place at the kettle, but he wasn't there for long. In 1957, less than ten years after People's modernized its facility to "keep up with demand," Carl Hanson decided to call it quits and closed the brewery. Carlson would later say that "People's Brewery [was] one of those which have disappeared due to overwhelming national competition." While competition and state and federal regulations ate away his profits in the beer business, he was doing quite well selling 7-Up. Hanson made the soda franchise People's parent company, so closing the brewery served as a tax write-off.

Luckow went on to work for Hamm's; whether Wollesen remained in the brewing industry is unknown. Hanson managed to sell the Olde English 600 label to

Spokane, Washington's Bohemian Breweries, which likely noted the malt liquor's Northwest following. Bohemian transferred rights to Spokane's Atlantic Brewing Co., who brewed the beer until 1962. In 1964 Blitz-Weinhard of Portland, Oregon, picked up the brand, and in 1973 its sales team tweaked the name to Olde English 800, which became the brewery's top-selling brand until it too fell to the big boys. The Pabst Brewing Co. purchased Olde English 800 in 1979, and the Miller Brewing Co. has been making it since 1999.

John Sorenson leased the People's facility from 1961 to 1969 for his Duluth Filter Company, which made industrial filters for large diesel engines used in the mining industry. Hanson kept his office at the brewery throughout the 1960s to look after his real-estate investments. He often visited with Sorenson sharing "stories of the good old days of the

BOTTOM LEFT: UNIDENTIFIED PEOPLE'S EMPLOYEES ENJOY A DRINK INSIDE THE BREWERY LIKELY IN 1956, WHEN THE MEN OF DULUTH WERE ENCOURAGED TO GROW FACIAL HAIR DURNG THE CITY'S CENTENNIAL CELEBRATION.

TOP LEFT AND BELOW: TIN SIGNS FROM THE 1950S ADVERTISIING PEOPLE'S REGAL SUPREME BEER. [P. CLURE COLLECTION]

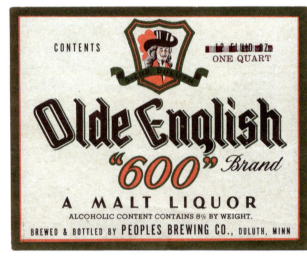

LABELS USED BY PEOPLE'S BREWING CO. IN THE 1950S FOR OLDE ENGLISH AND REGAL SUPREME BOTH FEATURED AN IMAGE OF "SIEUR DULUTH." A NUMBER OF BREWERIES MADE OLDE ENGLISH 600 AFTER PEOPLE'S CLOSED IN 1957. ITS NAME WAS CHANGED TO OLDE ENGLISH 800 IN 1973 AND IS STILL MADE BY THE MILLER BREWING CO. TODAY.

[STAG AND REGAL SUPREME (CENTER RIGHT): J. LEMKE COLLECTION; ALL OTHERS: C. OLSEN COLLECTION]

brewery business" and his connections with prominent local politicians. Hanson had the second floor of the office converted into "the Kitchen," outfitted with stainless-steel restaurant-quality equipment, seating for over fifty people, and a piano. Hanson used the room to host elaborate wild-game banquets twice a year—fundraising events for politicians such as John Blatnik (MN Senate 1940–1944; U.S. House 1947–1974), Francis "Frenchy" LaBrosse (MN House 1949–1964; MN Senate 1965–1970), and Arne "Painter" Wanvick (MN House 1932–1961). Every wall in the room was painted with murals, most depicting North Woods hunting and fishing themes. The murals and piano are still in the room, leading to the mistaken theory that the room was once the brewery's taproom.

Sorenson described Hanson as an honest and astute businessman who, although quite frugal, was also extremely generous to others. Hanson dressed "in a pinstripe suit and a wide-brimmed hat from the 1920s." He kept a Cadillac in his garage that he never drove, and instead had his daughter Dorothy chauffeur him to the brewery in a 1957 Chevrolet with a manual transmission and no radio, demanding she turn off the engine at stop lights to save fuel. Yet when Sorenson mentioned to Hanson his wife needed a car, Hanson gave him the Chevy.

In 1965 Sorenson and Hanson entered into a partnership to dismantle the brewing equipment and sell it as scrap.

Top: Carl Hanson (center) and friends in front of Hanson's Grumman "Super Widgeon" amphibious plane, which sported a Regal Supreme logo, ca. 1950. At far left is the plane's pilot; second from right is People's Brewing Company plant manager Octaaf Reiner.
[P. Clure Collection]

Bottom: The People's Brewing Co. facilities on December 5, 1961, after the brewery had been closed for four years.
[J. Lemke Collection]

Sorenson sold the brewery's glass-lined aging tanks and then hired a crew to use reciprocating saws to cut up most of the rest of the steel, brass, and copper equipment, including the massive brewing kettle. "It was sad to see this beautiful, historic equipment that had provided a living to so many being cut up for scrap," Sorenson recalled in 2018. The process took them nearly the entire winter.

Carl Hanson died in 1973 and was buried with his wife, Jennie, at Sunrise Memorial Cemetery just outside of Duluth in Hermantown, which Hanson developed on former farmland; the marble Hanson Family mausoleum is the cemetery's only above-ground marker. The wrecking ball tore down most of People's Brewery complex two years later. The office building still stands and today serves as the offices of Brock White Construction Materials. To the east, the original keg house has become the home to a Serv-Pro Restoration franchise. Some of the brewery's aging tanks, missed by Sorenson's 1965 cutting crew, still stand inside the building.

THE BREWERIES KEEP CLOSING (1961–1972)

People's Brewing Company was one of six Minnesota breweries to close in the 1950s, leaving just thirteen in the state. Wisconsin, down to thirty, had lost seventeen. The Twin Ports' remaining three breweries faced stiff competition. Northern's tiny 25,000-barrel capacity, the same as People's, ensured that it could never become more than a hometown

brewery. In Minnesota, Ostern had raised Duluth Brewing & Malting's output to 40,000 barrels a year, and Fitger's still annually produced 150,000, but that left them far behind Twin Cities brewers Gluek's (200,000), Schmidt (235,000), and Minneapolis Brewing Co. (800,000). Meanwhile Hamm's made 3,000,000 barrels in 1960, and 40 percent of beer sold in Minnesota came from out of state.

In June 1960 DB&M announced it had reopened the malt house because the demand for quality malt had increased. Ostern told reporters DB&M intended to again make its own malt and sell malt to other breweries, including "custom-made" blends for brewing various styles of beer. The move would add up to eight more names to the DB&M payroll, which regularly employed between thirty-five and forty people. Ostern withheld some information. The brewery had actually signed a three-year lease with G. Heileman of La Crosse, Wisconsin, which was growing

LEFT: DULUTH BREWING & MALTING ENGINEER CLARENCE JOHNSON (NOT TO BE CONFUSED WITH FITGER BREWING COMPANY HISTORIAN CLARENCE "COOPEN" JOHNSON) OUTSIDE THE DB&M BREWHOUSE IN 1962. THE SMALL DOOR NEXT TO THE STEP WAS USED TO TRANSFER MALT TO THE LOWER LEVEL OF THE BREWHOUSE.
[P. CLURE COLLECTION]

ABOVE: INSIDE THE DB&M TAPROOM, 1961.
[UMD MARTIN LIBRARY]

The Duluth Brewing & Malting facility in 1964.
[P. Clure Collection]

and needed more malt. The move came immediately after upgrades to DB&M's canning and bottling equipment and likely helped cover that expense.

Ostern's ideas for DB&M were placed in jeopardy in 1962 when the state highway department announced plans of its own. The Minnesota Highway Department intended to extend Interstate 35 through Duluth, and the brewery and malt house stood right in the proposed path. Ostern told reporters he hadn't determined if the company would fold or build a new facility. Beside's the brewery's forty-five employees, thirty other local jobs directly relied on DB&M. State officials said changing the plans to bypass the brewery was "impossible."

Ostern and his crew kept brewing, and the sales staff went to great lengths to keep promoting the brand, though its market had shrunk to just Minnesota and northern Wisconsin. Beginning in 1963, on the advice of local advertising executive H. E. Westmoreland, DB&M salesmen visited different taverns two or three times a week dressed in 1890s garb. They performed a few songs and skits while buying

rounds of beer and handing out six packs of Royal 58 until the practice ended in 1965. (Fitger's salesmen performed a similar act as the Foam Skimmers, named for the popular midcentury device bartenders used to skim the foam off the top of a glass of beer; pictured page 204.)

When Heileman's lease ended in June 1963, the La Crosse brewery agreed to buy the malt house outright for $49,000. That November Heileman's president Roy Kumm told reporters that when he made the deal, he had no idea the malt house was slated for demolition. He proposed that the Minnesota Highway Department shift I-35's path north of the brewery, but the state would not budge as the change would demolish other businesses. Kumm criticized the state for "a stubborn and ridiculous attitude." The plans did not change.

While DB&M's 1965 sales topped $1 million, the brewery's stockholders, most of whom lived out of state, voted to take the state's offer and close the brewery on April 14, 1966. Later that month DB&M and Heileman accepted offers from the state's condemnation board. Heileman received $193,000 for the malt house; DB&M got $517,000 for

the brewery. Both Heileman and DB&M later filed appeals, claiming the compensation was inadequate. Kumm wanted $800,000 for the facility that cost him just $49,000. Together the properties had been assessed at $597,291 and the state had paid $710,000—an amount it argued was already excessive. The U.S. District Court agreed with the state.

After seventy years of operation, Duluth Brewing & Malting closed its doors for good on July 11, 1966. Demolition began soon after. Ostern later recalled those final days. "We couldn't face up to it. We didn't want to see anyone kicked out of their job.... The brewery being torn down was the worst thing that could happen." At least Ostern and his crew could take some pride that failure hadn't closed their brewery. "We didn't shut down because of poor business," Ostern would say, "We shut down because of the Minnesota Highway Department."

LEFT: BOB OSTERN OF
DB&M INSPECTS GRAIN, 1962.

ABOVE: DB&M'S MALT HOUSE
(TOP) AND BREWHOUSE
(BOTTOM) IN 1964.
[P. CLURE COLLECTION]

In March 1963 *Duluth News Tribune* reporter George C. Flowers wrote an article headlined "House Haunted... by Memories." The story told the tale of a three-story "mansion" at 230 South Twenty-Ninth Avenue West in Duluth's Slabtown neighborhood. The neighborhood's colorful name came from its early history as a ghetto surrounded by lumber mills; residents used slabs of bark discarded by the mills as heating fuel. Duluth Brewing & Malting stood near its western border, and the house was built in 1897 by DB&M president Reiner Hoch. Flowers was inspired to write the article because much of the old neighborhood, including the Hoch house, was slated for demolition in order to make room for the expansion of Interstate 35.

Before the Hoch house was demolished, local teens entertained themselves by vandalizing the once-opulent home. Rocks had shattered the house's windows, and intruders had broken down doors and ripped apart imported woodwork. Flowers saw ghosts, writing that "when the moonlight reflects on these broken panes, you can see flitting images, as if the petticoated ladies of the past were waltzing to the hum of their own voices."

But while Flowers described a "haunted house," the story's subtext showed that the house haunted Roland Hoch, who had grown up within its walls. For years after his family left, he made a weekly habit of slowly driving by the place, remembering when it teemed with life.

Reiner and Mary Hoch had moved their family—Elsa, Frank, Walter, Albert, Carl, and Hugo—from Marquette to Duluth as construction commenced on the brewery. Roland was born not long after in 1898. Elsa, Frank, and Walter were the children of Hoch and Matilda Geele, his first wife, who died in 1887. Mary Trilling Hoch was Matilda's cousin.

Roland Hoch recalled that the house's interior woodwork consisted of oak and imported teak and mahogany, its fireplaces were surrounded in marble, and many of its window sashes once held stained glass. The first floor housed a library and a reception room and a grand dining room. The two-section parlor contained an opera-sized grand piano and was opened only when the Hochs held large parties, which was often; Elsa frequently played the piano for guests. A large butler's pantry led to a spacious kitchen. The second floor contained five bedrooms and a single bath, and the housekeeper lived on the third.

THE REINER HOCH HOUSE SHORTLY BEFORE IT WAS DEMOLISHED IN 1963.
[J. LEMKE COLLECTION]

The house was literally connected to the brewery—the steam that heated it was piped in from the plant. Hoch remembered that on Sundays, the brewery's stable master would hook a team to a fancy carriage and gently swat the horses on the rump, after which the horses would trot themselves down to the Hoch house where the family would climb aboard and go to church. Roland and his siblings hooked the family's goats to sleds or wagons and "drove them as if they were horses."

It wasn't all happy times in the Hoch house. In 1919 Reiner Hoch, after twenty-nine years of marriage, divorced Mary and left the house. He moved to another grand home at 1602 East First Street where he lived with divorcée Florence Davis, described by family members as his mistress, until his death on May 24, 1930. He was buried in the Hoch family plot in Milwaukee's Calvary Cemetery, and his passing was not noted in Duluth newspapers. Despite his 1919 divorce, the *Milwaukee Journal* reported Hoch was survived by "his wife, Mrs. Mary Hoch." Mary Hoch lived in the "Hoch mansion" until 1934. She died in 1948.

Roland "Rollie" Hoch was remembered for his sense of humor and love of practical jokes, but when he spoke to Flowers in 1963, he was feeling particularly sentimental. His parents and all of his siblings had died, and the family home—with all its memories, good and bad—would soon disappear. And he was two weeks away from retiring after twenty-five years as a liquor salesman, marking the end of his career.

Rollie commented about the house's impending demolition: "It makes me sick," he said. "It was another time. It was different. You had to be there to know it."

Ostern operated a Texaco station in Duluth before leaving town to return to brewing. After fielding offers from several small Wisconsin breweries, he ended up in St. Paul working for Hamm's. Two years later he moved to New Ulm, Minnesota, to serve as brewmaster at the August Schell Brewing Company. Ostern retired from brewing in 1973 and returned to Duluth, keeping himself busy as a caretaker of a nursing home and later as a bailiff in Duluth's district court. He died in 2000.

By the time DB&M closed its doors, Heileman had purchased the rights to Royal 58 and Karlsbräu, but stopped brewing both just six months later. (Minnesota's Cold Spring Brewery revived the Karlsbräu label in the 1970s and made it into the early 1980s.) The Wisconsin brewer also purchased the remaining DB&M buildings to use as a distribution center, but they sat vacant from 1967 to 1970. Beer distributor Better Brands used the bottling house and office from the mid 1970s until 2009, when the company was absorbed by Bernick's. Plumbing contractor Carlson Duluth then moved into the office and operates there today. Ribbon, another beer distributor, made the warehouse its headquarters in the mid 1970s. Ribbon became Michaud Distributing in 1990, and today Michaud drivers keep beer trucks rolling along Helm Street, a tradition that started with horses pulling beer wagons 120 years ago.

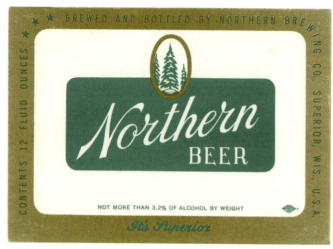

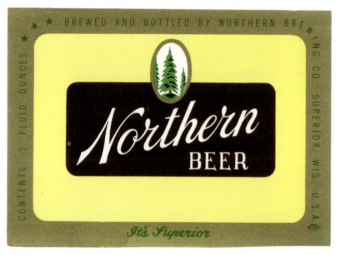

On the other side of the Interstate Bridge, the loss of president Robert Rooney and brewmaster Joe Hartel marked the beginning of the end for the Northern Brewing Company. Rooney died in July 1961, the same year Hartel suffered a stroke at the brewery. Two more strokes followed soon thereafter, and Hartel's entire right side was paralyzed, forcing him to retire. Peter Slomann took Rooney's place as president and tapped Harry Husold to replace Hartel in 1962. That year Husold had lost his job at Fox Head Brewery in Waukesha, Wisconsin, after Heileman purchased the brewery and shuttered the operation. Husold had taken a job as a circuit brewmaster connected with a brewing company in Detroit. Bob Byrne, Rooney's nephew and an employee at Northern from 1957 until six months before it closed, remembered that Husold visited the brewery every two or three weeks, spending two or three days in Superior before moving on to another brewery. Meanwhile, longtime Northern employee Joe Linsky handled the day-to-day brewing operation with help from Byrne and others.

To increase income, the brewery began bottling beer under private labels for specific accounts, including Community Club for the Community Liquor Store of Crystal, Minnesota, and Best Place by a Dam Site for a restaurant/nightclub/liquor store of the same name in Turtle Lake, Wisconsin. Husold also replaced the high-quality Bavarian hops with the least expensive hops he could find. The switch

CONTENTS   12 FLUID OZ.

COMMUNITY CLUB
STRONG BEER

BOTTLED EXCLUSIVELY FOR COMMUNITY LIQUOR STORE
CRYSTAL, MINN., BY NORTHERN BREWING CO., SUPERIOR, WIS.

did not go unnoticed, and many loyal Northern drinkers switched brands.

Other losses hindered profitability. Bob Byrne remembered the time he lost an entire batch of beer. One day he forgot to close the hatch of the wort tank. "Beer started pumping out of the hop jack like a fire hose," Byrne later said. He could do nothing but watch the entire 165-barrel batch of beer flow down the stairs and into the sewer.

Byrne recalled other changes that caused the brewery to struggle. Drinkers didn't return the brewery's returnable bottles, so Northern employees often drove to Duluth to buy Fitger's surplus bottles. When the brewery replaced its cypress fermenting vats with aluminum tanks, it meant that Byrne no longer had to scrape and varnish the aging redwood. But the change was ominous. A hole had to be cut into the brewery to get the large tanks inside, and during the process a worker was crushed to death.

At the time Northern's distribution included all of Wisconsin, Duluth, and the Twin Cities. Byrne also remembered that once a week two truckloads of Northern Beer was sent to Milwaukee. Sales dropped further after liquor stores and distributors returned a bad batch of beer "by the truckload." It cost Northern many loyal accounts—and Husold his job.

Slomann hired Henry Rothmann, for thirty years the brewmaster at the recently closed Wausau Brewing Company, as Northern's full-time brewmaster and plant manager. When Rothmann took over annual sales were already down from 25,000 to 18,000 barrels a year. The *Evening Telegram* announced Rothmann's hiring in June 1963, noting that sales had already increased based on the brewer's reputation and promising the current staff of seventeen employees would expand as sales increased. Instead, after Rothmann's changes sales declined substantially as local drinkers gave up on the hometown beer.

The sales staff countered the loss by trying to sell more beer elsewhere with lower prices. Dick Hartel noted that he could "go down to Wausau and buy [Northern] beer cheaper than I could working at the brewery in Superior." Dick's son Jim remembers that city employees would stop by the brewery's taproom each afternoon for free beer, but when his father saw the same people in taverns, they drank

LEFT: A LABEL FOR COMMUNITY CLUB BEER, BREWED BY NORTHERN BREWING CO. FOR THE COMMUNITY LIQUOR STORE OF CRYSTAL, MINNESOTA, IN THE 1960S.
[J. STEINER COLLECTION]

ABOVE: JOE AND DICK HARTEL OUTSIDE OF THE ORIGINAL 1890 KLINKERT BREWING CO., PREDECESSOR TO NORTHERN BREWING CO. THE 1914 STONE INDICATES THE YEAR AN ADDITION WAS MADE TO THE BUILDING.
[P. CLURE COLLECTION]

in the 1960s, leaving just sixteen at the end of the decade. Ten years later that number would be cut by more than half.

Minnesota's Cold Spring Brewing Company purchased the Northern label and accounts and kept the name alive until 1995. The brewery remained unoccupied for several years until various businesses, including a thrift store and an appliamnce recycler, tried to reuse it. Most of the brewery—including the office, taproom, cooperage, and part of the brewhouse—was demolished in the 1980s; the rest of the brewhouse came down in 2002. The glass-lined aging tanks installed in 1906 were left in the basement and remain buried today. Today the buildings sit empty.

Budweiser. Dick Hartel left the brewery after twenty years to work as a custodian at Superior Central High School. He would later tell researchers, "After my dad left the brewery, it wasn't the same. Corners were cut and the writing was on the wall." The same year Dick left the brewery, Joe Hartel died. He was seventy-five years old.

Northern stopped brewing in December 1966 and announced its closure the following February. The brewery retained a small crew until the inventory was depleted. Bob Byrne recalled that the last Superior bar to offer Northern on tap was his uncle's, Tommy Byrne's Tavern. Tracing its roots back to the original 1890 Klinkert Brewery, Northern had served Superior for seventy-seven years. It was one of fourteen Wisconsin breweries to call it quits

LEFT: A 1960S PRINT AD FEATURING THE SLOGAN "EVERYBODY HERE LIKES FITGER'S BEER!"

BELOW: A PLASTIC SIGN FOR FITGER'S BEER "BREWED WITH MATCHLESS LAKE SUPERIOR WATER" FEATURING A THERMOMETER. [P. CLURE COLLECTION]

after the death of J. Richard Beerhalter. Erwin Beerhalter replaced Johnson as vice president then stepped out of the Pop Shop to take over his brother's position managing sales. By then, longtime assistant brewmaster Otto Becker was in charge of Fitger's kettle.

Johnson reports that the remaining Beerhalter brothers tried various schemes to keep Fitger's afloat while conglomeration and national competition continued to close breweries across the country. In Minnesota, John Beerhalter Jr., pointed out, Fitger's competed for shelf space and tap lines with thirty-nine other brands. The brewery briefly distributed Dortmunder Union Beer, a German beer shipped to Duluth via the newly opened St. Lawrence Seaway, but

FITGER'S FALLS

Fitger's vice president Walter Johnson retired in 1960. Reaching seventy-five would be more than reason enough for anyone to retire, and after nearly sixty years in the business Johnson could see where the industry was heading, but Johnson may have left for other reasons. "Communication between [Johnson and Beerhalter Jr.] eventually became non-existent," Coopen Johnson wrote, "a sharp contrast to the earlier relationship between the senior Beerhalter and Johnson, who had worked very closely together for many years." Walter Johnson passed away in 1966, two years

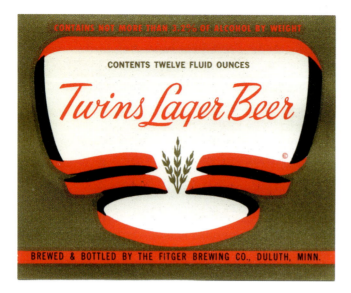

Two Fitger's Beer labels: "NATURALLY BREWED — NATURALLY BETTER / Fitger's / BEER / STRONG / BREWED & BOTTLED BY FITGER BREWING COMPANY, DULUTH, MINN. / CONTENTS TWELVE FLUID OUNCES" and "NATURALLY BREWED — NATURALLY BETTER / Fitger's / BEER / BREWED & BOTTLED BY FITGER BREWING COMPANY, DULUTH, MINN. / CONTENTS TWELVE FLUID OUNCES"

Top Left: Label for Fitger's Twins Lager Beer. [P. Clure Collection]

Right: Labels for Fitger's Beer used from the 1950s until 1972 featured an image of the Split Rock Lighthouse, an iconic landmark along the North Shore of Lake Superior. [C. Olsen Collection]

sales couldn't justify shipping costs. They considered product diversification ideas but never implemented any. Soon money was so tight the brewery asked distributors to pay in advance.

In a letter to stockholders in December 1966, Beerhalter Jr. reported the brewery's net profit for the year was $1,605.99, a little over $12,000 in 2017 dollars. "This is small, but BLACK not Red," he emphasized. The letter mentioned that, except for malt, the cost of supplies and packaging materials had doubled, In response, the brewery had tightened operations in the Pop Shop, dramatically cut the advertising budget, and consolidated delivery routes. Raising the price of Fitger's in Duluth helped, but Wisconsin sales dropped dramatically due to lack of advertising. Prices also went up for everything produced in the Pop Shop, and while the strategy increased income, the soft-drink department still operated at a loss.

Soon thereafter, Johnson reports, the brewery had to pay for grain before truckers would unload it—Fitger's had no credit. In 1967 longtime brewery chemist Johnny Hey died, and then the Beerhalters made a move that Hey, their father, and August Fitger would have greeted with disdain. Like many other struggling breweries, Fitger's turned to liquid hops to cut costs. For a brewery that had always prided itself on using the most modern equipment and finest ingredients, it was a desperate move—and poorly calculated. Liquid hops not only changed the beer's taste, but even when filtered left behind particles that looked like floating dandruff, which made the beer even more unappealing. Fitger's wasn't the only brewery making such mistakes. Milwaukee giant Schlitz suffered considerable damage to its reputation in the 1970s for, among other shortcuts, using pelletized hops and replacing malt with corn syrup.

According to Johnson, the brewery's "reputation and sales declined dramatically, forcing Fitger's to pull out of the Minneapolis market completely. Many loyal Fitger's customers became disgruntled and switched to other brands of beer." Some employees even refused to work in the bottle house. The practice ended swiftly, but Fitger's reputation "had already tarnished."

And then the Beerhalter family turned on itself. J. Richard Beerhalter's son Robert, a dentist, acted as agent for his mother Cecelia, who had inherited her husband's company stock. In 1968 Dr. Beerhalter joined a confederacy of minority shareholders who ousted his uncles. They named Dr. Beerhalter the brewery's new president, but his complete lack of experience in the brewing industry did nothing to vitalize the brewery.

The company ended its in-house distribution, subcontracting with Coopen Johnson to get its beer to the local market. Johnson remembered that two cold summers resulted in further sales losses. The dentist soon found himself up to his teeth in debt, with no cash for ingredients, advertising, or payroll. He closed the Pop Shop without any attempt to sell the Squirt or Lovit franchises. To generate cash he sold the property east of the Pickwick, including the brewery's icehouse, to the Wisocki family, who demolished the historic structure to create more parking for the restaurant.

Meanwhile, trust between the brewery and distributors outside of Duluth and Superior began to dissolve. If the

ABOVE AND LEFT:
PRINT ADVERTISEMENTS FOR FITGER'S BEER IN THE 1960S STRESSED ENJOYING THE NATURAL WONDERS OF NORTHERN MINNESOTA.
[P. CLURE COLLECTION]

brewery shipped out a bad batch of beer, the distributors would send it back—and then the brewery would ship that same bad beer right back to the same distributors. Further, many distributors could not pay their bills, compounding the mistrust.

On top of that, the Minnesota Pollution Control Agency (MPCA) had contacted the brewery, demanding that Fitger's stop dumping contaminated water leftover from the brewing process into Lake Superior. Since August Fitger's name first graced the brewery in 1885, the brewer took pride in keeping the facility up-to-date and using "pure" Lake Superior water to make its beer, and John Beerhalter Sr. had carried on that tradition. But by 1969, the once state-of-the-art brewery was polluting the very same Lake Superior water that made its beer so special. The problem could be solved by connecting the brewery's waste-water discharge to the city's sewer system, but that would be expensive.

In an attempt to raise funds to pay for the connection, Dr. Beerhalter entered into a complicated agreement with businessman John Ferris and his partner George G. Barnum that eventually gave the brewery to Ferris. Ferris had arrived in Duluth in 1948 to work as an engineer for U.S. Steel and belonged to the Duluth Chamber of Commerce. He had watched his father, a Boston banker, take a failing laundry, revitalize it, and then sell it for a profit. Ferris replaced Dr. Beerhalter as president after purchasing all of Cecilia Beerhalter's stock. Still, Dr. Beerhalter remained on the board as

TOP: FITGER'S STABLE/GARAGE
IN 1969.
[LIBRARY OF CONGRESS]

BOTTOM: THE BACK OF THE FITGER'S KEG RACKING
AND STORAGE FACILITY ON JUNE 19, 1974.
[J. LEMKE COLLECTION]

vice president, and other members included his uncles John and Erwin and former Fitger's executive Bert Jeronimus.

In September 1969 Ferris promised *Herald* readers he would initiate "an aggressive marketing program under additional working capital." Thirty-nine employees, nineteen of whom had worked for the brewery for twenty years or more, counted on Ferris to cover the company's $250,000 annual payroll. He also thanked the local brewers' union, which had allowed a moratorium on wage increases until the industry stabilized.

That December Ferris wrote the Minnesota Highway Department, who had surveyed the Fitger property earlier that month. Before he spent money fixing the discharge problem, he wanted to know what the state had planned for Fitger's as they continued with plans to extend I-35 even farther through Duluth. An agreement in May 1970 gave Ferris until the end of the year to fix the problem.

Some longtime employees of the brewery did not trust Ferris. Upon hearing about the Highway Department's potential plans, many suspected that Ferris had purchased the brewery never intending to keep it alive, but instead to realize a windfall after selling the property to the state. As Johnson describes it, employees felt Ferris spent more energy trying to buy Fitger's stock from shareholders than he did trying to improve the brewery's bottom line. Soon Ferris controlled 60 percent of the company, and the staff took note. "One by one," Johnson remembered, "the employees

began to leave Fitger's and seek other employment." In 1970 brewmaster Becker, recognizing that the end was near, took a job with Anheuser-Busch.

By then only six Minnesota breweries still made beer. Together Twin Cities brewers Grain Belt (formerly the Minneapolis Brewing Co.), Schmidt, and Hamm's enjoyed 68 percent of the Minnesota beer market, followed by national giants Schlitz, Anheuser-Busch, Heileman, Pabst, and Miller. Minnesota's Cold Spring and Schell's together owned less than 4 percent of the market. Fitger's sales made up less than 1 percent. Whether or not Ferris intended to keep the brewery open—and his investments suggest he did—the company had already been squeezed out by competition. And it would soon be squeezed between the MPCA and the Highway Department

In November 1970 the Minnesota Highway Department officially notified the brewery that plans to extend

THE EMPTY FITGER'S FACILITY IN THE EARLY 1980S.
[P. CLURE COLLECTION]

I-35 through Duluth indeed put the brewery right in the highway's path, just as it had with Duluth Brewing & Malt a decade earlier. Ferris filed for extensions with the MPCA, citing the "uncertainty" of the Highway Department's ultimate plans. The MPCA argued that the highway route may not be confirmed for five years, and it would not tolerate the brewery operating in its current state until that time. Ferris asked the MPCA to extend the deadline until September 1972, but it refused.

The following July an editorial in the *Herald* titled "Fitger Brewery Over a Barrel" made the brewery's case, arguing that the actions of the MPCA did not seem sensible. "Why require Fitger's to invest in rerouting some of its waste materials between now and next July when there is the possibility that the property will be condemned at the time?" As the paper suggested, it didn't make sense to modify a sewer system one year and then tear it up the next. Even the Highway Department wrote the MPCA, asking it to extend the brewery's deadline. The MPCA would not budge, and in the summer of 1972 Ferris signed an agreement with the state that demanded the brewery either "complete an expensive pollution abatement project or close down" no later than September 30, 1972.

Ferris told Duluth newspapers he planned to keep the Fitger's name alive by turning the brewery into a distributor and set up shop in a brand-new facility he intended to build in the developing industrial park near the airport (the plan never materialized). Fitger's staff, already down from thirty-nine to twenty since Ferris took over, would be reduced to just five including Ferris and his wife.

The last batch of Fitger's beer was brewed August 14, 1972. Bottle-house employees checked in for their final shift on September 14, and a dozen loyal employees filled the last cans of Fitger's beer on September 19. After 113 years, since Gottlieb Busch made his first batch of beer along Brewery Creek in 1859, the Twin Ports had no commercial brewer, marking the end of the longest-lived industry at the Head of the Lakes. And for the first time since 1881, there wasn't a beer on the market that contained even a single drop of Lake Superior water.

BREWING RETURNS
TO THE TWIN PORTS

AFTER FITGER'S PRESIDENT JOHN FERRIS SHUTTERED BREWERY OPERATIONS IN 1972, he contracted with Schell's Brewing Co. of New Ulm, Minnesota, to brew Fitger's beer. In 1981 Ferris and his crew dismantled the brewery's redwood fermenting and aging tanks, selling off the valuable wood. Meanwhile local citizens, including preservationists, had not approved of many aspects of the Minnesota Highway Department's plans to extend I-35 through Duluth, which would cut off public access to Lake Superior and cost the city many historic landmarks, including the brewery. Even the Minnesota State Historic Preservation Office got involved, pointing out the brewery's significance as "one of the last examples of an early American brewery left in the state." Other historic buildings stood in the highway's path, including the 1889 Endion Station and 1914 Hartley Building. The project would ultimately eliminate dozens of downtown buildings as well as homes along South Street.

An effort to preserve these buildings and lake access resulted in a new plan put together by the Mayor's Citizen Advisory Board. Tunnels would ensure lake access, and while many buildings indeed came down, the highway swerved between Fifth and Ninth Avenues East. Every structure on the lower side of Superior Street between Fifth and Eighth Avenues East was saved, including the Pickwick and the brewery complex. Endion Station was moved to Canal Park. Today Endion Station, the Hartley Building, and the Fitger's Complex all appear on the National Register of Historic Places.

Duluthians saved the facility, but Ferris and his fellow investors couldn't get back in the beer business without a major reinvestment. Instead he convinced the board to sue the State of Minnesota for losses the company incurred when the state forced the brewery to close and other related losses. The case would drag on for ten years and while the group

The Fitger's Complex
photographed in 2016 by
Dan Grandmaison.
[FITGER'S COMPLEX]

was awarded $5.3 million, the Minnesota Court of Appeals overturned the decision in 1987.

By then they had already sold the brewery and the rights to the Fitger name to Brewery Limited Partnership (BLP), an investment group led by Ron Jacobs. Jacobs planned to bring the facility back to life as Fitger's on the Lake, a retail complex with a hotel, shops, and restaurants. Renovations were underway in January 1985 when BLP began selling off the brewery equipment to make room. The pasteurizer went to the Point Brewery of Stevens Point, Wisconsin, and the malt mill to the Boulder Brewing Company in Colorado. Equipment that wasn't going to other breweries was sold as scrap metal.

Fitger's on the Lake opened in September 1985. Original plans called for an on-site brewery, but instead BLP contracted with Joseph Huber Brewing Co. of Monroe, Wisconsin, to brew beer labeled as "A Fitger & Co.'s Export Beer." That practice had ended by 1989 when BLP filed for bankruptcy and a local group led by William Papaik bought the complex from the bank that took over in receivership. In 1994 Papaik and his partners sold it to Fitger's-on-the-Lake LLC led by Duluthian Scott Vesterstein. The Fitger

label remained dormant until 2007 when a company led by Doug Donnelly, a grandson of Arnold Fitger, again contracted with Joseph Huber Brewing to produce "A. Fitger's Lager Beer." But Vesterstein argued he held the rights to the Fitger's name, and a lawsuit subsequently shut down Donnelly's operation. Vesterstein has since contracted with other breweries to make beer bearing the Fitger name.

Commercial beer brewing returned to both Fitger's and Duluth in 1994 when home-brewing enthusiast Bob Dromeshauser took a leap of faith and opened the Lake Superior Brewing Company, a brewery and home-brewing supply store, inside the Fitger's Complex. In those early days the tiny operation cooked just one six-barrel batch every Sunday with equipment obtained from a dairy, but it brought the craft-brewing renaissance that had begun to sweep the nation to the shore of Lake Superior. When this book went to press in the summer of 2018, sixteen breweries—nine in Duluth, two in Superior, two along the Wisconsin South Shore at Ashland and Washburn, and three along the Minnesota North Shore between Two Harbors and Grand Marais—were using that soft Lake Superior water to make naturally brewed, naturally better beer.

LAKE SUPERIOR BREWING CO.

ESTABLISHED: 1994
TYPE: 15-Barrel Microbrewery
LOCATION: 2711 W. Superior St., Duluth
TAPROOM: At Brewery
2016 PRODUCTION: 1,600 Barrels

The oldest microbrewery in Minnesota, Lake Superior Brewing Company began as a home-brewing supply shop within the converted Fitger's Brewery complex. It was established in 1994 by Bob and Laurie Dromeshauser with investors Don and JoAnne Hoag, John Judd III, and Karen Olesen. Don Hoag and Judd cofounded the Northern Ale Stars, Minnesota's oldest home-brewing club. A few months after the shop opened, Bob Dromeshauser, Don Hoag, and Judd began brewing one six-barrel batch of beer every Sunday. They were soon joined by volunteer brewer Dale Kleinschmidt, a home brewer himself since 1971. In 1996 the former hobbyists moved to a larger space within Fitger's and Kleinschmidt was hired as an official employee. Expansion forced LSB to change locations again in 1998, and they found a new home in Duluth's Lincoln Park business district. The Dromehuaser left LSB in 2001, and Kleinschmidt became a co-owner. By then, focusing on making British- and German-style beers, Kleinschmidt had refined LSB's flagship brands Kayak Kölsch, Lake Superior Special Ale, Mesabi Red, and Sir Duluth Oatmeal Stout, which are now distributed across Minnesota and Wisconsin. The brewery also cooks up a variety of seasonal beers and contracts with the Fitger's Complex to produce beer labeled and sold under the Fitger's name at the complex's in-house liquor store. In November 2017 Lars Kuenhnow and Lisa Blade became the brewery's newest owners. For Kuenhnow, it was more than an investment—it was a way to keep his all-time favorite beer, Kayak Kölsch, on the market. Kleinschmidt remained head brewer until the summer of 2018 when Ryan Woodfill, who brewed for Duluth's Canal Park Brewing Co. and the Crescent City Brewpub in New Orleans, came on to take over brew-ing operations. He is the first brewer hired by LSB with previous professional brewing experience.

FITGER'S BREWHOUSE

ESTABLISHED: 1995 (Brewing, 1997)
TYPE: 10-Barrel Brewpub
LOCATION: 600 E. Superior St., Duluth
2017 PRODUCTION: 1,400 Barrels

In 1994, Brainerd native Tim Nelson and Duluthian Rod Raymond returned from a ski trip inspired to open what was then a relatively new concept—a "brewpub," a restaurant that served up good food and craft beer, often made on site. They found an ideal location in the renovated historic Fitger's Brewery Complex but put brewing plans on hold as Lake Superior Brewing was already making beer within the building. Brewhouse bartender Mike Hoops was an avid home brewer, a hobby introduced to him by his brother Dave, and he volunteered at Lake Superior Brewing Company as an apprentice. When LSB left the complex, Nelson and Raymond gave Mike the green light to build a brewery. He found used equipment in Colorado and drove it back to Duluth in a rented truck. By April 1997 Fitger's was serving up its first batch of Hoops's Petroglyph Porter. Two years later he left, becoming head brewer for Minneapolis's Town Hall Brew Pub and has gone on to become Minnesota's most-decorated brewer. Dave Hoops, then working as a brewer in California, was willing to take over from his brother. The Hoops brothers were responsible for developing Fitger's flagship beers, including Witch Tree ESB, Big Boat Oatmeal Stout, Starfire Pale Ale, and El Niño IPA. Together with their assistants they earned the Brewhouse dozens of awards from regional and national beer festivals. Nelson and Raymond also established several other Duluth restaurants, all of which served Brewhouse beer. Nelson sold his portion of the business to Raymond in the fall of 2015, and Hoops left soon thereafter. Long-time Brewhouse brewer Frank Kaszuba briefly took over the kettle before Ted Briggs became brewmaster in December 2016. Today Alex "Coke" Chocholousek oversees brewing.

THIRSTY PAGAN BREWING CO.

ESTABLISHED: 1999, 2006
TYPE: 7-Barrel Brewpub
LOCATION: 1623 Broadway St., Superior
2017 PRODUCTION: 635 Barrels

Thirsty Pagan Brewing Company first opened within the tile-lined walls of Superior's historic Russel Creamery Company plant in 1999 as the Twin Ports Brewing Company. Owner Rick Sauer's two-barrel brewpub brought commercial brewing back to Superior for the first time since Northern Brewery closed in 1967. Sauer and his crew developed the flagship brands North Coast Amber, Derailed Ale, and Burntwood Black. In May 2006 Steve Knauss purchased the brewery and changed its name to Thirsty Pagan Brewing. Knauss told newspapers that he "recognizes our potential in focusing on just two things, pizza and beer. Do

LAKE SUPERIOR BREWING CO.'S DALE KLEINSCHMIDT.
[LAKE SUPERIOR BREWING CO.]

those two things correctly, and the world will come to us." Since then, TPB has indeed carved out a niche in the Twin Ports restaurant scene, and is known for its hand-tossed, deep-dish pizza. Knauss also expanded the brewing facility into a seven-barrel operation. Live music nearly every night of the week and an outdoor beer garden also help make Thirsty Pagan a popular nighttime haunt. Over the years brewmasters have included Nate MacAlpine, creator of the brewery's flagship IPA India Pagan Ale, and Allyson Rolph. During her five-year tenure with the brewpub, Rolph helped Thirsty Pagan gain a reputation for making outstanding mixed-fermentation sour beers, including Maku Amber, Yukon Red, and Mumford Red. Today Knauss keeps a variety of beers on tap, including Reinhold Berlin(er) Weisse, Birne Sage Pils, Velo Saison, and Oktoberfest. When this book went to press in the summer of 2018, Kathleen Culhane, founder of St. Paul nanobrewery Sidhe Brewing Company, had just been hired as Thirsty Pagan's head brewer.

CARMODY IRISH PUB & BREWERY

ESTABLISHED: 2006 (Brewing 2009)
TYPE: 5-Barrel Brewpub
LOCATION: 308 E. Superior St., Duluth
2017 PRODUCTION: 100 Barrels

Rick Boo and Eddie Gleeson hadn't considered starting a brewery when they opened Carmody Irish Pub inside the historic 1905 Burrell & Harmon Metal Works, but Gleeson couldn't get away from his family's history. The bar itself is named after his grandmother Margaret (Carmody) Gleeson and his cousin Agnes Carmody, and his grandfather Michael Gleeson served as vice president of Duluth's People's Brewery, established in 1907 by a group of independent "liquor retailers" including Gleeson himself, who operated saloons and hotels in Duluth's notorious St. Croix District, once home to the Zenith City's brothels and gambling and opium dens. (Today it is part of the Canal Park Business District.) Carmody first began brewing in 2009, with Gleeson's wife, Liz, heading brewing operations (she now

owns the facility). Carmody has had several brewmasters since then, including Jason Baumgarth, former Thirsty Pagan brewmaster Nate MacAlpine, and Thirsty Pagan/Twin Ports Brewing's original brewer Rick Sauer, Carmody's current brewmaster. The brewpub's flagship brands include People's Pub Ale, Agnes Irish Red, Scanlon IPA, and Black 47 Irish Stout, made with potatoes. Despite its status as a brewpub, Gleeson explained to the University of Minnesota Duluth *Statesman* in 2012 that his original vision for Carmody was as "an Irish Heritage center" and a "community center for the dispossessed," but instead it became known as a live-music venue. Considering Boo's

EDDIE GLEESON OF CARMODY IRISH PUB & BREWERY, THE TWIN PORTS' SMALLEST BREWERY, GRANDSON OF PEOPLE'S BREWING CO. FOUNDER MICHAEL J. GLEESON. [KIP PRASLOWICZ]

background, in retrospect live music seems as inevitable as brewing beer: Boo ran Duluth's iconic NorShor Theatre during its glory years as the unofficial home of Duluth's music scene, incubating local acts and helping to develop the Homegrown Music Festival. Carmody's beer is also available at Boo and Gleeson's Carmody 61 up the North Shore in Two Harbors, Minnesota.

DUBRUE

ESTABLISHED: 2011
TYPE: 15-Barrel Microbrewery
LOCATION: 211 E. Second St., Duluth
CLOSED: 2014

Former Fitger's Brewhouse employees Bob Blair and Nicholas Cameron opened Dubrue—a contraction of "Duluth Brewing"—inside an old Gold Cross Ambulance garage in 2011. The pair of Duluth East High School graduates had spent two years gathering funding for their dream, with Blair working as brewmaster while Cameron, who also had experience as a financial analyst, handled sales. They assembled their facility using equipment bought at auctions and farms and started brewing. Soon their flagship Pub Ale, an English-style session ale, and India Black Ale were being sold on tap in over a dozen Twin Ports bars and restaurants, and they were anticipating producing one thousand barrels during their first year. Unfortunately, the brewery was short lived. Fire struck the facility in 2014, destroying equipment and forcing Dubrue out of business.

DUBH LINN IRISH BREW PUB

ESTABLISHED: 2006 (Brewing 2011)
TYPE: 2.5-Barrel Brewpub
LOCATION: 109 W. Superior St., Duluth
2017 PRODUCTION: 150 Barrels

Dubh Linn Irish Brew Pub takes its name from the Old Irish word for "dark tidal pool," used to identify a spot along Ireland's River Dodder that was once the site of

FROM LEFT: COLIN AND LAURA MULLEN AND KAREN AND BRYON TONNIS, FOUNDERS OF BENT PADDLE BREWING, THE TWIN PORTS' LARGEST BREWER BY VOLUME.
[BENT PADDLE BREWING CO.]

a Viking village and later became Dublin, Ireland's principal city. Owner Mike Maxim Jr. chose the name because it reflected "the Scandinavian heritage of Northern Minnesota and the Irish traditions of fine spirits, good company, and a comfortable atmosphere." Maxim himself is a mix of Irish and Scandinavian ancestry, as is his brother Seth, Dubh Linn's head brewer. Seth learned to brew from Mark Dexter, a member of the Northern Ale Stars home-brewing club and one of the most-decorated homebrewers in Minnesota. It was Dexter who first suggested that Maxim offer beer brewed on site after the pub began serving homestyle food inspired by his Irish-immigrant grandmother. That's when Seth, a biologist by training, joined the team. Dexter and Seth created a brewing system using two forty-gallon soup kettles and computer-controlled fermenting tanks. Flagship brands include Cobh Harbor IPA, Maple Amber Ale, Wandering Druid Trippel, Peach Radler, and Harmon's Killer Brew, a bourbon-barrel stout aged six months that comes with all the slugging power of its namesake: a 10.5 percent alcohol content. In 2016 Dubh Linn added a rooftop hop garden to grow fresh hops

not only for its beer, but also to season its food and cocktails. Much of the harvest is set aside to brew Dubh Linn's Rooftop Hop. Seth has also tried to replicate Guinness Stout using a recipe Mike found in book allegedly published by a disgruntled member of the Guinness family. The experiment was certainly appropriate: legend has it that the waters of that "dark pool" first inspired brewer Arthur Guinness to create his famous black porter.

BLACKLIST ARTISAN ALES

ESTABLISHED: 2012
TYPE: 20-Barrel Microbrewery
LOCATION: 211 E. Second St., Duluth
TAPROOM: At Brewery
2017 PRODUCTION: 1,300 Barrels

Childhood friends Jon Loss and Brian Schanzenbach have spent much of their lives scheming up adventures for themselves, such as piloting a catamaran made of canoes and plywood down the Mississippi River from their hometown of Brainerd to St. Cloud (they nearly made it). Their plans for Blacklist Artisan Ales have been much more successful. While Loss studied graphic design in Minneapolis, Schanzenbach headed to Duluth to learn biology but ended up brewing, first as an intern for Lake Superior Brewing Co. He then spent six years brewing at Fitger's Brewhouse. Their idea to open their own brewery became much more than an adventure after Schanzenbach attended the Siebel Institute while Loss studied marketing

and increased his brewing knowledge by becoming a cicerone, the brewing industry's equivalent to a wine sommelier. They began brewing as Blacklist in 2012 using a 2.5-barrel system within the same facility used by Dubrue (see page 182) and ended up taking over the facility after fire forced Dubrue to close. Attorney T. J. Estebrook came onboard as co-owner in 2015. By then Blacklist was moving into the last place anyone anticipated, the historic 1908 Delray Hotel—better known as the last home of the Last Place on Earth, a notorious head shop shut down by federal agents for selling synthetic marijuana. The Blacklist crew is proud of turning the location—which today includes a 5,700-square-foot taproom with a stage for live music—into a vital part of Duluth's Historic Arts & Theater District. And of course, they are equally proud of their product, which is highly influenced by Belgian brewing traditions without "following a strict dogma." Besides a constant stream of new releases, Blacklist's flagship brands include a Belgian-style IPA labeled simply BIPA, Classic WIT wheat ale, and Or de Belgique Belgian-style strong ale.

CANAL PARK BREWING CO.

ESTABLISHED: 2012
TYPE: 15-barrel Brewpub
LOCATION: 300 Canal Park Drive, Duluth
2017 PRODUCTION: 1,047 Barrels

As the first brewpub to set up shop in the Canal Park Business District, the Canal Park Brewing Company's location adjacent to the Duluth Lakewalk gives it boasting rights to the best view of Lake Superior enjoyed by a Twin Ports brewery. To get that view, Duluth's Kavajecz family spent nearly $1 million cleaning up a former industrial site before building their brewpub. The Kavajecz's come from a beer-brewing bloodline: their uncle Maximillian Hernberger worked for Fitger's in the 1940s and often brought his employer's beer to family gatherings, which they say "inspired a long-lasting love of great beer." Canal Park Brewing sources its ingredients as locally as it can, buying malt from Breiss Malt in Chilton,

TIM WILSON, TIM NELSON, FRANK KASZUBA, AND ALLYSON ROLPH OF EARTH RIDER BREWING, SUPERIOR'S NEWEST BEER MANUFACTURER [EARTH RIDER BREWING]

Wisconsin, and hops from St. Croix Valley Hops in St. Croix Falls, Wisconsin. Many have taken their turn at the kettle for CPBC, including original and current brewmaster Dan Aageness, former lead and head brewers Matthew "Badger" Colish, Jeremy King, and Ryan Woodfill. As this book went to press Austin Clem was assisting Aageness as the brewpub searched for a new head to oversee production of the brewery's "Northcoaster"-style beers, including flagship brands Stoned Surf IPA, Pack Sacker Oatmeal Stout, Ankle Deep Pilsner, and Nut Hatch Nut Brown Ale, winner of the silver medal for English-Style Brown Ale at the 2014 World Beer Cup. That Northcoaster style reflects the brewpub's guiding philosophy: "We are inspired by the wild beauty of Lake Superior, the steadfast nature of our community, and the epic adventures right outside our back door. Perhaps that's why we've always called it home, and probably why we've always wanted to share it with others.

What better way to share our tales and reminisce than to sit down together over a couple craft beers and real food?"

BENT PADDLE BREWING CO.

ESTABLISHED: 2013
TYPE: 30-Barrel Production Brewery
LOCATION: 1912 W. Michigan St., Duluth
TAPROOM: 1832 W. Michigan St., Duluth
2017 PRODUCTION: 16,705 Barrels

A mutual love of craft beer and canoeing connected Bryon and Karen Tonnis with Colin and Laura Mullen in 2010. At the time Bryon worked as head brewer for Minneapolis's Rock Bottom Brewery, while Colin was head brewer for Barley John's Brew Pub in nearby New Brighton. Moreover, Karen's and Laura's business experience meshed with the needs of operating and promoting a commercial brewery. They organized in 2013 as the Bent Paddle Brewing Company, adopting the name from Bryon's preferred tool for mixing mash: a bent-shaft canoe paddle. The four chose Duluth, Laura's home town, for the location of their brewery not just for its proximity to canoe country, but also so they could make their beer with that legendary soft Lake Superior water, which they say "mimics the water of Pilsen, Czech Republic, the birthplace of pilsners." They leased a warehouse in what has since become known as the Lincoln Park Craft District and began brewing. Sales outgrew capacity within six months—and continued to climb. Bent Paddle famously reached its ten-year goal within two years and has continued to grow ever since. The brewery strives to produce beers that "bend the tradition of the classic style[s]" while remaining "drinkable, balanced beers...for all beer lovers to enjoy." The brewers of Bent Paddle craft a wide variety of beer, including flagship brands Kanu Session Pale Ale, Venture Pils Pilsner Lager, Bent Hop Golden IPA, 14° ESB Extra Special Amber Ale, Black Ale, and Cold Press Black

Coffee Ale, made with a unique blend of beans from the Duluth Coffee Company. In 2016 Bent Paddle moved its offices to another historic warehouse a block away at 1832 West Michigan Street, which became home to the brewery's taproom in 2018.

EARTH RIDER BREWING CO.

ESTABLISHED: 2017
TYPE: 20-Barrel Microbrewery
LOCATION: 1617 N. Third St., Superior
TAPROOM: 1715 N. Third St., Superior
PROJECTED 2018 PRODUCTION: 2,500 Barrels

After walking away from Fitger's Brewhouse in 2015, Tim Nelson couldn't walk away from brewing. As a founding member of the Minnesota Craft Brewers Guild, he had fought for off-site sales and helped legalize refillable growlers. So he teamed up with former Brewhouse brewmaster Dave Hoops and others to form BevCraft, a "craft beverage think tank" that "incubates and consults breweries from idea to thriving business." Frank Kaszuba, another former Brewhouse brewmaster, later became BevCraft's director of brewing operations, and Nelson's brother Brad pitches in as director of brands. Both Nelson and Hoops also entertained plans to open their own breweries, and building them would be good experience for the young company. Nelson chose to set up shop in Superior for several reasons: his Swedish and Norwegian great-grandfathers had both immigrated to Superior, he wanted a historic waterfront location, and he preferred Wisconsin's laws governing beer sales to those of Minnesota. Appropriately enough, BevCraft moved into the upper floor of the Cedar Lounge, first built by Northern Brewing in 1912 as a tied-house saloon. Nelson planned to build his brewery on vacant land east of the Cedar, but instead leased the nearby Leamon Mercantile building and turned it into the Earth Rider Brewing Co. Allyson Rolph, formerly of Thirsty Pagan Brewing, and Tim Wilson, who brewed for both Bent Paddle and Fitger's Brewhouse, were brought on as lead brewers. Kegs of Earth Rider beer were first tapped in October 2017 and cans of their flagship brands—Superior Pale Ale, Precious Material Helles Lager, North Tower Stout, and Caribou Lake IPA—landed on store shelves the following March. The Cedar Lounge now serves as the brewery's taproom and features live music sometimes played by BevCraft executives: both Nelson brothers are veterans of the Twin Ports' vibrant music scene.

HOOPS BREWING CO.

ESTABLISHED: 2017
TYPE: 15-Barrel Microbrewery
LOCATION: 325 Lake Ave. S., Duluth
TAPROOM: At Brewery
ANTICIPATED 2018 PRODUCTION: 2,000 Barrels

Inspired by the emerging craft brewing industry, Duluth native Dave Hoops began brewing in his San Francisco kitchen in 1992. His passion for craft beer lead him to Chicago's Siebel Institute and an apprenticeship with nearby Goose Island Beer Co. He then returned to San Francisco and began brewing for the Pyramid Brewing Company before replacing his brother Mike as brewmaster at Fitger's Brewhouse. When Hoops left Fitger's in 2015, he joined Tim Nelson at BevCraft (see Earth Rider, facing page). One of BevCraft's early projects was Hoops Brewing Company, and once the brewery was up and running, the companies severed ties as Hoops's focus turned to his new operation. The Hoops Brewing Company opened in June 2017 within Duluth's historic Marshall-Wells Hardware Building, built in 1900 as a warehouse and office complex to serve what became the world's largest hardware wholesaler. When it first opened, the brewery's taproom was the largest in the state, with seating for over 250 people. Floor-to-ceiling windows provide customers with a view of the brewery. Hoops tapped Melissa Rainville as his head brewer and brought Casey Tatro and Pete Bystrowski on board to assist her—both Rainville and Tatro had built their experience working with Hoops at Fitger's Brewhouse. Hoops Brewing likes to mix it up, brewing "three to four batches a week" to make up to one hundred unique recipes each year, enough that the brewers have developed a numbering system to identify their different brews. Standard offerings include "Hoops-centric" pales and IPAs, barrel-aged beers, sour beers, American- and German-style lagers and pilsners as well as wheat beers and fruit beers. Beer lovers who have followed Hoops since his Fitger's Brewhouse days will also recognize carryovers Daisy Ale and Finn's Finest, pale ales named for his children.

URSA MINOR BREWING CO.

ESTABLISHED: 2018
TYPE: 5-Barrel Microbrewery
LOCATION: 2415 W. Superior St., Duluth
TAPROOM: At Brewery
ANTICIPATED 2018 PRODUCTION: 500 Barrels

Brothers Ben and Mark Hugus feel that they found their way home through craft beer, and that's why they named their brewery for Ursa Minor, a constellation also known as the Little Dipper. It contains the North Star, which has provided travelers a guiding light for eons. "Craft beer is our guiding light," Ben Hugus explains, "and we have fallen in love with the community that surrounds the craft beer industry." The Hugus brothers spent four years planning their brewery. While Ben and his wife were teaching abroad in Bangladesh and Ecuador, Mark earned a marketing and business degree and gained brewing experience with Red Eye Brewing Company in Wausau, Wisconsin, their home town. Mark then moved to Duluth and worked for both Castle Danger and Fitger's Brewhouse while he and Ben raised the funds to build their own brewery. Duluth native and UMD graduate Andrew Scrignoli joined the team as general manager months before they first opened in September 2018. Ursa Minor's limited brewing capacity is intentional, as it allows them to brew small handcrafted batches of a variety of beers that will rotate on tap from week to week. One of the first to pour in the Ursa Minor taproom was a double IPA called Big Bad John, named for the Hugus brothers' father John, who passed away in 2013; like their father the beer is bold, strong, and persistent. The Ursa Minor crew would love to see their taproom, which will include a wood-fired oven to cook up artisan pizzas, become a gathering place. "We want people to come to our taproom and feel at home and welcomed and allow our beer to serve as the medium to new connections. We love people, people love beer, and beer loves us!"

BEN HUGUS, MARK HUGUS, AND ANDREW SCRIGNOLI OF URSA MINOR, DULUTH'S NEWEST BREWERY, IN FRONT OF LAKE SUPERIOR.
[URSA MINOR BREWING]

OTHER REGIONAL BREWERIES* ESTABLISHED SINCE 1994

BOATHOUSE BREWPUB & RESTAURANT

ESTABLISHED: 2008
LOCATION: 47 E. Sheridan St., Ely, MN
TYPE: 3.5-Barrel Brewpub
OWNER: Mark Bruzek
BREWMASTER: Ben Storbek
2017 PRODUCTION: 280 Barrels

BOOMTOWN BREWERY

ESTABLISHED: 2018
LOCATION: 531 E. Howard St., Hibbing, MN
TYPE: 7-Barrel Brewpub
OWNERS: Jessica & Erik Lietz
BREWMASTER: Dennis Holland
ANTICIPATED 2018 PRODUCTION: 1,000 Barrels

BOREALIS FERMENTERY

ESTABLISHED: 2012
LOCATION: Knife River, MN
TYPE: 3-Barrel Nanobrewery
TAPROOM: None
OWNER/BREWMASTER: Ken Thiemann
CLOSED: 2017

CASTLE DANGER BREWERY

ESTABLISHED: 2011
LOCATION: 17 7th St., Two Harbors, MN
TYPE: 30-Barrel Production Brewery
TAPROOM: At Brewery
OWNERS: Jamie & Clint MacFarlane, Mandy & Lon Larson
HEAD BREWER: Bjorn Erickson
2017 PRODUCTION: 14,900 Barrels

CUYUNA BREWING CO.

ESTABLISHED: 2017
LOCATION: 1 E. Main St., Crosby, MN
TYPE: 5-Barrel Microbrewery
TAPROOM: At Brewery
OWNERS: Nick and Laura Huisinga
BREWMASTER: Nick Huisinga
2017 PRODUCTION: 200 Barrels

GUNFLINT TAVERN & BREWPUB

ESTABLISHED: 1998 (Brewing 2014)
LOCATION: 111 W. Wisconsin St., Grand Marais, MN
TYPE: 5-Barrel Brewpub
OWNERS: Susan & Jeff Gecas
BREWMASTER: Paul Gecas
2017 PRODUCTION: 200 Barrels

KLOCKOW BREWING

ESTABLISHED: 2017
LOCATION: 36 SE 10th St., Grand Rapids, MN
TYPE: 8.5-Barrel Microbrewery
TAPROOM: At Brewery
OWNERS: Tasha & Andy Klockow
BREWMASTER: Andy Klockow
ANTICIPATED 2018 PRODUCTION: 300 Barrels

SOUTH SHORE BREWERY

ESTABLISHED: 1995
LOCATION 1: 808 Main St. W., Ashland, WI
TYPE: 10-Barrel Brewpub
LOCATION 2: 532 W. Bayfield St., Washburn, WI
TYPE: 15-Barrel Production Brewery
TAPROOM: At Washburn Brewery
OWNER/BREWMASTER: Bo Bélanger
2017 PRODUCTION: 1,800 Barrels

VOYAGEUR BREWING CO.

ESTABLISHED: 2015
TYPE: 20-Barrel Microbrewery
LOCATION: 233 W. Highway 61, Grand Marais, MN
TAPROOM: At Brewery
OWNERS: Ritalee & Bruce Walters, Sue & Mike Prom
BREWMASTER: Stuart Long
2017 PRODUCTION: 1,900 Barrels

CLINT MACFARLANE (LEFT) AND MASON WILLIAMS OF CASTLE DANGER BREWERY IN TWO HARBORS, MINNESOTA, THE SECOND-LARGEST BREWERY IN THE WESTERN LAKE SUPERIOR REGION, POSE IN LAKE SUPERIOR WITH A STRINGER OF GROWLERS.
[CASTLE DANGER BREWING CO.]

*Located in the same region covered in parts 1–4: On Minnesota's Iron Range and along the Minnesota North Shore and Wisconsin South Shore of Lake Superior.

TWIN PORTS BREWERIANA

MANY OF THE IMAGES THAT ILLUSTRATE THIS BOOK ARE THOSE OF "BREWERIANA," memorabilia associated with the brewing industry that is collected by enthusiasts: product labels, bottles and cans, packaging, advertising signs, advertising novelties, and rare items such as delivery truck driver uniforms. Many collectors seek hard-to-find items of ephemera including print advertisements, stock certificates, corporate letterhead, and much more. They sell and trade their items online and at breweriana shows. The majority of breweriana that appears in this book comes from two members of a group called the Nordlagers, named after a beer first produced by the Fitger Brewing Co. in the late 1930s, Chris Olsen and this book's coauthor Pete Clure. On a Saturday in August 2016 Olsen and Twin Cities breweriana collector Jody Otto brought the best Twin Ports' breweriana from their collections to Clure's house, where photographer Brian Rauvola of Duluth's HBR Studios had turned the living room into a makeshift photo studio and publisher Tony Dierckins had set up a flatbed scanner.

For nineteen hours over the next two days, Rauvola photographed everything that couldn't fit into the scanner. The result was a collection of over five hundred images, many of which were used to help illustrate the main body of this book—all of the book's modern color photographs of breweriana were made by Rauvola. The following pages contain the pictures that we couldn't fit in. Please note that while this is an impressive collection of breweriana, it does not constitute a complete collection of items associated with the four major breweries that served the Twin Ports from 1885 to 1972—an objective collectors themselves recognize as unobtainable. In fact, it doesn't even include all of the breweriana collected by Clure, Olson, and Otto. We include the following samples to further illustrate the story told on previous pages.

KEGS, ETC. FOR TWIN PORTS BREWERIES, CA. 1900–1965

FAR LEFT: A RARE STEEL KEG USED BY PEOPLE'S BREWING CO.; SECOND COLUMN, MIDDLE: A KEG BRAND FOR DULUTH BREWING & MALTING; SECOND COLUMN, BOTTOM: A FITGER'S COOLER TAP, WHICH COOLED BEER ON ITS WAY FROM A KEG TO A GLASS.

WOODEN BEER CASES, CA. 1909–1950

DULUTH BREWING & MALTING BOTTLES, CA. 1934–1966

THE PHOTO OF FITGER'S REX BOTTLES FROM THE 1940S (LEFT COLUMN, CENTER) INCLUDES ONE BOTTLE (FAR LEFT) FEATURING THE LABEL USED BY DULUTH BREWING & MALTING CA. 1910 WHEN IT OWNED THE REX NAME. FITGER'S PURCHASED DB&M'S PRODUCT NAMES IN 1930.

TOP LEFT: SQUIRT WAS BOTTLED BY THE FITGER BREWING COMPANY; BOTTOM LEFT: THE NOVELTY PENCIL WAS ACTUALLY A PACKAGE FOR CHOCOLATE HASH, MADE BY FITGER'S DURING PROHIBITION; CENTER TOP CENTER: FITGER'S PRODUCTS MADE DURING PROHIBITION; BOTTOM CENTER: SODA BOTTLED BY FITGERS IN THE 1950S AND 1960S; TOP RIGHT: TWO OF PEOPLE'S PROHIBITION PRODUCTS; BOTTOM RIGHT: PEOPLE'S BOTTLED 7-UP AND ROYAL CROWN COLA FROM THE LATE 1940S UNTIL 1957.

COASTERS FOR TWIN PORTS BREWERIES, CA. 1934–1965

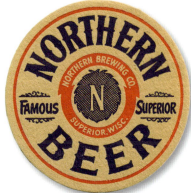

THE FITGER'S CARDBOARD REPLICAS OF LAKE SUPERIOR'S SPLIT ROCK LIGHTHOUSE (TOP LEFT) WERE LIT FROM WITHIN BY A LIGHT BULB; THE DULUTH BREWING & MALTING ROYAL 57 AND ROYAL 58 ITEMS (BOTTOM LEFT) ARE LAMPS AND LAMP SHADES; THE PLASTIC PEOPLE'S REGAL SUPREME BOTTLE (BOTTOM CENTER) IS A RADIO.

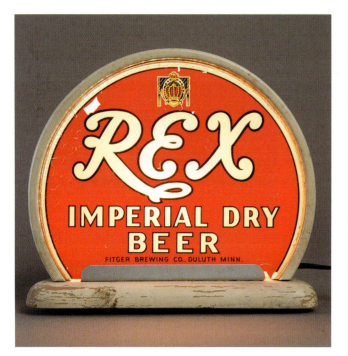

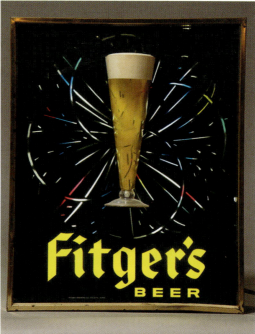

A GEL INSIDE THE FITGER'S "GALAXY" SIGN (TOP CENTER) ROTATED, CREATING THE ILLUSION OF BURSTING FIREWORKS IN SEVERAL COLORS.

CLOCKS FOR TWIN PORTS BREWERIES, CA. 1939–1960

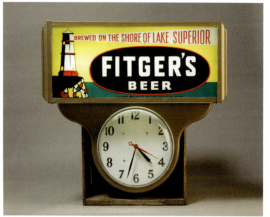

THE ROYAL BOHEMIAN SIGN (TOP LEFT) IS GLASS; THE REX SHIELD (TOP LEFT CENTER) IS WOOD; THE REX CROWN SIGN (TOP CENTER RIGHT) IS PLASTIC AND DESIGNED TO FIT ON THE COLLAR OF A KEG TAP; THE CIRCULAR REX SIGN (TOP RIGHT) IS STEEL AND GLASS.

THE POSTER AT BOTTOM RIGHT, MADE IN THE 1930S, ILLUSTRATED THE LYRICS OF A GERMAN DRINKING SONG.

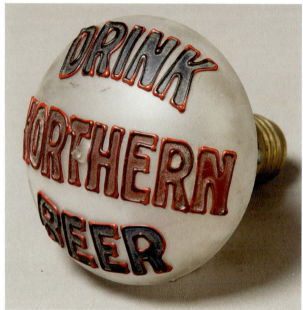

TOP LEFT: GLASSES, CA. 1898; TOP RIGHT: A WAX-PAPER DISPENSER; BOTTOM LEFT: A FOAM SCRAPER, A DEVICE BARTENDERS ONCE USED TO SKIM THE FOAM OFF THE TOP OF A GLASS OF BEER.

INDEX

FITGER BREWING CO. LETTERHEAD, CA. 1905. [C. OLSON COLLECTION]

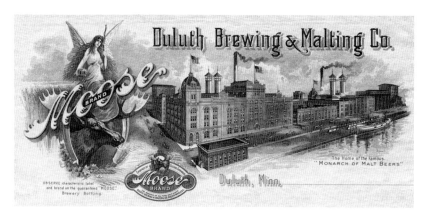

DULUTH BREWING & MALTING CO. LETTERHEAD, CA. 1900. [C. OLSON COLLECTION]

PEOPLE'S BREWING CO. LETTERHEAD, CA. 1945. [P. CLURE COLLECTION]

FITGER BREWING CO. LETTERHEAD, CA. 1940. [C. OLSON COLLECTION]

DULUTH BREWING & MALTING CO. LETTERHEAD, CA. 1945. [C. OLSON COLLECTION]

DULUTH BREWING & MALTING CO. LETTERHEAD, CA. 1962. [C. OLSON COLLECTION]

A FITGER BREWING COMPANY BEER TOKEN, CA. 1946.
[P. CLURE COLLECTION]

REFERENCES

Akin, Ron and Lee Reiherzer. *The Breweries of Oshkosh: Their Rise and Fall*. Oshkosh, Wisc.: Self-published, 2012.

"Anneke, Mathilde, 1817–1884." Wisconsin Historical Society. www.wisconsinhistory.org. Accessed February 4, 2017.

Anderson, Bonnie S. *Joyous Greetings: The First International Women's Movement, 1830-1860*. New York: Oxford University Press, 2001.

Apps, Jerry. *Breweries of Wisconsin, Second Edition*. Madison, Wisc.: University of Wisconsin Press, 2005.

Armour, Robert E. *Superior, Wisconsin: A Planned City*. Superior, Wisc.: Self-published , 1976.

— —. *Superior, Wisconsin 1857–1885*. Superior, Wisc.: Self published , 1994.

Baago, Jay. "They Rolled Out the Barrels." *Lake Superior/Port Cities Magazine*. Spring, 1985.

Beerhalter, John Jr. "Letter to Stockholders of the Fitger Brewing Company." December 21, 1966.

Berg, Bob. "Building a Better Beer: There's a New Wave of Regional Craft Brewers." *Lake Superior Magazine Guide*. 2013.

Brewer's Register. Supplement to the *American Brewer's Gazette*. January 15, 1873.

Bull, Donald with Manfred Friedrich and Robert Gottschalk. *American Breweries*. Trumbull, Conn.: Bullworks, 1984.

Byrnes, Robert. Interviews with Tony Dierckins, December 12, 2017; February 28, 2018.

Clure, Pete and Doug Davis. "Duluth Brewing & Malting Company: Good Leadership and Smart Marketing Delivers Beer." *American Breweriana Journal*. Vol. 96, January–February 1999.

— —. "Northern Brewing Company: If at First You Don't Succeed, Try, Try Again." *American Breweriana Journal*. Vol. 87, July–August 1997.

Cornell, Martin. "How Milwaukee's Famous Beer Became Infamous: The Fall of Schlitz." *The Beer Connoisseur*. www-.beerconnoisseur.com. Originally posted January 10, 2010.

Commemorative Biographical Record of the Upper Lake Region. Chicago, Ill.: J. H. Beers & Co., 1905

Davis, Doug. "History in a Bottle...or a Tray, or a Clock." *Lake Superior Magazine*. October-November 2002.

Dick, Charles E. "A Geographical Analysis of the Development of the Brewing Industry in Minnesota." Graduate Thesis, University of Minnesota. Minneapolis, Minn.: Self published, 1981.

Dierckins, Tony, and Maryanne C. Norton. *Lost Duluth: Landmarks, Industries, Buildings, Homes, and the Neighborhoods in Which They Stood*. Duluth, Minn.: Zenith City Press, 2012.

Duluth, Minnesota: The Zenith City of the North-West. Duluth, Minn.: North American Industrial Review, ca. 1901.

Fawcett, Gil. "Diary of Duluth." Radio teleplay transcript of a broadcast of August 12, 1948, on the pioneer breweries of Duluth, Minnesota, and Superior, Wisconsin.

Flower, Frank A. *Eye of the Northwest: First Annual Report of the Statistician of Superior, Wisconsin*. Milwaukee, Wisc.: King, Fowle & Co., 1890.

Fieldhouse, Ron ed. *Bottles, Breweriana and Advertising Jugs of Minnesota 1850-1920. Volume 1: Beer, Soda, Household*. Self published 1986.

"Fitger Brewing Company Logs March 21, 1930–September 1, 1931." From the Coopen and Rockne Johnson Collection.

"Fitger Brewing Company Files." Correspondence of the Fitger Brewing Company from November 1934 until April 1942, bound in six volumes. From the collection of Douglas Fitger Donnelly.

Forstall, Richard L., ed. "Population of the United States and Counties of the United States: 1790–1990." Washington, D.C.: Department of Commerce, 1990.

"Gentlemen of the Brewery." Transcript of a speech given to employee's of the Fitger Brewing Company on the retirement of Charles "Spike" Uden, n.d. (ca. 1940). Located in the clippings files of the Duluth Public Library.

Gettelman, Nancy Moore. *A Gettleman Brewing Company: One Hundred and Seven Years of a Family Brewery in Milwaukee*. Milwaukee, Wisc.: Procrustes Press, 1995.

Governor's Message and Accompanying Documents of the State of Wisconsin, Vol. 2. Madison, Wisc.: Democratic Printing Co., 1893.

Gravel, Russell. Letter to Peter Clure September 21, 1998.

Hanson, Dorothy Decker. "Letter to Otto Wieland, president of the St. Louis County Historical Society about the life of her grandfather, Nicholas Decker." November 25, 1940. Located in the clippings files of the Duluth Public Library.

Hartel, Jim. Interview with Tony Dierckins February 6, 2018.

Hoch, Rolan F. III. "Roland O. Hoch." Unpublished manuscript dated January, 2013.

Horsley, Joe. "A German-American Feminist and Her Female Marriages: Mathilde Franziska Anneke (1817–1884)." *FemBio Online*. Accessed October 24, 2017.

Hoverson, Doug. *Land of Amber Waters: The History of Brewing in Minnesota*. Minneapolis, Minn.: University of Minnesota Press, 2007.

— —. *The Drink that Made Wisconsin Famous*. Minneapolis, Minn.: University of Minnesota Press, forthcoming 2019.

"Hugo." *Washington County History Guide*. Washington County Historical Society. www.projects.wchsmn.org/communities/ hugo/. Accessed January 29, 2017.

Ice & Refrigeration Illustrated. Vol. 27, Nos. 1 to 6, July to Dec. Chicago: Nickerson & Collins Company, 1904.

Johnson, Brooks. "The Boom Ain't Over: Northland Brewing Scene Just Starting to Mature." *Duluth News Tribune Extra*. April, 2017.

Johnson, Coopen. *Fitger's: The Brewery and Its People*. Duluth, Minn.: Fitger's Publishing, 2004.

— —. "Reiner Hoch." Unpublished, undated manuscript from the Coopen and Rockne Johnson Collection.

Kay, Bob. "Labelology: Dating Beer Labels." *The Breweriana Collector*. Summer, 1998.

— — *U.S. Beer Labels: 1950 and Earlier Volume Three—Central States*. Batavia, Ill.: Bob Kay Beer Labels, Inc., 2007.

Kroll, Wayne L. *Badger Breweries Past & Present*. Jefferson, Wisc.: Wayne L. Kroll, 1976.

Leggett, William. *Duluth and Environs: An Historical, Biographical, Commercial and Statistical Record*. Duluth: Leggett and Chapman, 1895.

Lilligard, Robert. "The Beer Age: Duluth-Superior is Brewing Up a Storm." *Duluth~Superior Magazine*. September, 2013.

Makki, Lisa. "Annual Duluth-area beer production hits one million gallons." *Perfect Duluth Day* website. www.perfectduluthday.com. Posted May 1, 2017.

Magnaghi, Russell M. "Breweries in the Lake Superior Basin: An Essay." *Upper Country: A Journal of the Lake Superior Region.* 2014.

——. *Upper Peninsula Beer: A History of Brewing Above the Bridge.* Chicago, Ill.: Arcadia Publishing, 2015.

Maury, James. "A History of Brewing in Duluth." Unpublished manuscript dated 1965 located in the University of Minnesota Duluth Kathryn A. Martin Library Archives and Special Collections.

Melton. Lori C. "Crafting a Living: Bulldogs Pivot toward Careers in Craft Beer." *University of Minnesota Duluth Bridge.* Vol. 35, No. 1, Spring 2018.

Memorial Record of the Northern Peninsula of Michigan. Marquette, Mich.: Lewis Publishing Company, 1895.

Mershart, Ronald V. *Pioneers of Superior.* Roseville, Minn.: Park Genealogical Books, 1996.

——. *They Remembered Superior.* Superior, Wisc.: Douglas County Historical Society, undated (ca. 1995).

Michols, J. M. with Coleman F. Naughton and Ray D. Handy. *Duluthians in Cartoon: Being a Most Successful Attempt at Portraying Representative Business Men of Duluth, Minnesota, in Their Respective Professions and Trades.* Duluth, Minn.: Publisher unknown, undated (ca. 1909).

Minnesota State and Territory Census (1855-1895). State of Minnesota. Retrieved from ancestry.com.

Minnesota State Gazetteer and Business Directory. Detroit, Mich.: R. L. Polk & Co., 1872–1873 and 1878–1879.

One Hundred Years of Brewing: A Complete History of the Progress made in the Art, Science and Industry of Brewing in the World, Particularly During the Nineteenth Century. New York: Arno Press, 1974. (Originally published in 1903 by H. S. Rich & Co.)

Ostern, Robert (Bob). Interview with Pete Clure, February 3, 1998.

Page, Herb with Bob Kay, Tye Schwalbe, and John Steiner. *Wisconsin Beer Labels: The First Seventy-Five Years.* La Crosse, Wisc.: Tye Schwabe, 2005.

Pen and Sunlight: Sketches of Duluth, Superior and Ashland. Chicago: Phoenix Publishing Co., 1892.

Powers, Madelon. "Women and Public Drinking, 1890-1920." *History Today,* Feb. 1995.

Piepke, Susan L. *Mathilda Franziska Anneke (1817–1884): The Works and Life of a German-American Activist.* New York: Peter Lang Publishing, 2006.

R. L. Polk's & Co.'s City of Detroit Directory. Detroit, Mich.: R. L. Polk & Co., 1870–1900.

R. L. Polk's & Co.'s City of Duluth Directory. Duluth, Minn.: R. L. Polk & Co., 1884–2017.

R. L. Polk's & Co.'s City of St. Louis Directory. St. Louis, Missouri.: R. L. Polk & Co., 1860–1885.

R. L. Polk's & Co.'s City of Superior Directory. Superior, Wisc.: R. L. Polk & Co., 1889–2017.

Refrigerating World, Volume 31, Issue 2, Feb. 1906. New York: Ice Trade Journal Co.

"Reiner and Mary Hoch House." Unpublished manuscript dated February 27, 1965, from the Coopen and Rockne Johnson Collection.

Sanborn Fire Insurance Maps: City of Duluth. Sanborn Map Company. Pelham, New York: 1883–1954.

Sorenson, John. Interview with Tony Dierckins, April 20, 2018.

Stack, Martin. "A Concise History of America's Brewing Industry," *EH.Net Encyclopedia*, edited by Robert Whaples. July 4, 2003.

"The Fitger Brewing Company Story." Unpublished manuscript dated May 25, 1973. St. Louis County Historical Society. Located in the University of Minnesota Duluth Kathryn A. Martin Library Archives and Special Collections.

United States Census (1830–1960). United States Census Bureau. Retrieved from ancestry.com.

Van Brunt, Walter. *Duluth and St. Louis County, Minnesota: Their Story and People, Vols. 1–3.* New York: The American Historical Society, 1921.

Van Wieren, Dale P. *American Breweries II.* West Point, Penn.: East Coast Breweriana Association, 1995.

Wahl, Robert and Arnold Spencer. *American Brewers' Review,* Vol. 18. Chicago: WahlDer Braumeister Publishing Company, 1904.

——. *American Brewers' Review,* Volume 20. Chicago: WahlDer Braumeister Publishing Company, 1906.

Winchell, H. N. with Edward D. Neil and J. Fletcher Williams. *History of the Upper Mississippi Valley.* Minneapolis: Minnesota Historical Company, 1881.

Wisconsin State and Territory Census (1855-1895). State of Wisconsin. Retrieved from ancestry.com.

Woodbridge, Dwight E., and John S. Pardee, eds. *History of Duluth and St. Louis County, Volumes 1 and 2.* Chicago: C. F. Cooper & Company, 1910.

STORIES REFERENCED FROM *ZENITH CITY ONLINE*:

The following sources were all originally published on *Zenith City Online* (zenithcity.com) between 2012 and 2016. By Heidi Bakk-Hansen: "Nicholas & Benjamin Decker," "Philadelphia Roughs & Duluth's First Murder," "Prohibition in Duluth (1916–1933)." By Tony Dierckins: "A Killing at the Beer Garden," "Duluth's Post-Prohibition Liquor Laws," "Lakeside/Lester Park and Liquor," "The Temperance Movement in Duluth."

STORIES REFERENCED FROM *THE GROWLER*:

The following sources were all originally published on the *Growler* website (www.growlermag.com) between 2012 and 2018: "Blacklist Artisan Ales Opens Taproom in Downtown Duluth," "Canal Park Brewing with Fresh Hops from Local Farm," "Earth Rider Brewery Announces Lead Brewers," "Fitger's Co-founder Announces Plans to Open New Brewery in Superior, Wisc.," "New Owners Take the Helm at Lake Superior Brewing," "Sneak Peek of Bent Paddle's New Taproom and Pilot Brewery," "Ursa Minor Brewing to Open in Duluth's Lincoln Park 'Craft District'."

NEWSPAPERS:

Research for this book included thousands of articles and advertisements found in the following newspapers:

Ashland Daily Press, Ashland Wisconsin
Daily Mining Journal, Marquette, Michigan
Detroit Free Press, Detroit, Michigan
Duluth Budgeteer Duluth, Minnesota
Duluth Evening Herald, Duluth, Minnesota
Duluth Herald, Duluth, Minnesota
Duluth Minnesotian, Duluth, Minnesota
Duluth Minnesotian-Herald, Duluth, Minnesota
Duluth Morning Call, Duluth, Minnesota
Duluth News Tribune, Duluth, Minnesota
Duluth Weekly Herald, Duluth, Minnesota
Duluth Weekly Tribune, Duluth, Minnesota
Lake Superior News, Duluth, Minnesota
Lake Superior Review & Weekly Tribune, Duluth, Minnesota
Minneapolis Tribune, Minneapolis, Minnesota
Saint Paul Daily Globe, St. Paul, Minnesota
Superior Chronicle, Superior, Wisconsin
Superior Citizen, Superior, Wisconsin
Superior Evening Telegraph, Superior, Wisconsin
Superior Gazette, Superior, Wisconsin
Superior Inland Ocean, Superior, Wisconsin
Superior Inter Ocean, Superior, Wisconsin
Superior Times, Superior, Wisconsin
Wisconsin Jewish Chronicle, Milwaukee, Wisconsin
Wisconsin State Journal, Madison, Wisconsin

About the Images

Many individuals and organizations generously conributed to the collection of images that illustrate this book.

Images of and access to breweriana and historic photos were provided by Noel Boelter, Pete Clure, Coopen and Rockne Johnson (credited herein as C&R Johnson), Ken Malz, Chris Olsen, Jody Otto, Terry Post, John Steiner, and Jeff Lemke of Twin Ports Rail History.

More historic images came from the the Duluth Public Library, the Douglas County Historical Society, American Breweriana Association, Fitger's Historic Brewery Complex (credited herein as Fitger's Complex), Library of Congress, the Minneapolis Streetcar Museum, and the University of Minnesota Duluth Kathryn A. Martin Library Archives and Special Collections (credited herein as UMD Martin Library) as well as the archives of the book's publisher, Zenith City Press.

Brian Rauvola of Duluth's HBR Studios photographed all of the images that appear in the book's appendix (see page 187), and images created using Rauvola's photos also appear on pages 59, 63, 101 (Silver Spray sign), 106, 115, 116, 121, 123 (Gold Shield sign), 126 (Fitger's Natural sign), 128 (Lovit sign), 133 (Nordlager's sign), 136 (J. F. Kernan print), 143, 144 (Vic's Special sign), 146, 150, 151, 153 (Royal 58 sign), 154 (Royal Bohemian sign), 156 (Royal 58 sign), 157 (Northern meat tenderizer), 161 (Regal Supreme signs) 173 (Fitger's thermometer sign), and 212–214.

Those who generously shared images of their family include Jeff Andrews (Ernst Klinkert), Eddie Gleeson (Gleeson family and People's employees), Roland F. Hoch III (Reiner Hoch), Bill Ralph (Mary and Benjamin Decker Jr.), and Joan Wilson (Joseph Hennes).

The breweries of the Twin Ports, Minnesota's Arrowhead, and Lake Superior's North and South Shore supplied the logos and photographs that illustrate this book's epilogue, except for the photograph of Eddie Gleeson, which was made by Kip Praslowicz.

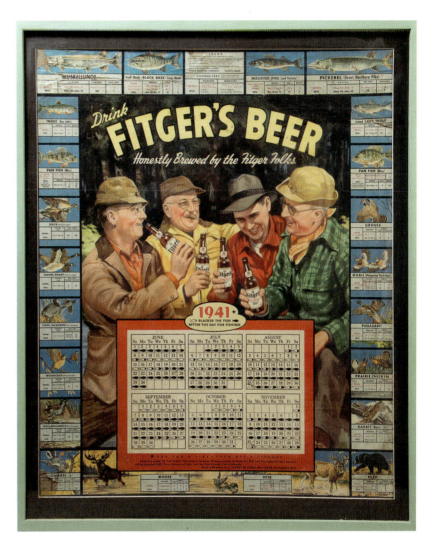

ABOVE: A 1941 Fitger's Hunting & Fishing Alamanc featuring an image of the brewery's corporate officers (from left) Walter Johnson, John Beerhalter Sr., John Beerhalter Jr., and Arnold Fitger.

Facing page: A pre-Prohibition tray for People's Brewing Co.

[P. CLURE COLLECTION]

A FITGER BREWING CO.
DELIVERYMAN'S HAT, CA. 1950.
[P. CLURE COLLECTION]

ABOUT THE AUTHORS

Duluth author (and St. Paul native) Tony Dierckins has written or cowritten more than two dozen books, from the ridiculous *Duct Tape* books to the fun and informative *Mosquito Book*. His regional history books include *Crossing the Canal: An Illustrated History of Duluth's Aerial Bridge* and, with Maryanne C. Norton, *Lost Duluth: Landmarks, Industries, Buildings, Homes, & the Neighborhoods in which They Stood*—both finalists for the Minnesota Book Award—as well as *Glensheen: The Official Guide to Duluth's Historic Congdon Estate* and, with Nancy S. Nelson, *Duluth's Historic Parks: Their First 160 Years*, both winners of the Northeastern Minnesota Book Award. Dierckins is a past recipient of the Duluth Depot Foundation's Historic Preservation and Interpretation Award and the publisher of Zenith City Press, celebrating historic Duluth and the Western Lake Superior region at www.zenithcity.com.

Duluth native Pete Clure has been collecting memorabilia related to and researching the history of brewing in the Twin Ports for more than forty years. He has coauthored histories of Northern Brewing Co. and Duluth Brewing & Malting for the *American Breweriana Journal* and is a member of the American Breweriana Association, the National Association of Breweriana Advertising Collectors, the North Star Chapter of the Breweriana Collectors of America, the Hamm's Club, and Duluth's own Nordlager Club. He works seasonally for Sea Service, shuttling ship pilots to oceangoing vessels docked outside of the Duluth-Superior Harbor, who in turn navigate the salties through the Duluth Ship Canal as required by law. But most days you'll find him working as a sales representative for the Zenith City's Michaud Distributing, making sure that Superior, Duluth, and Proctor, Minnesota, never run out of beer.